Let's Get Civil

Let's Get Civil

Healing Our Fractured Body Politic

By
Patrick Conroy

E-BookTime, LLC
Montgomery, Alabama

Let's Get Civil
Healing Our Fractured Body Politic

Library of Congress Control Number: 2019937397

ISBN: 978-1-60862-752-3

First Edition
Published April 2019
E-BookTime, LLC
6598 Pumpkin Road
Montgomery, AL 36108
www.e-booktime.com

Printed on acid-free paper.
Printed in the United States of America.

To My Parents:

Cecilia Veronica Leary Conroy
Daniel William Conroy
Sis and Dan

Acknowledgments

In the spring of 2017, my wife Barb found me yelling at the television. She told me to stop yelling and write the book. So I did. She also endured hours of my talking about it, gave me valuable feedback, and, by the way, had taught me about Kohlberg's work in moral development.

Ron Messina read the fourth draft. Ron helped me transition from the casual language and stream of consciousness style I use to put my rough ideas into words and get them on paper where I can study them. Ron encouraged me to keep at it.

Roger Fillion is a journalist. He chimed in around the eighth draft and made helpful editing suggestions. He also suggested that I provide brief introductory paragraphs to help readers anticipate what they are going to read. That suggestion led to my writing Pat's Notes as both introductions and conclusions.

Megan Moye Zacher designed the front and back cover and spine. Our work on the front cover reminded me to help readers believe that the goal of the book is realistic.

John Moye and I were classmates at Notre Dame. John is an attorney and once again had my back when I started sending manuscripts out.

Allan McNichol edited the 15th draft. Allan was raised Republican and is disenchanted with what the Republican Party has become, but he maintains considerable respect for what it has been and what it can be. He schooled me on financial markets and demonstrated a keen eye for detail when editing. But most of all he helped me refine my language regarding capitalism and conservative politics, reminding me that there are millions of Americans who will like what I write if I am smart enough not to insult them and their beliefs. Which of course is the whole point of the book. We all need to be smart enough not to insult each another so that we can argue productively.

Contents

1 Introduction xv

PART I
THE SCIENCE OF COGNITIVE AND
MORAL DEVELOPMENT
Pat's Notes... 1

2 Cognitive Development.. 3
  Piaget's Stages of Cognitive Development 5
  Pre-Operational and Concrete Operational Levels 6
  Formal Operations 7
  Formal Operations in General.. 8
  Kuhn and Formal Operations.. 10
  Paradigms and Scientific Revolutions............................... 11
  Formal Conceptual Frameworks 13
  Thinking About How We Think.. 13

3 Moral Development... 15
  Level II Stage 3 – Tribal Moral Reasoning 15
  Level II Stage 4 – Organizations 19
  Level II Stage 5 – We the People 21
  Elliot Turiel on Learning and Moral Development............. 23
  The Domains of Full Human Development 25
Pat's Notes... 29

PART II
RELIGION, HUMANISM AND PUBLIC DISCOURSE
Pat's Notes... 33

4 Public Theology and American Politics.................................. 35
  What is Religion? 36
  A Formal Conceptual Framework for Public Theology 38
  Anti-Intellectualism in American Religions...................... 41
  Public Engagement and Responsibility in Evangelical
  Christianity 45
  How Status Christianity became Political 48

The Political Alliance of Republicans and Status
Christians 50

5 Religious Humanism and the Long Sixties............................ 58
    The Amazing and Tragic 60s... 59
    Origins of 1960's Activism.. 61
    The Civil Rights Movement... 64
    The Vietnam War Protests, 1964 – 1973 66
    The Free Speech Movement... 68
    The End Game – Victory and Defeat, Hope and Despair ... 71
        1967: Race Riots and Vietnam War Protests 72
        1968: National Tragedy... 74
            The Democratic National Convention................. 76
        The Draft, Cambodia, Student Riots, and the
        End of the War 79
            The Vietnam War Hangover 80
Pat's Notes 83

PART III
CHALLENGES IN MORAL PHILOSOPHY
AND SOCIAL SCIENCE
Pat's Notes 85

6 Early Western Moral Philosophy and Social Science............ 87
    The Rejection of Reason in Islam 90
    The Ascendance of Natural Science 92
    Religious Wars and Religious Moral Philosophy 94

7 Modern Western Moral Philosophy and Social Science......... 98
    The Divorce of Moral Philosophy and Social Science 98
    Moral Philosophy Today.. 100
    Social Science and the Interface of Moral Philosophy
    and Science 103
        Understanding Today's Moral Philosophers............. 105
        Phenomenology... 107

8 Integrating Moral Philosophy and Social Science 110
    The Epistemology of Moral Philosophy 112

Contents

The Teleological Structure and Standards of
Moral Reasoning.. 114
The Morally Grounded Purposes of America's
Liberal Democracy 116
The Source of Knowledge in Moral Philosophy 122
Social Science Method and Epistemology 124
The Source of Knowledge in Social Science............. 125
The Structure and Standards of Knowledge in
Social Science.. 125
The Organization of Knowledge in Social
Science.. 126
Natural Science, Social Science, and Moral
Philosophy 127
Pat's Notes.. 130

PART IV
USING MORAL PHILOSOPHY AND SOCIAL SCIENCE
Pat's Notes.. 133

9 Economic Justice.. 137
A Formal Conceptual Framework for Economics............ 139
Mercantilism.. 141
Capitalism.. 144
Communism.. 146
Socialism 147
Analyzing and Evaluating Economic Theories 149
The Morally Grounded Pragmatic Dialectic of
Capitalism and Socialism 151
Capitalist Issues that Confront We the People 153
Competition 153
Employment and Unemployment............................ 154
Rights of Inheritance.................................... 156
Just Taxes and the Distribution of Wealth............... 156
Controlling the Distribution of Profits.................. 157
Fiduciary Responsibility and the Distribution of
Profits.. 163
Capitalism and Free International Trade 164

10 Education Justice 167
   Professional Leadership in Education 170
   Conroy's Education Paradigms CP 1.0 and CP 2.0 175
   Paradigms vs. Theoretical Models 176
   The Story Behind Conroy's Paradigm 1.0 177
   Using CP 1.0 180
      Fundamental Assumptions 180
      Advantages and Disadvantages that Students
      Bring to Learning 181
      Feuerstein's Theory of Structural Cognitive
      Modifiability 182
      Advantages and Disadvantages as a Formal
      Conceptual Framework 185
      Methodology 187
   The Stories Behind Conroy's Paradigm 2.0 189
   Using Conroy's Paradigm 2.0 192
      Methodology 192
      Instrumentation 195
      Laws and Intellectual Authority in Education 196
   Evaluation in Education 197

11 Women's Reproductive Rights 201
   The Supreme Court and Religious Moral Arguments
   on Abortion 202
   Before Roe v. Wade 206
   Catholic Arguments against Artificial Birth Control 208
   Political Arguments against Birth Control 210
   Abortion – Women's Rights and Public
   Responsibilities 212
   Catholic Moral Arguments against Abortion 213
      The Soul and Abortion 215
      A Woman's Capacity to Make Moral Decisions 221
   Early Term Abortion and the Phenomenology of
   Pregnancy 225
   Early Term Abortion and Mature Public Moral
   Reasoning 229
      A Priori Assumptions (APA) of Public Moral
      Arguments Regarding Abortion 232

Contents

Using Our A Priori Assumptions 234
Fetal Viability and the Morality of Abortion 235
Mature Religious and Public Moral Reasoning and
Late Term Abortions 236

12 Social Justice 244
Social Justice Challenges that Demand Capitalist
Solutions 246
Advance Long and Productive Lives 246
End Homelessness 247
Build Financial Capability for All 248
Reduce Extreme Economic Inequality 249
Social Justice Challenges that Demand Socialist
Solutions 249
Ensure Healthy Development for All Youth 249
Physical Health of All Children 250
Social Health of All Children 251
Mental Health of Children 251
Close the Health Gap 252
Promote Smart Decarceration 253
Social Justice Challenges that Demand Individual and
Community Solutions 257
Eradicate Social Isolation 257
Stop Family Violence 258
Achieve Equal Opportunity and Justice 259
Social Justice Challenges that Require Capitalist,
Socialist, and Individual/Community Solutions 263
Create Social Responses to a Changing
Environment 263

13 Conclusion 266

Bibliography 278

1
Introduction

"What should we do?"

"Wrong question."

"What's the right question?"

"What should I do?"

"But I already know what I should do. The question is, 'What should we do?'"

"Impossible to answer. We can only answer, 'What should I do?'"

It may seem obvious that We the People must answer the question, "What should we do?" But "What should we do?" is a moral question, and there is fairly widespread popular and intellectual agreement that the only valid moral statement that any of us can make is one that applies only to one's self.

We also know that We the People must make laws and all laws are moral laws because they tell us what we can and cannot do. When we agree about our laws, we agree about what We should do in public life, not just what I should do.

So We the People must be able to agree about what we should do. But we can't. We are a fractured body politic. We face big moral questions. Some of those questions are easy to answer and some seem impossible. How have we answered the tough questions? We turned them over to the big guys. How did that turn out? Congress passed and the President signed the Civil Rights Act and the Voting Rights Act, but that did not bring us together. It divided us more deeply. The Supreme Court ruled in favor of Roe v. Wade, but that divided us more deeply. Clearly, if We the

People cannot agree, our government and courts cannot unite us. We have got to unite ourselves. We have got to agree about what we should do, what we believe about ourselves, and then we can leave our government and courts to work out the details.

We need to be able to talk about these things in families and towns, in the public square.[1] We the people must heal our fractured body politic. And that means that we must agree on our core values, agree who we are as a nation. We must have a shared identity. We must be able to complete the sentence: We hold these truths to be self-evident. It's one of the defining statements in our Declaration of Independence. It defined our core values as a new nation. And it must continue to define our core values. It must continue to form the foundation of our identity as Americans, as members of our democracy. But to do that, we must be able to agree on the list of truths that we hold as self evident.

We the People must face challenging issues, argue about them, come to agreement, and guide our government. We can't do that if we can't argue productively. We can't be Americans if we can't argue productively. Our democracy can't survive if We the People can't argue productively.

"I may be ignorant, but I'm not stupid." Usually, when I have heard that said, it has sounded more like "Ah may be ignrant, but ah ain't stoopud." When I first heard it said like that, I assumed that the speaker was both ignorant and stupid, but that was because of my sheltered upbringing and my own ignorance. Pope Francis recently said that abortion is like "hiring a hit man to resolve a problem." The Pope isn't stupid, but damn, that's ignorant.[2] And that's the problem. Way too many really smart

---

[1] The public square was the square or park in front of the Town Hall. Social media provides a virtual Town Square where people can meet and argue and agree. The quality of those arguments and the information brought to them matters.

[2] It's unfortunate that Pope Francis used such extreme, volatile language regarding the choices women make regarding abortion. In Chapter 11, Women's Reproductive Rights, we consider the different experiences women have with pregnancy and their attitudes toward abortion. We also subject the Catholic Church's arguments against both birth control and abortion to rational scrutiny.

people are too danged ignorant to conduct productive discourse in the public square. Like all those academics who believe "The only valid moral assertion that any one of us can make is one that applies only to one's self." That is just flat ignorant. We have some work to do to help those academics develop the capacity to argue and reach agreement about what we all should do. Along the way, we will help regular Americans do it too.

When We the People engage each other in public arguments, reach agreement, and direct our politicians; we act as our nation's Body Politic. Body is a great image. One mind, one body, many parts.

We know that we aren't talking and acting together as a body politic. What's at stake? If we don't protect our democracy, we won't revert back to a monarchy, but we could very well descend into a democratic oligarchy. Democratic Oligarchy: an authoritarian government run by an authoritarian president with a group of very rich individuals for their own benefit. Strictly speaking the United States does not have oligarchs, but it does have very rich radical capitalists who use their wealth and power to advance their goals, to benefit themselves. I use the term "radical capitalists" throughout this book and distinguish it from traditional capitalists. However, I don't explain the term and the full power and threat of radical capitalists until Chapter 9, Economic Justice. There I praise capitalism, suggest ways to improve it, and expose the dangers of radical capitalism.[3]

How does this book help heal our body politic? First, I explain how We the People became fractured: The forces that drove us apart and the innocent intellectuals and politicians who could have stopped it but did not because they got mixed up intellectually. They were smart, but ignorant. Second, I develop the intellectual solutions needed to heal our body politic. That may sound impossible. Let me indicate what we will do.

---

[3] Readers uncomfortable with the term "radical capitalist" should go to Analyzing and Evaluating Economic Theories in Chapter 9 Economic Justice. There I make an argument for the complete rejection of radical capitalism and a better understanding of traditional capitalism.

We the People can't complete the sentence: We hold these truths to be self-evident. These truths are moral truths: All men are created equal. That's a moral assertion. They're endowed by their Creator. That's both a religious and a moral assertion. With certain unalienable rights. What's unalienable cannot be taken away or denied. That's a philosophical and moral assertion. Among these are life, liberty, and the pursuit of happiness. That's a moral assertion. Our country was founded on moral assertions.

But we have stopped thinking morally as a body politic. We don't know how to conduct public moral arguments and that's why we can't agree on the moral truths we need to bind our nation together. To unite us, unite We the People, as a body politic with all of our differences. That's a complex problem. I make it simple and solve it.

I need to expand upon this point. We get it that we rely on intelligent solutions that allow us to conduct moral arguments. Also, these arguments deal with public morals, what We the People should and should not do in public life. We don't deal with personal or private morals. However, what we do privately can't hurt others. Whenever we hurt others we stop acting privately.

In order to develop and use intelligent solutions, we must improve how We the People think, how we think as a group, the mind politic, and how we think as individual members of the body politic. We must think about what we think, but more important, we must learn to think about how we think. None of this is obscure. After all, I am talking about how all of us think. We recognize all of this. Some of the terms I use might be new, but the experiences they name are not new.

For example, we all think in "Doctrines felt as facts."[4] Think about that for a second. What do I just believe? Is it a fact or a doctrine? Some of our doctrines felt as facts are obvious. Do we believe that "All men are created equal" applies only to men, or only to white men and women? Or only to men and women who agree with us? Or do we believe that "All men are created equal" applies to all men and women, all races, all religions, all sexual

---

[4] Basil Willey, *The Seventeenth Century Background: The Thought of the Age in Relation to Religion and Poetry.*

orientations, all nationalities? Which of those doctrines we believe has a huge impact on how We the People think about ourselves and each other. Can two people conduct mature, rational arguments using contradictory doctrines felt as? Yes, if both are willing to examine his or her doctrines felt as fact. "Doctrine felt as fact" may be a new term, but what it talks about is not at all new to us. Even if we have not thought about it before, we immediately understand it. Well, immediately after just a brief example.

Some of our doctrines felt as facts are obvious as soon as we begin to think about them. Others require a lot of work, a lot of self reflection, and sometimes a lot of study. We inherit our doctrines felt as facts. We learn them within our family, church, and community without noticing that we have learned them. They become a part of whom we are, habits of mind that direct how we view the world and other people. They also direct how we feel.

How we feel. Most of us have been told that our feelings are true. Stick to your feelings. Be true to your self. Well, kind of. What we feel is indeed what we feel and there's a kind of truth in that. But much of what we feel results from what we think. That's an important fact that's too often overlooked. Some feelings are physical, tied to our genetic makeup and our biology. Others result from how we think. How we think leads to feelings that help us solve problems or feelings that make problems worse. We become empowered as individuals when we learn to control our thoughts, words, feelings, and actions. Being a grownup has a lot to do with taking control of our thoughts. And that involves discovering, among other things, our doctrines felt as facts and subjecting them to critical reflection.

We will notice doctrines felt as facts often in this book. Noticing them helps us understand ourselves and others and the tasks we face as we strive to argue productively.

Many of us have heard someone end an argument by saying something like, "Well, be that as it may, I just disagree." No matter the other side of the argument, we all get to just disagree. We're entitled to our own opinions. That's absolutely true. In our private lives. But it's only true, can only be true, in our private lives. We totally frustrate the purpose and demands of public argument if we rely solely on our personal opinions. If we're unable or unwilling to subject our personal opinions to argument. The whole purpose of public argument is to move beyond personal opinions and build shared opinions in the public square, opinions grounded in grown up reasoning.

John Henry Newman defined assent as the individual's right to just believe in God or to believe anything else. We get to do that and no one can take that right away from us. It defines our freedom in our private lives. But he demonstrated that assent, the right to individual opinions, does not work in public argument. His language is a bit old fashioned, so let me paraphrase it:

> Assent is appropriate to the individual. But it undermines productive arguments. It confines itself to its own evidence and its own standard. It cannot be anticipated or accounted for because it is the accident of this person or that.[5]

Any way of thinking that's based solely on the views of the individual and disregards any other evidence or standards of knowledge make public argument impossible. We will give a lot of attention to the challenge of developing methods and standards of thinking that guide public arguments. But for now, we must agree or at least open our minds to the proposition that We the People cannot rely on individual opinions if we want to conduct productive public arguments. We all must work to grow our personal opinions into shared opinions.

Let's not underestimate the challenge we face. Richard Rorty was an esteemed American philosopher. Years ago, I called him to discuss concerns I had regarding education leadership. He took my call, was respectful and congenial, and listened while I explained the problems I was trying to solve:

> When principals hold faculty meetings to discuss with their teachers how their children learn and how best to teach, they need their teachers to come to agreement. Their students need their teachers to agree, especially

---

[5] *An Essay in Aid of a Grammar of Assent*, p. 82-83.

that vast majority of students who need good teachers if they're going to learn. But, I explained, education research is all over the place. Education researchers and teacher educators don't agree, so there is no way that teachers can work toward agreement. No matter how hard principals may work, it's impossible to get teachers who disagree to learn to agree. As a result, principals end up with divided faculties who can't even speak to each other, and their students – who move from classroom to classroom and grade to grade – encounter contradictory, incompatible teaching and motivation.

When I finished, Rorty replied, "But Pat, if principals end their faculty meeting and none of their teachers agree, they can be confident that they have done something right." Rorty was a brilliant man, no doubt about that, but he was flat ignorant about intellectual leadership in public education.

That was a few years before he died in 2007, and I am confident that at that time Rorty would have said that one of the best features of our democracy is that people don't agree. I'm not sure he would have said that like teachers it's a good thing if they can't reach agreement, but it seems so.

And now as we face the fact of our fractured body politic, it's fair to blame him and all the philosophers and other intellectuals who followed or did not challenge his views. But I must admit, I didn't challenge him. I realized that I had no chance of even discussing my concerns with him and turned my attention to getting off the phone gracefully. But that story helps us appreciate the challenges we face. Esteemed intellectuals don't share our goal of building agreement in the mind politic and the body politic. They cannot even think about our building agreement in the public square. Instead, they teach views that undermine our goal.

What's our goal?

To conduct discourse in the public square that allows us to agree on what is right and what is wrong in public life so that we can make laws and develop public policies that support what is right and reject what is wrong.

Right now, we can't do that. We can't agree on anything as We the People, to say nothing of agreeing on what is right and what is wrong in a way that guides us when making laws. Let's get started figuring out how we must think so that we can do that. We may be ignorant, but we ain't stupid.

Now let me introduce a useful way of thinking about our challenge.

In the mid-19th century, scientists discovered that although it takes energy to heat something; it takes no energy for it to cool. Holy cow! If it takes energy to generate heat and no energy for heat to dissipate, the whole universe must be in a process of cooling. They realized that this process of moving from hot to cold consists of moving from order to disorder. They called this process entropy and it meant that the whole universe was caught in a process of moving from order to disorder. That was a terrifying prospect.

But in the 20th and 21st centuries, scientists discovered a remedy to entropy: information. Information creates order without using energy. So we have two fundamental processes at work in the universe:

ORDER ==> ENTROPY==> DISORDER
DISORDER ==> INFORMATION ==> ORDER[6]

Scientists have been interested in information technology, computers, the awesome power of digitalized information moving at the speed of light. But we can understand information differently.

We keep in mind the power of entropy to create disorder. We recognize that our society, our body politic, We the People, are an organized group of citizens, working together. But our order, our being organized, is subject to entropy. It can dissipate without the use of energy if we don't take care of it. And we understand what scientists believe about information, but we take it further. We know that it is not enough to think about and pursue information.

---

[6] Jim Al-Kahlili; BBC's Big Science Season documentary "Order and Disorder."

We must think about and pursue knowledge. Scientists can think about and study the information that underlies the order of the universe, of all things physical. That information already exists in the physical world.

But humans have created societies. Our Founding Fathers invented our democracy. They bequeathed order to us, an organized political system that depends upon the ongoing vigilance of We the People to maintain it, to fight entropy. Our Founding Fathers' intellectual achievements were enormous. Maintaining them requires knowledge, and developing that knowledge requires serious intellectual attention. It doth not fall like rain from heaven.

The fact that our body politic has fallen into disorder is proof that We the People have failed to do the intellectual work required to maintain order in our body politic, public square, and government.

The good news is that we have not collapsed into chaos. The bad news is that we're headed in that direction. Our challenge is to reverse our direction. We must redirect ourselves to order.

Not all of us need to solve intellectual problems. One person or just a small group of people can solve an intellectual problem. Everyone else only has to learn the solution and use it. Learning takes attention and work, but lots of Americans are willing and able to learn and work. We just need a critical mass of Americans to learn these solutions and put them into practice. We need leaders to lead using these solutions. We need these solutions to become the way we do things as a body politic. And we do not just need leaders in great leadership positions. They can certainly help, but we also need leaders throughout all of society. They exist and they know who they are. We need them to get on board.

Now let's take a quick look at what we're going to do to improve our thinking.

In Part I we learn about cognitive and moral development. We have all gone through stages of cognitive and moral development, so learning about them has to do, for the most part, with understanding what we have already experienced. That makes it easy. But since we have experienced them and everyone else has experienced them, there are a lot of "doctrines felt as facts" that deal with cognitive and moral development. That can make learning about them a bit more challenging.

Understanding cognitive and moral development provides the foundation to everything else we do in this book. The reader cannot duck or skim through this discussion. This one must be mastered. Cognitive development and moral development define what it means to be a grownup in the public square and in our relationships with each other. It's the key to everything this book sets out to do and is the key to healing our body politic. Acting out doctrines felt as fact rather than understanding what we think is a luxury that We the People can't afford. It represents a stupid commitment to ignorance.

Cognitive development refers to our capacity to reason. Moral development refers to our capacity to reason morally. We're interested in how we reason regarding public moral issues, not personal moral issues. Our goal in this discussion is to see the difference between immature reasoning and mature reasoning, and to develop the skills required to conduct mature moral reasoning in the public square. That can't be a hard sell. Certainly no one wants to argue that they would rather be immature than mature. The challenge will be that we all will have to abandon some immature doctrines felt as fact. Don't think about it as a teenager being grounded. Think about it as getting a driver's license. Empowering. We get to do things and go places that used to be impossible.

While learning about moral development, we find out that Learning Leads Development. That Learning Leads Development is not a doctrine. It is demonstrably true. Demonstrably, demonstrate, prove. We will demonstrate that it is true in Chapter 3 when we discuss the work of Kohlberg and Turiel. It's a big deal because it puts us in charge of our development. We the People can develop mature reasoning and mature moral reasoning.

Monarchies and dictatorships operate on the assumption that their subjects need to be ruled because they can't rule themselves. Democracy assumes that those who govern must be guided and controlled by the people who are not their subjects. In a democracy, the people, to an important extent, rule themselves. Democracy assumes that the body politic operates at mature levels of cognitive and moral development. The whole assumption that democracy is the best form of government depends upon our understanding how humans learn and develop. With that understanding established, we move on to learning how our body politic became so fractured.

Part II is titled Religion, Humanism, and Public Discourse. We all think that we remember or know all about the 1960s, but in fact, an enormous amount of money has been spent waging a propaganda campaign that mocks 60s social activists and opponents of the Vietnam War. We must get to the truth behind the 60s so that we can recapture its spirit and its moral certitude.

Religion has both contributed to and disrupted our body politic. We need a common understanding about the role of religion in private lives which must be protected. That understanding protects religion in families, churches, and religious communities. And we must understand, build agreement about, the role of religion in the public square. We have a particular challenge because many Americans have no interest at all in theology and little interest in religion. On the other hand, many other Americans are interested in religion and fight to assert their religious views in the public square. Indifference to religion coupled with religious activism has helped fracture our public square. We need a general knowledge about religion in the public square so that We the People can deal with the moral questions that lie at the heart of all public arguments.

Understanding religion is not just about putting religion in its place. Religious humanism has an impressive history in American culture and played an important role in the civil rights movement and the social activism of the Long 60s[7]. The Long 60s witnessed a powerful combination of religious humanism and secular humanism. I give this unique marriage enough attention for the reader to develop indignation if not anger that fundamentalist Christians successfully rejected the "secular humanism" of the Long 60s for their astonishingly un-Christian, dehumanizing politics that followed the Reagan presidency. I provide that

---

[7] "Long 60s" is discussed in Chapter 6, Religious Humanism and The Long Sixties.

background in the chapter, Religious Humanism and the Long Sixties. That chapter also allows us to witness three things that seem to have been lost in our sense of the recent past. First, religious and secular humanists sought to expand human rights during the Long 60s but were met with massive indifference. Second, 60s activists' tactics were peaceful: Peaceful marches and peaceful sit ins and peaceful civil disobedience. Third, their peaceful activism was met with violence, violence that was condoned and protected and perpetrated by politicians, most of the media, and virtually the entire legal system. The Long 60s must be understood for their enormous human achievements and tragedies. We want to regain the spirit and moral certitude of the 60s, the religious and secular humanism and activism, without the institutional violence.

We then move to Part III Integrating Moral Philosophy and Social Science. The challenge here is that few Americans know anything at all about moral philosophy. We don't have to know a lot, but we must know a little. And we must know a lot about the relationship between moral philosophy and social science. One of the challenges I took on in writing this book was to lead the reader through interesting steps that help them learn what otherwise would be difficult. The steps:

First, we briefly review the history of moral philosophy and social science,

Second, we look at their rather messy divorce,

Third, we discover the harm the divorce caused both disciplines,

Fourth, we realize that the divorce contributed to the fracturing of our body politic, and

Fifth, we reunite them, which is one of the major intellectual achievements of this book.

I will tell you that the fifth is the most difficult. But the preceding steps make it easily accessible. Years ago, my principal visited my classroom of smart high school seniors. Later, he stopped one of the kids in the hall and asked him, "Lon, did you have any idea what Mr. Conroy was talking about?" Lon replied, "Of course." Then after a slight pause Lon added, "Oh, but I can see how someone who had not been in his previous classes would not know what he was talking about." The point is, attend all the classes, read all of the previous material, and the last step will make sense and be quite accessible.

Just start rested and relaxed, with a favorite beverage at hand, when you take on the last step: Chapter 8 Integrating Moral Philosophy and Social Science. Actually, it's really cool, and it makes all of the work we do in Part IV possible.

In Part IV we use all the work we have done in Parts I through III to frame major issues that confront us today in the public square. I start with Economic Justice because we must achieve economic justice if we're going to have any opportunity to conduct productive discourse on anything else that confronts us in the public square. Not only do I help the reader reject radical capitalism, I also argue for the complete rejection of communism. Having eliminated those extreme and deeply flawed economic theories, I am able to place capitalism and socialism in what I call a morally grounded pragmatic dialectic that promotes productive discourse on economic justice. In this discussion we realize that one of our major tasks as a body politic is to decide which areas of our economy are best met with capitalist enterprises and which are best met with socialist enterprises.

Then I turn to Education Justice because education is America's oldest and largest socialist enterprise. That discussion allows us to unveil the enormous flaws in education leadership and how it has harmed that entire socialist enterprise. We see that education's most esteemed leaders maintain astonishing indifference to the capacity of education to achieve its goals and we note the stakes at play in allowing this massive socialist enterprise to fail. Of course, then I offer solutions.

The next topic is Women's Reproductive Rights. I have been thinking and writing on this topic for years but did not intend to include it in this book until Justice Kennedy announced his retirement from the Supreme Court. Now it's impossible to ignore.

Finally, I talk about Social Justice. This topic is somewhat difficult to address because our general inability to conduct mature rational discourse about economic justice has left our nation bereft of social programs. After many drafts and a ton of work, this chapter took on a useful shape.

All of this may seem impossibly complex, but it's actually quite simple once we remove the intellectual barriers to developing a mature body politic. Such a project may seem off-putting to some readers. Too challenging. Kind of scary. But remember. Solutions are much more difficult to discover than to learn. With the help of many others, I have done the hard work.

That being said, every reading of the final draft left me concerned that the book will be too damned hard to read for too many people who I hope will read it. So I have gone back and added some help, a kind of CliffsNotes within the text. Critics have complained that students read CliffsNotes instead of the original works. CliffsNotes has defended their work, claiming that they help many students read and understand the original works.

I have provided Pat's Notes, introductions and summaries in Part I through Part III, and included them in the table of contents. I hope they help many readers get access to this book.

Good people, people with good hearts and great hope for our country live everywhere in America, and we must unite. Martin Luther King Jr. and Robert F. Kennedy were the last great American leaders who believed that we all could be united and who actually worked to that end. But they were assassinated within two months of each other in 1968, and we have not recovered that faith and that goal since. We must if we're to heal our fractured body politic.

Let's get to work, together.

PART I

THE SCIENCE OF COGNITIVE AND MORAL DEVELOPMENT

Pat's Notes

Becoming grownups. That's what we're talking about. And a big part of becoming grownups involves intellectual development. Not becoming intellectuals, whatever that means. But developing our intellects, our ability to think and talk and act like grownups.

Intellectual development consists of both cognitive development and moral development. That is not a doctrine felt as fact. It is demonstrably true and we will demonstrate that it is true when we integrate moral philosophy and social science in Chapter 8. In the meantime, the reader can recognize that it just makes sense. Operating at high levels of cognition is impossible if we cannot tell right from wrong.

Cognitive development supports mature reasoning. Moral development supports mature moral reasoning. Both cognitive development and moral development are related to biological development. As children get older, they go through increasingly advanced phases of biological development that make cognitive and moral development possible. But biological development only permits cognitive and moral development, only makes it possible. It doesn't assure it. Learning leads development. Learning is the key to actual development and good teaching is the key to learning.

Virtually all humans have attained the biological maturity required for both mature reasoning and mature moral reasoning by around the age that American students graduate from high school. And yet the majority of American adults haven't achieved the highest level of cognitive development and the vast majority haven't achieved mature moral development. Many adults are smart, but few can make mature arguments, arguments that use mature reasoning. And even more smart adults are good, but cannot make mature moral arguments, arguments that employ mature moral reasoning. We use our arguments in the public square to decide on the laws we make. We the People need to operate with mature reasoning and mature moral reasoning. We need to get good at both.

2
Cognitive Development

We have two goals in this and the next chapter. First, we will learn about cognitive and moral development as they occur in individuals. How each of us grows up, as it were, matures cognitively (how we think and reason), and morally, (how we think and reason morally). Second, we will learn about how we as a society, as a body politic, mature cognitively and morally. It's obvious that we don't want to be immature adults or an immature body politic. It's not so obvious how we can become mature and more important, how we can attend, as a society, to the full cognitive and moral development of our mind politic, how We the People think, and our body politic, how We the People conduct arguments in the public square.

We're talking about the majority of Americans who can develop cognitively and morally but too often don't. And the more we learn about human development, the more shocking it is that so many adults don't fully develop and that our society remains indifferent to that failure. Indeed, some members of our society undermine the full development of our people. That's an important point. We can't sit back as a society and ignore the full development of our people, and that includes taking on the forces that work against that development. And here's the real kicker. We can't allow people who find it in their interests to make arguments at low levels of cognitive and moral development to go unchallenged. People can say anything they want, but not with impunity. Not all arguments are equal just because the right to speak is equal. So we all get to participate, we all get to speak.

But those who are stuck at immature levels of cognitive and moral reasoning cannot be allowed to prevail.

Why do we care? Give a state a critical mass of ignorant citizens and it gets stuck on stupid. They do not solve problems. They make a stupid commitment to ignorance. Give a state a critical mass of grownup citizens, and they can solve problems, meet challenges, prepare for the future. Everything is at stake for our body politic, for our nation, and for our constitutional democracy.

There is an old saying: You can't argue with stupid. There is some truth to that, but it's not the whole story. Many people are ignorant but not stupid; they lack cognitive and moral development. They haven't had the learning experiences they needed to achieve cognitive and moral development. We show insight into these people by recognizing that they may be immature but that does not make them stupid. Indeed, they may have been so exploited that they have developed doctrines felt as facts that inhibit their cognitive and moral development.

We will see that humans live in three domains: the individual, the person, and the self. That's true of immature people as well as mature. One does not lose one's humanity by being immature. That's rarely just the fault of the person who is immature. It's both wrong and ineffective to disdain people who are immature. They aren't stupid and they aren't deplorable. They're humans with all of the dignity and rights inherent in human beings, and we're here to help them become fully developed human beings.

Additionally, there is no reason to bother learning about cognitive and moral development if we're not going to act on that knowledge, if we're not going to make decisions based upon mature thinking and reasoning. This is not elitism. Elitism is out there and we will talk about it. But this ain't elitism. It's common sense. We want to think and act like grownups. But we must give intellectual attention to understanding the difference and social attention to making that difference.

We start with cognitive development because we must understand it to understand moral development. Cognitive psychology studies both how we think and reason and how we develop the capacity to do so. I confine this initial discussion to Piaget who was interested in early development. Eventually, I use Thomas Kuhn, whose research helped me understand the highest level of cognitive development, formal reasoning.

Piaget's Stages of Cognitive Development

Piaget identified four stages of cognitive development which are listed below. We have no interest in the sensory motor stage because it has nothing to do with moral development. We're interested in the pre-operational stage to the extent that understanding it helps us understand the concrete-operational stage. Adults who are able to find their way to the public square operate at least at the concrete-operational stage.

Piaget's Stages of Cognitive Development
Stage 1: Sensory motor, birth to age 2.
Stage 2: Pre-Operational, age 2 to 7.
Stage 3: Concrete-Operational, age 7 to 11.
Stage 4: Formal Operational, age 11 to 15.

Importantly, the ages associated with each stage of development refer to the ages at which the majority of children become capable of that level of development. They're ranges that apply to virtually all children. There's a lot of time within those ranges, but we're not concerned here with children. We're interested in adults and their capacity to reason. Four things interest us.

First, humans become capable of high levels of both cognitive and moral development at an early age.

Second, although all adults are old enough to have attained high levels of cognitive and moral development, their actual development covers a wide range. Age allows development. It does not guarantee it. Many adults operate at low levels of cognitive and moral development.

Third, learning leads development at every stage of cognition. Learning determines both development and the content of development, the fullness of development at every stage. Two people can operate in concrete operations, for example, and one can have vastly greater knowledge and skill than the other.

Learning ===> Development ===> Learning

Learning allows us to develop new, higher levels of cognition. Once we have developed a new capacity, learning with that new capacity determines how much we actually know and are able to do.

Fourth, formal operations are tricky. Most adults operate in concrete operations. And the vast majority of adults who do operate in formal operations do so in areas of their work where they have been taught a specific formal operation that applies to their work. They may work within the formal operation, benefit from it, without knowing that it is a formal operation. A formal operation represents an intellectual achievement. They do not grow on trees and we do not mature into them. We either learn them or learn to work within them. All this will become clearer when we get into our discussion of formal operations.

Pre-Operational and Concrete Operational Levels

A classic example of the difference between pre-operations and concrete-operations involves a teacher and students. The teacher has two containers of equal size and shape each containing an equal amount of water. Kids look at both and see that they're the same. Then she pours the water from one into a big container and the water from the other into a much smaller container. Tricky! Then she asks the children, Which of the new containers has more water in it? Young children, children still in the pre-operational stage of cognitive development, almost always choose the smaller container because it looks more full. Once children reach the stage of concrete operations, they remember that equal amounts of water were poured into the two containers and know that they hold the same amount of water, regardless of how full or empty the containers may appear. They remember that the original containers held the same amount of water and apply that knowledge to the question regarding the second set of containers. They think about what they saw and apply it to what they now see. Similarly, children who have reached concrete operations can go outside, walk some blocks from home, turn around, and follow the path they took away from home back home. They can remember where they went and apply that knowledge to what they see on their return trip and use that information to find their way back home. These children can find a toy or book by thinking about where they left it. There is a huge difference in the mental capacity of children when they move from pre-operations to concrete operations. The vast majority of adults operate in concrete operations. It's the content of their knowledge and skills they have developed within concrete operations that vary.

Concrete operations are operations on things that are physically present, whether we can see them right now or not. According to Piaget, children become able to perform concrete operations from around age 7 to 11. They become able to perform formal operations as early as age 12.

Formal Operations

Formal operations dominate our attention here, in moral reasoning, and throughout the book. Everything we do in this book and everything required to heal our fractured body politic depends upon our capacity as individuals and as a body politic to operate in formal operations. Not in all facets of our lives, but clearly in moral reasoning. We the People must achieve formal operations in moral reasoning.

With formal operations, we become able to think about how we think. If we're going to argue about laws, we must be able to think about how we think about laws. And all laws are moral laws, so we must be able to think about how we think morally. Theo Epstein demonstrated that the brain grows physically in stages that correlate closely with Piaget's stages of cognitive development.[8] So we're talking real physical and psychological

---

[8] Epstein, "Growth Spurts during Brain Development: Implications for Educational Policy and Practice."

growth. But when we talk about formal operations, we must focus on intellectual growth, even more, intellectual achievements. In order to think in formal operations, one must employ a formal conceptual framework. A formal conceptual framework represents an intellectual achievement. We need them, but they're far easier to use than to invent. I use formal conceptual frameworks throughout this book.

We need formal reasoning to operate at Kohlberg's Level 3, his highest level of moral reasoning. But formal reasoning receives little attention in education or psychology. We need to give it considerable attention because we must use it. Thomas Kuhn[9] helped me understand it. First let's just talk in general about formal reasoning, then we can begin to see how Khun helps us understand it.

Formal Operations in General

With concrete operations, we can think about things we have seen even if we can no longer see them. But we can only think about things we have seen or touched or weighed or heard. Thus the term "concrete."

With formal operations, we can think about what we have never seen. Here is a fun example. Vygotsky and his colleague A.R. Luria studied the impact of literacy on adult cognitive development. They visited Russian farming communities that were still populated entirely by illiterate adults.[10] They presented the adults of these towns this question:

> In the far north where there is snow year round, the bears are white.
> Novaya Zemlya is in the far north.
> What color are the bears in Novaya Zemla?

The leaders of the towns invariably laughed and replied, "None of us has ever been to Novaya Zemlya. How could any of

---

[9] Kuhn, *The Structure of Scientific Revolutions.*
[10] Luria, *The Making of Mind.*

us know what color the bears are there?" They laughed, thinking it was silly that anyone would ask them to think about a place and things they had never seen. They were not capable of formal reasoning. Although being illiterate virtually guarantees that one cannot think formally, one can be literate and still not have developed the capacity to reason formally. But I have always liked this story and find it useful to introduce formal reasoning.

The term formal comes from the role of the form of a deductive argument, the most famous of which is the syllogism. The form matters because in a syllogism, if the form is followed correctly, and the premises are true, then the conclusion must be true. If these illiterate Russian farmers were capable of formal reasoning, then they would have known:

A. If all of the bears in the far north where it snows year round are white,
B. And if Novaya Zemlya is in the far north where it snows year round,
C. Then all of the bears in Novaya Zemlya must be white.

But notice, even such a syllogism represents an intellectual achievement. We must learn about syllogisms, and practice constructing them in order to be able to invent one. Syllogisms are invented. They do not occur in nature. Formal operations allow us to think about what we haven't seen or touched. We think using formal logical operations. In her wonderful little book, *Children's Minds,* Margaret Donaldson insists that children aren't capable of success in school after a fairly early age if they can't solve the problem:

If $A > B$
And $B > C$
Then $A > C$

In other words, students must learn to think formally to succeed in school. Her example has the added benefit of using symbols which takes us immediately into mathematics where of course formal reasoning is essential.

Notice that this syllogism does not work:

If A > than B
And C is > than B
Then . . . Nothing.

All we know is what we have stated, both A and C are greater than B. But we do not know which is greater, A or C. We do not have to have been trained in logic to see the difference between the two syllogisms, especially once their difference has been pointed out.

Now this is all well and good as an introduction to formal reasoning, but it does not get to what finally allowed me to understand formal reasoning and develop the formal intellectual tools that contribute to this book. Deductive reasoning has been around since before Aristotle and he pretty well perfected the syllogism. So what did I have to figure out?

Kuhn and Formal Operations

My insights into formal operations began to emerge when I read Kuhn's *The Structure of Scientific Revolutions*. For a few years I had been baffled by Piaget's claim that formal operations allow us to account for all of the hypotheses that can be constructed around a topic. What does that mean? *"Account"* for all the hypotheses? How does it do that? I wondered. Piaget, as far as I can tell, did not explain what that means, not in any of his works that have been translated into English.

First let me answer the question about what *account* means. Now remember, Piaget was a brilliant natural scientist, a biologist, before he became a developmental psychologist. It's fair to assume that he knew what Kuhn was talking about, even if he had never read Kuhn. Kuhn accounts for various questions or hypotheses with these responses:

Yes, we know that's true; and no, we know that's not true.

Interesting, and we're studying that expecting to find an answer, either that it's true or not true.

And finally:

Sorry, we don't know if that's true or false and there's no way we can study it at this time, within our current paradigm.

That's what "account for" means. Yes we have answered it, yes we're studying it, no we can't even study it. But jump back? What do you mean you can't even study it? How do you account for something if you can't even study it?

We have noticed that to move from concrete operations to formal operations someone needs to invent a formal conceptual framework. Kuhn studied scientific revolutions. As I read Kuhn's descriptions of these revolutions, what he called paradigm shifts, I noticed that they were not just scientific revolutions, they were also cognitive revolutions. By understanding how science advances knowledge, I was able to understand how we can advance our understanding of cognitive development. Scientists learn new stuff, stuff that's so new and so big that it causes a revolution in how they think. We also need to learn new stuff to advance from concrete operations to formal operations, to change how we think. The more we understand the structure of scientific revolutions, the more we can understand the structure of formal operations. Cool! Don't you think? So let's talk about Kuhn and paradigms. We will learn about the structure and content of paradigms.

Paradigms and Scientific Revolutions

The first scientific revolution that Kuhn describes is the Copernican Revolution. You know, Copernicus and Galileo rejected the Ptolemaic view of the universe, the Ptolemaic paradigm, in which the earth was the center of the universe. Copernicus argued and Galileo proved that the earth rotates around the sun.

Let's explain how not being able to study something accounts for it. Imagine 15th century astronomers studying the sun and planets and one asks, "How long does it take for the earth to travel around the sun?" Within the 15th century astronomy paradigm it was impossible to think about or study that question. So they could account for it as being impossible to study or answer within that paradigm. That is a big deal. Knowing what they cannot study let's scientists focus on what they can study and ignore what they cannot study. Scientists can study evolution and ignore creation stories. Why? Because there is no way to study creation stories within a scientific paradigm.

But back to astronomy. As 15th and 16th century astronomers gathered more and more data on the movement of planets, they began to encounter more questions than answers. And a few, Copernicus in particular, began to consider the possibility that they didn't even know how to think about some of these questions. Copernicus began to think differently about the fundamental assumptions of the Ptolemaic paradigm. Copernicus changed those assumptions and thereby destroyed the old paradigm and invented a new one. Not everyone agreed right away, but as astronomers used it, this new theory allowed them to answer questions about the movement of the planets that they had not been able to answer. And Galileo knew a lot. He also employed the newly invented telescope to develop the evidence required to prove the new paradigm.

Notice, the new scientific paradigm which was developed by Copernicus and Galileo did not come fully developed. It won out over the old paradigm for two reasons: First, the old paradigm was exhausted; it created more problems than solutions, more questions than answers. Second, the new paradigm immediately allowed astronomers to explain things in new and better ways. The new paradigm did not have all the answers immediately, but it provided a new way of thinking that researchers could use to investigate questions they had been unable to investigate, solve problems they had been unable to solve.

According to Kuhn, a paradigm is an intellectual achievement that provides the organizing principles that unite (organize) a scientific discipline's knowledge into a coherent whole and its members into a unified community of scholars. The Copernican Revolution was, first of all, an enormous intellectual achievement. It did not win out immediately, but when it did, it united the community of astronomers. Copernicus crafted the theory, Galileo proved it, and Newton developed the whole system of scientific reasoning that has propelled scientific progress that continues to this day. Kuhn made no scientific discoveries. All Kuhn did was figure out and set down in writing the structure and content of scientific revolutions by reflecting on what had happened. But Kuhn's work helps us. For it helps us understand formal operations and formal reasoning in a whole new way.

Formal Conceptual Frameworks

I learned about conceptual frameworks from Piaget. He was interested in how the brain works and how it develops. He taught us that the brain organizes information into different files, what he calls schema. A formal conceptual framework is a schema that organizes a bunch of schema, a bunch of files. They let us think about how we think about the information in different files. How are they similar? How are they different?

Paradigms organize all of the knowledge in a discipline. Formal conceptual frameworks organize a bunch of information on a topic. I have developed formal conceptual frameworks that help us think about what I call Public Theology and economic justice. We the People must be able to think about how to think about these topics in order to participate in rational conversations in the public square.

Thinking About How We Think

Knowing about syllogisms helps us think about the arguments we make that are fundamentally syllogistic. We know we cannot argue productively by just focusing on conclusions. We must ask two questions: 1. Are our premises, our assumptions, correct? 2. Is there a necessary logical relationship between our assumptions and our conclusions? When we ask ourselves those questions, we're thinking about how we think. And when we argue about

13

those questions, we can argue productively. The premises are either demonstrably true or not. We can argue about that. The arguments are either logically necessary or not. We can argue about that. We cannot argue about conclusions. What we can argue about are the premises and the logic. Those arguments tell us if we can agree on the conclusions or not.

When we have developed or learned a formal conceptual framework, it helps us think about how we think about its topic. We need an example. Let's keep it simple for now. We will use more complex ones in the text.

Years ago I coached middle distance runners, I knew that I needed to develop their strength and speed, but I was not sure how to balance the two. So I asked Bill Bowerman, the brilliant track coach at the University of Oregon. He told me to watch runners in races or time trials. If they had trouble running their pace, could not get up to speed, give them more speed work. If they handled the pace comfortably but faded, give them more strength work. If they can do both, begin to train them at a faster pace. Unbelievably simple. He taught me in an instant how to think about my runners' total training system. It's a glimpse at what was known as the Oregon System. It was a nifty formal conceptual framework.

Paradigms help entire disciplines think and think about how they think. Biologists use the scientific theory of knowledge developed by Newton and the scientific method. But they also use evolution and genetic theory. Chemists use the scientific theory of knowledge and the scientific method but also use the periodic table of elements, atomic theory, and quantum mechanics. I will defer to philosophers of science to distinguish formal conceptual frameworks from paradigms. My guess is that the periodic table of elements is one of the most powerful formal conceptual frameworks in all of science, but not a paradigm.

But here is the key for all of us. We the People need to be able to think about what we think and how we think in order successfully to operate as a body and mind politic, in order to solve the moral challenges we face. To do that, we must be able to think about how we think about moral development and moral reasoning. We turn to that topic now.

3
Moral Development

We've talked about how moral development matters. Entropy threatens our democracy. It's aided by some powerful Americans who seek their own ends over the ends that benefit society. In order to enjoy the benefits of a constitutional democracy, We the People must fight to keep our democracy alive and well. And we need tools to fight with. Mature moral reasoning is one of the most important tools we have at our disposal. We must pursue it and use it and shame those who ignore or oppose it. But first, we must make sure we have it in our tool box.

Lawrence Kohlberg described three levels of moral development. Each of Kohlberg's three levels correlates roughly with Piaget's three highest stages of cognitive development. Kohlberg described two stages of moral development within each level. "Levels with Stages" is new.

We will focus on Kohlberg's Level 2, Stages 3 and 4 which are common among adults, and on Level 3, Stage 5, which is rare among adults. Stage 5 must be the stage We the People seek in our moral development so that we can conduct productive public arguments. Achieving that goal will not be easy, but we make it realistic. Does it take a little work? Yes. Is it impossible? Not at all. Is it worth it? You bet!

Level II Stage 3 – Tribal Moral Reasoning

Stage 3. . . . Did you read it below? This is an important developmental stage. It's important for children to enter and it's important for children to mature out of. All of the growth we talk about in Level II is vitally important to the child's development,

---

LEVEL II CONVENTIONAL[11]
Stage 3: Mutual Interpersonal Expectations, Relationships, and Interpersonal Conformity Ages 8-12
Piaget's Stage 3, Concrete Operational, Ages 7-11

What is Right: Living up to what's expected of you by people close to you or what people generally expect of people in your role as son, daughter, friend, etc. "Being good" is important and means having good motives, showing concern about others who are close to you. It also means adhering to relationship norms such as trust, loyalty, respect, and gratitude within your group.

Reasons for Doing Right: The need to be a good person in one's own eyes and those of others who are close to you. Caring for others who are close to you. Belief in the Golden Rule – treating others in a way you want to be treated – as it applies to you and those close to you. Desire to maintain rules and authority which support stereotypical good behavior.

Social Perspective: Perspective of the individual in relationship with other individuals. Aware of shared feelings, agreements, and expectations within your group which take primacy over individual interests. Relates points of view through the concrete Golden Rule, putting one's self in other person's shoes within your group. Does not yet consider generalized system perspective.

---

[11] Conroy, Barbara J.; *Teachers' Moral Reasoning and their Attitudes and Behaviors Regarding Discipline.* I took these summaries of Kohlberg's levels and stages from Barb's dissertation. She used a handout she had received at a Kohlberg training program at Harvard in the early 1970s. I restructured them to make them easier to read.

important for them to mature into and out of. Stage 3 is fun to watch kids mature into but can also be maddening. Parents benefit from recognizing the growth and development that occur at this stage. They can encourage their children when they enter it and then help direct them through and out of it. But to our task of healing our body politic, this stage destroys public discourse if adults get stuck in it. Adults must mature beyond Stage 3. Adults must outgrow their tribes and become members of We the People.

The focus of children and adults who operate at Stage 3 can be summarized as "me and mine" vs. "others." Stage 3 is tribal and relies on Piaget's third stage of cognitive development, Concrete Operations, ages 7-11. With the development of concrete operations, children become capable of abstract thinking (not formal operations, but abstract thinking). They can think about what they have seen and done and talked about even if it's not present.[12] At Stage 3, children adopt the norms established by their parents or teachers or friends. And they apply those norms beyond themselves.

Stage 3 Tribal moral reasoning lets children make a huge leap in social perspective. They move from thinking primarily about themselves to thinking about themselves as members of a group, their tribe. They think about their friends and all the other kids who are not their friends. Think cliques and gangs. What is important for us to notice is that these cliques and gangs have one set of rules for themselves, another set for everyone else. These rules benefit the clique or gang and disadvantage others. They contradict all mature concepts of justice.

This level of moral development is disruptive enough in junior high schools. Among adults, it supports racism, misogyny, and most other economic and social problems. It lies at the heart of social and economic injustice. When it dominates how We the

---

[12] At this stage, children become capable of abstract thinking, but they're just learning to do it. Some children use this new capacity to remember all the fabulous things they have seen on the internet, in magazines, and in their neighborhood. They remember them and combine them into images of a perfect life for themselves. It's a kind of magical thinking. There it is, so clear. Why don't they have it? They blame their parents for not providing it. Maddening in children, dangerous in adults.

People think, this stage of moral development fractures our body politic, and replaces the body politic with tribes.

Adults operating at Stage 3 belong to tribes with strong identities. They know who belongs to their tribe and they know who is targeted by their tribe. Some are benign: Alabama and Auburn football fans. Some are harmful, even malignant. When Stage 3 is malignant, the "we" are always more powerful than the "they." Think white racists who had all the power, and black civil rights activists in the 1950s and early 1960s who had none. "We" decide what is right and what is wrong and if "they" attempt to challenge what is right or do what is wrong, our entire tribe retaliates. And our retaliation can have few boundaries.

These adults can be mean and even violent in how they treat others while being enormously loyal within their tribes. That's why members of tribes invariably talk about each other in glowing terms: Great person, good person, sincere person, trustworthy person. We need to stop and think and feel this point. Often, members of these tribes treat each other well. They come to each others' aid. They're willing to risk their lives and make great sacrifices for each other. All of which contributes to their powerful tribal identity. At the same time, they ignore the indefensible ways they treat others.

Racism depends on Stage 3 moral reasoning and the profound social experiences that support the tribe. Those experiences unite the tribe both as a tribe and in their rejection of their targeted "others."

Whole police forces can get stuck in Stage 3 Tribal moral reasoning. Obviously, the military benefits from Stage 3 moral reasoning when soldiers face combat – which is reason enough for the military to be subjected to civilian control.

That's the short of it. And what we must remember is that these adults operate at a level of moral reasoning that supports each other's thinking and behavior. They hold dear their doctrines felt as facts that their tribes share. One can point out to Southern racists that the North won the Civil War and that they should join the Union, become part of our democracy, and adopt and adhere to its values. But to no avail. The North has still not won the argument. What racists do is justified by what they think and the fact that the only people they care about agree with them. Their doctrines felt as facts are wrapped up in what they call the unique and special Southern tradition and culture. They can't think differently. They're rationally incapable of questioning each other. We will talk about our fellow citizens who are stuck in Stage 3 moral reasoning when we revisit the civil rights movement and the Americans who brutally attacked peaceful activists. But we'll also talk about it when we discuss radical capitalist and economic justice. That discussion will reveal American oligarchs for what they are and the forces they apply to their goal of controlling our democracy for their benefit.

Level II Stage 4 – Organizations

Unlike Stage 3, Stage 4 has significant strengths in adult society, but it's still in Level II. When young adults achieve Stage 4, they know that family and school rules are important – indeed, more important than the norms set by friends and peers. Almost shockingly, these young adults can call out other students or friends for doing something they know is wrong. How's that possible? That shift in loyalty. Now students evaluate family and school and social norms in ways that go far beyond their earlier sense of fair – "What me and my friends want (sic)." Instead, they focus on whether or not these norms work or don't work for the institution. This represents a huge change, among high school students and adults.

We need to take a deep breath. Maybe get up and walk around. We have just moved from the moral reasoning that supports deeply loyal and mean tribes whose members aren't capable of questioning each other even when they're engaged in mean or even violent behavior, to moral reasoning that allows members of groups to call each other out if they have violated the norms of organizations or institutions[13] to which they belong. And that development can occur while students are still in high school.

---

[13] It might be useful to differentiate organizations and institutions (O/Is): organizations as capitalist enterprises and institutions as socialist enterprises. Google is a capitalist organization. The Securities and Exchange Commission (SEC) is a socialist institution.

Level II Conventional
Stage 4: Social System and Conscience, Ages 12-16
Piaget's Stage 3, Concrete Operational, Ages 7-11

What is Right: Fulfilling the duties to which one has agreed. Laws are upheld, except in extreme cases where they conflict with other fixed social duties. Right is contributing to the organization or institution (O/I).

Reasons for Doing Right: To keep the O/I going as a whole, to avoid the breakdown in the system that would occur "if everyone did it," or the imperative of conscience, to meet one's defined obligations.

Social Perspective: Differentiates societal point of view from interpersonal agreement or motives. Takes the point of view of the system that defines roles and rules. Considers individual relations in terms of place in the system.

At Stage 4, adults adopt the rules made by the organization or institution (O/I) they belong to, not the rules made by them and their friends, their tribe. Stage 4 adults don't reject rules because they aren't what "we" want but because they're stupid. Why are they stupid? Because they don't support, or even undermine, the O/I's goals.

By fairly obvious logical extension, we realize that laws made in the public square must have a rational connection to the public's goals. But what are the public's goals? Just the goals of O/Is? Here we encounter the problems with Stage 4. As we will see, the public's goals are prior to, have priority over, the goals of O/Is.

The goals of an O/I can be great for that O/I, but they may not be great for other O/Is or for the local community. It's great for a corporation to set cities in competition to win their new factory or corporate headquarters. They use the competition to get leverage when negotiating taxes and the acquisition of land and preparation of sites. But that's not so clearly in the interest of the city. It can be, but questioning the norms of the corporation does not shed light on the benefits to the city. Kohlberg's Stage 5 moral reasoning allows us to think about goals and norms that are larger than O/I goals?

Level II Stage 5 – We the People

LEVEL III POST-CONVENTIONAL OR PRINCIPLED
Stage 5: Social Contract or Utility and Individual
Rights Ages 16 and older
Piaget's Stage 4, Formal Operational, Ages 11-15

What is Right: Being aware that people hold a variety of values and opinions, that most values and rules are relative to your group (culture, large group). These relative rules should usually be upheld, however, in the interest of impartiality and because they are the social contract. Some non-relative values like *life* and *liberty*, however, must be upheld in any society and regardless of majority opinions.

Reasons for Doing Right: A sense of obligation to law because of one's social contract to make and abide by laws for the welfare of all and for the protection of all people's rights. A feeling of contractual commitment, freely entered upon, to family, friendship, work, and community obligations. Concern that laws and duties be based on rational calculations of overall utility, "the greatest good for the greatest number."

Social Perspective: Prior to "my society" perspective. Perspective of a rational individual aware of the values and rights of individuals *prior to social attachments and contracts*. Integrates perspectives by formal mechanisms of agreement, contract, objective impartiality, and due process. Considers moral and legal points of view; recognizes that they sometimes conflict and finds it difficult to resolve such conflicts.

Kohlberg had trouble conducting research on this level of moral reasoning because so few adults operate at it with enough consistency to be studied. The problem is that Stage 5 is the first of his stages to require formal operations, formal reasoning. As I will discuss later, that was a problem for Kohlberg because he did not fully understand the nature of formal operations and its impact on moral reasoning.

As we have seen, when young adults begin to think formally, they enter a whole new structure of reasoning, new forms: syllogisms, formal conceptual frameworks, and paradigms. Kohlberg did not understand the full development of formal reasoning which is why he had trouble understanding why adults could not operate at it consistently. But he did capture the key elements of Stage 5 moral reasoning.

In Stage 5 We the People moral reasoning, adults take a social perspective that's larger than our tribe or our organization or our institution. They take the perspective of a rational individual aware of the values and rights of individuals *prior to social attachments and institutional attachments*. Prior to, we give priority to rational standards over social standards. We think about and treat everyone as equal. There is no "we versus them," no "others." There is only, We the People. See why We the People must operate at Stage 5? See why each of us must work to gain the maturity of Stage 5 moral reasoning to participate as full members of our body politic? See why insisting on lower levels of moral reasoning reduces the intelligence of the mind politic?

If We the People don't operate at Stage 5 moral reasoning, we can't complete the sentence, "We hold these truths to be self-evident . . .," That's the bad news.

The good news is that if We the People operate at Stage 5 moral reasoning, we can complete the sentence, We hold these truths to be self evident. We can agree on and list those truths.

We will talk a lot about Stage 5 moral reasoning and we will do the work that needs to be done in moral philosophy to develop the intellectual tools we need to function consistently at Stage 5. That work will represent a major intellectual achievement that will impact how we think about the nature of inquiry in the social sciences as well as how We the People conduct discourse in the public square. We will teach the public mind what it must know to develop and use Stage 5 moral reasoning.

I have claimed that learning leads development and referred to Kohlberg's blind spot regarding formal reasoning and how it limited his understanding of his work on moral development. Now we can give these topics our attention.

Elliot Turiel on Learning and Moral Development

When Elliot Turiel was one of Kohlberg's doctoral students, he decided to confirm that children move sequentially through Kohlberg's stages of moral development, that they're actually developmental stages that all children must pass through and not just various ways of thinking. In order to conduct his project in a reasonable time frame and not have to wait for all of his subjects to develop naturally, he provided instruction to aid their development. It worked. His subjects moved along, through the stages, and he noticed that offering instruction at one stage above their actual development was more effective than reviewing previous stages or instructing at two stages above their current level.

His findings were important: Children develop sequentially through all stages, in order. But he didn't follow up on his other important finding – that instruction aids development. Kohlberg had known that learning aids development, that when children encounter moral crises and are forced to think differently about moral issues, they use their current level of moral development and if that level does not work, they often advance their thinking. They learn to think at a higher level. But that interpretation of events left Kohlberg in the behaviorist theory of learning, for behaviorists acknowledge the role of experience in learning.

Turiel seems to have overlooked the important new information he verified: that instruction aids development. He assumed that it fit in his old schema that said learning through experience aids development, but just as stimulus and response. He assumed that in providing instruction, he had just provided a stimulus. He remained stuck in behaviorist theory of learning, that learning is a natural process of stimulus and response. The fact that instruction aided the development of his subjects' capacity to reason was not interesting to him.

This is important for us to understand. His instruction aided his subjects' development because he influenced how they think. He did not just offer rewards. He did not threaten grounding or offer trips to the ice cream store. He engaged how they thought, and he found that by instructing them in how they think at a higher level of reasoning than they currently used, he impacted their development. Learning leads development. Obvious to us. Not obvious to Turiel.

Since many adults operate at Stage 4 moral reasoning, many adults can help young people and other adults learn to operate at Stage 4.

Virtually every O/I has norms and employees can learn to follow those norms, to work for the good of the O/I. O/Is can include training in Stage 4 moral reasoning as part of their personnel development programs. Clubs like the Lions Club are famous for teaching Robert's Rules of Order which provides skills that aid the use of Stage 4 moral reasoning in various settings.

But Stage 5 requires that we think beyond O/I, beyond any social arrangements. As powerful as Stage 4 is, it does not lead naturally to Stage 5. Indeed, one might argue that most O/Is have a vested interest in keeping everyone focused on their needs and not the needs of the larger society. Setting aside that rather interesting argument, the question at hand is, Who cares enough about a system of moral reasoning that operates at Stage 5 to do the work required to achieve it? Turns out, no one. We will, which is interesting and exciting.

We have talked about cognitive and moral development, their stages and even how to aid their development. But that does not tell the whole story of human development. Before we leave this topic, we must build a stronger foundation in moral reasoning by thinking about what it means to be a fully developed human being.

The Domains of Full Human Development

Each of us lives, experiences our lives, in at least three domains, and we're fully developed human beings to the extent to which each of these domains is fully developed and properly ordered.

> **Individual:** The biological human, the DNA and physical makeup which is unique to each human and distinct from all other species.

> **Person:** The individual in society, all of the commitments and relationships the individual has developed living in society, in the family, with friends, at work, in school, and so on.

> **Self:** The psychological human: the intellectual, moral, emotional, aesthetic, and spiritual inner life of the human, all that the individual has become through intent and accident, hard work and luck, all of one's life's experiences and how one has responded to those experiences.

We can express this as a major principle, an *a priori* assumption, if you will:

> Full human development occurs in three domains: The individual, the person, and the self.

The individual is tied to the biological, physical nature of humans. It's important. A strong, healthy body is a sine qua non to everything else. The older I get the more I understand that health is everything. But our bodies are meant to be lived in and to make everything else possible. They don't provide us with what we think of as the fullness of our humanity. The history of humans has played out most obviously in our families and social/political activities and engagements.

The Person is our domain that engages other persons in society. To achieve full development as a person, we and our society must develop. It's difficult for any human to be better than

25

his or her society, but it's not at all difficult to be unworthy of one's society, one's family or friends or craft or profession or community, state or nation. Each of us must learn the virtues that make us worthy members of our social relationships and commit to do them. And we must learn the vices that undermine our social relationships, and commit to not do them.

Merely acting in society does not reveal virtues and vices. The capacity to discern virtues and vices resides in our selves, our inner selves, our reason and will. Our reason reveals virtues and vices. Our will allows us to control our animal instincts and do what is right and not do what is wrong. But of course our inner lives have to do with far more than controlling our social behaviors. Our self allows us to properly order our bodies and mind. Our inner lives have a whole wonderful world of their own. The self is the deepest domain of our humanity.

We have talked about cognitive and moral development. Both are huge parts of our selves, our inner lives, and the full development of our human capacity must be a major interest for each of us and for our society. We will return to this topic often as we use mature cognitive and moral development as criteria for our evaluation of how we speak and act in the public square.

Each of us has enormous capacity to develop as human beings, but most of us have limited capacity to pursue that development alone. Just as most of us benefit from assistance when learning anything, we benefit from assistance in learning to develop our full humanity. Parents and teachers are obvious mediators for children, but so are coaches, other children, relatives, and other influential adults. That's important to mention so that we understand how children develop their humanity.

But more important to this discussion is to identify the mediators who influence the full development of adults when they join the public square. Adults shape the public square, for good or ill. Which takes us back to our primary concern, our fractured body politic. We will look at religion, moral philosophy, and social science. All three have contributed to the fracturing of our body politic and public square and all three can help heal it.

Readers may find all this interesting but doubt that most Americans are capable of full cognitive or moral development. In the chapter Education Justice, I discuss learning theory and demonstrate that students and adults are capable of learning far more than they do. That's why I wrote a chapter on education justice. But to relieve the readers' concern now, let me just say that when we establish an education or training program, we have to decide if we're going to ask people to change what they do as a way of getting them to change how they think or are we going to ask people to change how they think as a way of getting them to change what they do. The first is called behavior modification, the second cognitive modification, and they represent the two major theories of learning.

In Education Justice, I explain that behavior modification works both to change what people do and what they think if what we want them to think is concrete and simple. But if we want them to think and act with formal operations, we must help them change how they think. We must use cognitive modification, and to do that we must use the learning theory of Reuven Feuerstein. So yes, virtually all students and adults can learn to reason formally and to operate at Stage 5 moral reasoning, but not if our instructional methods are grounded in behaviorism.

In this project we identify a lot of things in our society that we have to fix. But some of them we must fix in the university in order to fix them in society. Fixing how we educate and train our people is just one of them. And when we learn how to fix education we see that once we institutionalize those solutions, educating our students and adults becomes a realistic goal. It's not simple and it's not easy, but it becomes realistic, and I should add, affordable.

The reader can be confident that we know how to achieve our goal:

> To conduct discourse in the public square that allows us to agree on what is right and what is wrong in public life so that we can make laws and develop public policies that support what is right and reject what is wrong.

However, we need:

A critical mass of Americans to show up in the public square and support our arguments. Religious humanists who believe that social responsibility is a prerequisite to redemption. Secular humanists who believe that a good life requires that they help others. Americans who believe that they're members of and responsible for our community and our democracy.

Pat's Notes

We are interested in the two highest levels of cognitive development: Concrete operations and formal operations. Concrete operations let us think about what we have experienced: Seen, heard, touched, tasted, smelled. We can think about these things because we can remember them. We can think about what we have messed around with. Most adult thinking uses concrete operations. And although virtually all adults use concrete operations, there is a huge difference in how much different adults know and are able to do using concrete operations. Obviously, different adults know more about different things. We all know people who know more about some stuff than we do. And we know more about other stuff than they do.

Formal operations allow us to think about what we have not experienced and most important for our purposes, formal operations allow us to think about how we think. Very few adults think in formal operations. That's why it's so difficult to think about our doctrines felt as facts. More on that later. We will discuss formal operations throughout this book. For now, we can learn a lot about cognitive development by looking at moral development.

Four stages of moral development interest us because they explain each other when we compare and contrast them. They also explain a whole lot about how adults think and talk and act in the public square. Some immature, some mature. Stage 2 Individualism is typical of very young children. They're mainly interested in themselves and their needs.

Stage 3 Tribal, Me and My Friends, is typical of junior high children. These kids form powerful groups, cliques and gangs. And here is the key: They have one set of rules for their group and another set of rules for everyone else. Their rules benefit themselves. The rules that they impose on others puts the others at a disadvantage when dealing with their group. Sound familiar? Monarchs. Dictators. Oligarchs. Tribes. Any group of powerful adults who use their power to create laws that work for them and against everyone else operates at Stage 3 moral reasoning. And they learned it in junior high school. Certainly, We the People can agree not to use or tolerate Stage 3 moral reasoning in our body politic.

Stage 4 Organizations or Institution. We become capable of this Stage in high school. This is when kids begin to challenge their parents or teachers because the rules the adults make are dumb, because they undermine the goals of the family or school. This is a useful stage of moral reasoning when applied within organizations. Labor unions can fight management decisions that distribute profits to share holders instead of making needed investments in the organization. But those are mature labor unions, not stage 3 unions that fight for their own benefit without any regard for the organization. See how powerful this stuff is?

The problem with Stage 4 is that We the People are interested in the needs of society, not just the needs of various organizations or institutions. We are interested in what is good for our country, for everyone. We learn to think in those terms in Stage 5.

Stage 5, We the People. We hold these truths and they apply to everyone. The technical term is the Social Contract. It's the contract under which everyone in society agrees to be governed. Since everyone agrees, the contract guarantees the dignity and rights of everyone. That's the level of moral reasoning that We the People must use when we think about what we should do, when we talk about what we should do, and when we make laws that tell us what we must do and what we must not do.

Here is the killer. Stage 3 and Stage 4 can function with Concrete Operations. Stage 5 requires Formal Operations and the vast majority of adults do not operate in formal operations.

This is not about adults being dumb. It's about our not having learned to operate with formal operations. Formal operations occur in three forms (thus the term formal): syllogisms, formal conceptual frameworks, and paradigms. Most adults do not know the rules required to construct syllogisms. But they can learn them and they can learn to analyze and evaluate syllogisms. Adults can learn to judge for themselves the truth or validity of syllogisms.

Formal conceptual frameworks are typically created by adults who have experience in and have thought a lot about a topic. They're not so easy to create, but they really help others learn and think about a topic. When we use a formal conceptual framework, we're able to think about what we have not experienced and think about how we think about the topic. We can think in formal operations by learning the formal conceptual frameworks that others have designed.

Both the stages of cognitive development and moral development are formal conceptual frameworks. They help us think about how we think about cognitive and moral development. In the next chapter, I provide a formal conceptual framework that helps us think about Public Theology.

PART II

RELIGION, HUMANISM AND PUBLIC DISCOURSE

Pat's Notes

Because We the People argue about what laws and policies our government ought to make, we argue about what We the People should and should not do. All religions are also interested in what people should and should not do. As a result, religious beliefs are often used in the arguments that We the People conduct in the public square. The First Amendment of the U.S. Constitution prohibits the government from establishing a religion. It makes sense that We the People cannot use religious beliefs when creating public laws. To do so would be to establish a religion. But nothing is ever quite that simple. We the People must be able to think, talk, and make decisions regarding the place of religion in our public arguments.

Many Americans have no interest in religion which is not a problem unless they're confronted by deeply held religious beliefs that have made their way into the public square. Or when large and powerful religious groups like Catholics and Baptists have joined a political party and received financial backing by its major financiers to advance shared political agendas. How do the rest of

33

us even have a conversation, let alone productive arguments, with such an alliance? We all need to understand enough about religion to think, talk, and decide what its role is in the public square. That is what we do in Chapter 4.

Religious and secular humanism share common roots and have contributed a great deal to American government and public life. Humanism is indispensable to the social contract. In Chapter 5 we look at attacks on humanism and reestablish its place in public life as one step in healing our fractured body politic.

4

Public Theology and American Politics

So here I sit, working on a chapter about religion in America, quite confident that many of my readers have little interest in religion. Let me make this whole discussion more simple by clarifying what we're talking about and what we're not talking about. We're talking about arguments that We the People make in the public square in our attempt to identify the laws we will make that tell us what we must and must not do in public life. Representatives of different religions often want to make religious arguments that impact the arguments that We the People conduct. We must decide what kind of religious arguments have a place in the public square and what kind of religious arguments have no place in the public square.[14]

Ultimately, we must demand mature moral reasoning in the public square, and work to establish a place for it. That demand allows us to establish Stage 5 We the People moral reasoning standards for religious communities that wish to participate in discourse in the public square. If they can't meet or abide by those standards, they must confine their teaching and preaching to

---

[14] Full disclosure: I was raised in an Irish Catholic family. That's where I first learned about religion and Catholicism. My mother taught me to ask questions. I attended grade schools taught by the Sisters of St. Joseph of Newark and the Sisters of the Holy Names, a Jesuit high school, and the University of Notre Dame which is run by the Congregation of the Holy Cross. John Dunne, CSC, taught me to think about and study my religion and other religions. I did not ask Catholic bishops for permission to publish this book.

their own community, or to what I call the religious square. They're protected by the First Amendment. They're free to practice their religion and adhere to their beliefs in private and in their religious communities. And they must adhere to the American tradition of the separation of church and state. They must agree not to try to impose their religious beliefs on the public and certainly not attempt to make laws that impose those beliefs on the public.

We can't be satisfied with kicking religion out of the public square. The Constitution prohibits the government from establishing a religion. But it also guarantees religious freedom. We seek to find an appropriate place for religion in the public square. Religion, not a religion. We must create the principles that separate religion from the public square and the principles that include it. To do that, we figure out how to think in what I call Public Theology. But to understand Public Theology, we have to know a bit about religion in America. To assist that understanding, I have constructed a formal conceptual framework for Public Theology. Formal conceptual frameworks help us think about how we think. Importantly, our formal conceptual framework will help those of us who have no interest in religion, as well as those of us who are religious, to think about Public Theology.

What is Religion?

"Religion" means many things to many people. What interests us is religion's capacity to answer questions regarding the meaning of life, especially in the face of death, and tell its members what they must do and not do to fulfill that meaning. Some might argue that religion is most important in teaching people to do good and avoid evil. It also provides the motivation to do good and avoid evil. Most religions in the West promise the ultimate reward of eternal life in heaven. Eternal life provides the meaning of this life as we live it and as we face death. Religion's promise of eternal life motivates us to do what is right and not do what is wrong.

However, not all religions agree on many of the moral questions that most demand our attention in the public square. Birth control and abortion. They do not agree. The death penalty. They do not agree. LGBT rights. They do not agree. Use of the military. They do not agree. Civil rights. They do not agree. We could go on. And it's more than the mere fact that they disagree. They rely on different sacred texts or different interpretations of the same sacred texts to assert their views. Arguments can't be productive if they're grounded in fundamental disagreement. That's a huge point. I better support it. John Courtney Murray is one of America's most influential moral philosophers. Here is what he had to say about agreement and productive arguments:

> The whole premise of the public argument . . . is that the consensus is real, that among the people everything is not in doubt, but that there is a core of agreement . . . We hold certain truths; therefore we can argue about them . . . . There can be no argument except on the premise . . . of agreement . . . . This is true of scientific, philosophical, and theological argument. It is no less true of political argument.[15]

If there is no basis for agreement, no matter the content and context of our arguments, there is no chance of conducting productive discourse. We can express our different opinions, but if there is no basis of agreement, we can't get anywhere. And this is true, *mutatis mutandis,*[16] regardless of the topic or the discipline in which it occurs. That's why so much political argument is unproductive. Why it ends in hardening and widening positions and not a real consensus. That's a major reason why our country is so divided with what appears to be no hope of reuniting. We haven't established the foundation of agreement required to conduct productive arguments. We're going to fix that. Fr. Murray, being a good Jesuit, offered Catholic solutions. We produce American solutions.

---

[15] *We Hold these Truths: Catholic Reflections on the American Proposition,* (p. 10).

[16] *Mutatis mutandis* is Latin and is used when we're saying the same thing about different topics and recognize that there are unnamed differences that don't change our point. I sneak it into the text one more time.

But to fix it, we need to be able to think in Public Theology, and we must be able to think about how we think. Thinking about how we think requires a formal conceptual framework.

A Formal Conceptual Framework for Public Theology

I have developed a targeted conceptual framework. I have not tried to account for all of the hypotheses possible when thinking about public theology. This is not a paradigm. Rather, I have identified major concepts that impact how different religions might participate in public arguments and organized them in a

A Formal Conceptual Framework for Public Theology
Intellectual Tradition:
Anti-intellectual.
Intellectual tradition in which moral theology is the focus.
Intellectual tradition in which moral theology and moral philosophy are the focus.
Basic Concept of the Nature of Humans
Humans are fundamentally corrupt, unworthy of redemption.
Humans are born innocent and learn to seek either good or evil.
Basic Concept of Redemption and Spiritual Fulfillment:
Redemption is a status, it occurs as an event in the relationship between the person and God.
Redemption is a process that begins with the person committing to God but is completed in spiritual fulfillment and living the good life.
Public Engagement and Responsibility
Has nothing to do with redemption and a spiritual life.
Is an extension of redemption, a key to living a good life and to spiritual development.

way that helps us think about them. It is designed to help We the People think about how we think about different religious assertion that are made in the public square.

Various religious traditions have different intellectual traditions, basic concepts regarding the nature of humans, basic concepts of redemption and spiritual fulfillment, and different expectations of their members' engagement in society. Our formal conceptual framework allows us to think about these differences independent of the teachings of any one religion. We don't look at religion from the point of view of any religion. We look at all religions from a public point of view.

Using our formal conceptual framework, it's pretty easy for us to make judgments about different religious views. Some are incapable of participating in the public square. Being anti-intellectual undermines full intellectual development. Believing that humans are by nature corrupt and unworthy of redemption, undermines a commitment to the dignity and worth of all humans. Believing that redemption has nothing to do with helping others, undermines any sense of citizenship. Americans who hold such beliefs undermine the work We the People must do in the public square. I call these Christians Status Christians[17] and distinguish them from evangelicals who do have an intellectual tradition, who believe that all humans are inherently good, and most of all believe that their religion challenges them to bring Christ's message into this world, to the benefit of all mankind.

Status Christians have little to contribute to discourse in the public square. We the People can agree without hesitation or apology to tell these people that we defend their right to their beliefs and that we have no interest in any arguments they wish to make in the public square based on those religious assumptions. They have a secure place in their religious communities but no place in the public square so long as they only speak from those religious views.

---

[17] I am indebted to Stanley Hauerwas, *Truthfulness and Tragedy*, P. 83, for his insight into the language of status in theology and religion. This usage of "status" has nothing to do with "status quo."

And we must do more that acknowledge their right to exist. That's a bit cold and impersonal. They too are our fellow Americans, and if we're going to tell them to keep their religious beliefs to themselves, the least we can do is demonstrate respect and care for their experiences and their beliefs. Hymns provide a great window into their experiences of God in their lives. I will cite just a few.

Amazing Grace

Amazing grace! how sweet the sound,
That saved a wretch; like me!

For those of us who have sinned or debauched or lived lives that shame us in our own minds, this genre of spiritual music describes religion that can heal the sin sick soul. It's to be admired.

How Great Thou Art

And when I think of God, His Son not sparing
Sent Him to die, I scarce can take it in
That on the Cross, my burden gladly bearing
He bled and died to take away my sin.

God so loves the world that he sent his only begotten son to die for us. If that's what someone believes, it's only to be admired, maybe envied. Like Camus, we can wish that we could believe even though we cannot. Those are universally known hymns. This one maybe not so much, but it's worth knowing so that we can connect with believers.

What a Friend We Have in Jesus

O what peace we often forfeit,
O what needless pain we bear,
All because we do not carry
Everything to God in prayer!

> Do thy friends despise, forsake thee?
> Take it to the Lord in prayer;
> In His arms He'll take and shield thee,
> Thou wilt find a solace there.

These hymns resonate with all Christians, regardless of their intellectual traditions, definition of redemption, and so on. Still, We the People must establish rules of engagement in the Public Square. We cannot tolerate Stage 3 Tribal moral reasoning and we cannot tolerate religious beliefs that have no foundation in reason. We the People must think and act like grownups. We must insist upon mature cognitive development and mature moral development. Both are impossible for any religion or group that is anti-intellectual for to be anti-intellectual means that one rejects mature reasoning and mature moral reasoning.

There is a long history of anti-intellectual religious communities staying out of American politics. Working in their communities, but outside of politics. We're interested in when and why they changed and got into politics. Let's get to know a bit about anti-intellectualism in American religion and then we will look at:

Public Engagement and Responsibility in Evangelical Christianity.

Status Christianity and How It became Political.

The Political Alliance of Republicans and Status Christian.

Anti-Intellectualism in American Religions

America was not founded as a Christian nation, but the colonies were founded as Christian colonies. The colonies established religion. By 1702, all 13 American colonies provided some form of state support for religion, from tax benefits to religious requirements for voting or serving in the legislature. Seven of the thirteen colonies had established churches. These colonies not only supported their churches, they prohibited religious practice or proselytizing by other religions within their colonies.

The Pilgrims, who were Calvinists, established the Congregational church in Connecticut, Massachusetts and New Hampshire. Later colonists enjoyed financial backing from England and not surprisingly established the Anglican Church (the Church of England) in their colonies: New York, Virginia, Maryland, and the Carolinas. These colonies levied taxes that supported their parishes, ministers, and priests.

The major established religions were Anglicanism and Congregationalism. Anglicanism is part of the Church of England with its intellectual ties to Oxford and Cambridge. Congregationalism grew out of John Calvin's highly intellectual theology.

Evangelical Christianity emerged much later than Congregationalism and Anglicanism, during the 18th century, but before the American Revolution. Evangelicals relied on John Wycliffe's claim that everything anyone needs to gain salvation is contained in the bible. Evangelical preachers took bible in hand and preached to frontier communities. Their influence grew during what has come to be called the First Great Awakening. They were fervent, fundamentalists Christians. They rejected the established churches, their ministers, and their wealth for not being adequately Christian and sought to restore individual piety and religious fervor.

Evangelicalism came to stay, but the political control of the established religions in the colonies limited its spread. All of that changed with the American Revolution, the Declaration of Independence, the U.S. Constitution, and especially the Bill of Rights' First Amendment. The First Amendment forbids the government from establishing religion. The First Amendment forced states (former colonies) to disestablish, to remove public support for, their established religions.

Baptists were the most persecuted of the unestablished churches. By the time the Colonies revolted against the King of England, Baptists supported religious liberty and the separation of church and state. Evangelicals supported and benefitted from the separation of church and state. It provided the legal protection they needed to grow and expand.

What a break for evangelicals! Now free to preach and practice anywhere, evangelicalism witnessed the Second Great Awakening. Baptists and Methodists led the movement, and by 1820 evangelical membership had risen rapidly. It's a bit ironic that in the 21st century, evangelicals insist that America was founded as a Christian country, their kind of Christian, and seek to undermine the First Amendment and establish their religious beliefs in America. The First Amendment saved them from the seven colony's established religions. How can they ignore their own history? Of course, a handy effect of anti-intellectualism includes not knowing one's own history and not having any need to incorporate such history into one's doctrines felt as facts.

That's the political story. Importantly, 18th century evangelical preachers did not reject the Anglican and Congregationalist intellectual traditions on any intellectual grounds. They just ignored them. They were more a-intellectual than anti-intellectual. They did not have enough in common with Protestant theologians even to argue with them. They read their bibles and gave rousing sermons that were easily accessible to the rough and tumble pioneers and settlers who were their major audience. They enjoyed the unconscious habits of mind that had persisted in England and America since John Wycliffe (mid 1320's – 1384) taught that each person, each individual, has access to salvation through the study of scripture.

The anti-intellectualism came later, as an unintended consequence, and for us in a dramatically unexpected place. Princeton University was associated with John Calvin and the Presbyterian Church. In the late 19th century, theologians at Princeton's divinity school engaged in arguments with Congregationalist scholars at Yale's divinity school and New York's Union Theological Seminary about the nature of the bible and the best way to interpret it. Scripture scholars at Yale and Union had been influenced by German scholars who used a kind of literary method to study scripture. They believed that the bible is written in symbolic language that must be studied, like literature, to be properly interpreted. They sought to understand who wrote various biblical text and in what historical context. It made for really interesting scholarship, but it also raised questions about the authority and authenticity of the bible.

The boys at Princeton would have nothing to do with it. They insisted that the bible is the word of God and must be interpreted literally,[18] that every word is true and if one word is proved wrong the whole edifice collapses.[19] It bears noting that Princeton was tied to Calvinism.[20] The defense of Calvinism is entirely biblical, both Old and New Testament. It postulates a cruel and unmerciful God and defies human reason. It hangs its hat entirely on scripture. Such dependence on scripture requires the absolute truth of scripture. Princeton's theologians understood that they had to stick to their fundamentalist guns or give up their entire theology.

The usual arguments arose: Which bible is absolutely and completely true? Which translation? In which language? Obviously, replied the Princeton authorities, the original texts, those that were first written down. And they stuck to that conclusion. The problem was that virtually none of the original texts of the various books of the bible exist. So the boys at Princeton hung their claim to the absolute, literal interpretation of the bible on imaginary texts. No wonder Princeton soon abandoned both its Calvinist ties and fundamentalist beliefs. To maintain them, they would have had to abandon any claim to reason.

Conveniently, fundamentalist preachers did not participate in these arguments. They were a-intellectual. And that indifference to their intellectual history and to intellectual arguments allowed them to insist upon the literal interpretations of the bible to their flocks without having to deal with their inability to support their

---

[18] Let that settle in. In the late 1800s, less than 50 years before Einstein moved to Princeton, the Princeton divinity school was obdurately fundamentalist Christian.

[19] Well, at least that's consistent with the grand tradition of mathematics at Princeton and the Mathematics School in the Institute for Advanced Studies in Princeton, New Jersey.

[20] For more on Calvinism, see: Steele, David N. and Curtis C. Thomas; *The Five Points of Calvinism: Defined, Defended, Documented*, 1963. The story of Yale's theological journey is too long to tell here, but today it's clear that both Yale and Princeton have moved on from Calvinism. Many fundamentalists have not.

view on any rational, scholarly grounds. It's important to remember how ironic it is that fundamentalist preachers bring their bibles into the public square and, supported by the voting block they represent, insist that laws be written that support their fundamentalist views of scripture. It would be profoundly hypocritical if they knew how they distort and abandon their own history.

We tend to think that Jerry Falwell and the Moral Majority marked the beginning of fundamentalist Christians being active in the public square. But it's actually a longer story which We the People benefit from knowing and which Jerry Falwell conveniently both ignored and exploited. He ignored it in his preaching and exploited it in his strategies and tactics.

Public Engagement and Responsibility in Evangelical Christianity

During the Second Great Awakening, evangelicals divided into two branches. One branch thought of and experienced redemption as a personal event, a status: Have you accepted Jesus Christ as your personal savior? We're all sinners, but once we call upon Jesus to save us, accept Jesus as our personal savior, we're saved. Period. Done. Scripture supports this view. Romans 10:13, "For whosoever shall call upon the name of the Lord shall be saved." However, We the People must be aware of this unique development in Christianity: The language of redemption became an experience of status rather than a revelation of what individuals and the church must do to bring Christ into this world. Status: this is who I am. I am saved.

The other branch of evangelicals thought of and experienced redemption as a process. First, I get baptized (and/or declare that Jesus is my personal savior), but then I must live a life that brings Christ into the world. Dallas Willard taught me the importance of this view in evangelical religions. Here is how he described it:

> Through the Grace of the Holy Spirit I have been welcomed into the family of Christ and I must live my

life in a way that brings Christ into the lives of others, now, in this life.[21]

This view also has a scriptural source, The Lord's Prayer: "Thy kingdom come, Thy will be done, on earth as it's in heaven." On earth. God's kingdom is not just for the hereafter. It's to be realized by the spread of Christianity on earth. Huge challenge! Not only are we saved by baptism or accepting Jesus as our personal savior, we have a duty to do the work required to bring God's kingdom, God's will, to earth. To remake this life into the life God wants for all of us.

This branch of evangelical Christianity provides an archetype of Christian humanism. These Christians charged themselves with improving social conditions in their communities. They cared for the poor; helped children, widows, and orphans; reformed prisons; built hospitals; and most telling of all, they opposed slavery. The abolition movement in the north was led by Christian humanists, both from major Protestant denominations and among these evangelical Christians.[22]

These two branches of evangelical Christianity lived side by side and indeed prayed together in the same denominations. Baptists and Methodists included both of these branches of evangelical Christianity. Until the mid eighteen hundreds when slavery and abolition divided the country and these denominations.

The Southern Baptist Convention (SBC) emerged in slave states and left the Baptist Church. Whatever their previous stance had been on social engagement, Southern Baptists stood for slavery. The same divide occurred among Methodist, another large national congregation. Some have called Methodists the Liberation Theologians of the Industrial Revolutions, comparing them to

---

[21] *The Divine Conspiracy: Rediscovering Our Hidden Life in God*, 1998. Willard not only talks of bringing Christ into this world, he illuminates the transformative power of Christ and the Holy Spirit in our lives in this world. He was kind to me.

[22] In 1850, Catholics made up only five percent of the total U.S. population.

the late 20th century Catholic humanists in South America. A separate and different southern Methodist tradition took its stand in support of slavery, but did not rename itself.

Supporting slavery requires a theology that denies the full humanity of those who are enslaved. That's how slavery and racism are justified: They aren't really human. We understand the depth of this denial of the full humanity of African Americans. First supporters of slavery reduced African Americans to just their biological domains and insisted that they were not fully human biologically. After that, they refused, simply could not admit at all to the other domains of their humanity, to the person and the self of each and every African American.

With this in mind, we can begin to sense the full horrors of slavery and racism that these religious groups justified throughout the South. They did not just brutalize these human beings, they destroyed families and friendships, and prohibited basic civil rights. Segregation separated the races, which made it impossible for whites to have the relationships with blacks that would allow them to experience the person of blacks. It crushed their awareness of social, psychological and spiritual domains of black people, no matter how well developed they were. That African Americans have thrived in all of these domains of humanity is a testament to their nobility and endurance, and to their moral and psychological superiority over those who oppressed them.

Virtually all Southern Baptists and southern Methodists came out of the redemption tradition that was instantaneous, personal, gave them a special status; that did not require that they engage in public life. These are the Status Christians, the same Christians who supported slavery and Jim Crow laws and joined the Ku Klux Klan. And they're the same Christians who in the 1950s and 60s opposed civil rights, voting rights, free speech, the right to assemble and protest. And they're the same Christians who from the 1970s on have opposed gay and lesbian rights, women's rights, and the integration of public schools. They did not take these stands in support of the status quo. They took them from their position of Stage 3 Tribal moral reasoning that endowed their group with the status of being saved and set their group in opposition to everyone else whom they considered damned. These they viewed as others.

America has two major strands of evangelical Christianity that interest us: Status Christians and Christian Humanists. It's important to recognize these two groups. The evangelical tradition has thrived throughout Christianity: "Go forth and teach all nations," (Matthew, 28:19). We will talk about Christian Humanists in the next chapter. But now let's look at the politicization of Status Christians who are fundamentalist, anti-intellectual, evangelical, and deny any social responsibilities in their status as fully and permanently redeemed.

How Status Christianity became Political

In Lynchburg, Virginia, Jerry Falwell, a Southern Baptist preacher, made an interesting discovery. He had built a successful church and enjoyed the radio station he had created to spread the Word. He enthusiastically accepted the challenge of raising funds needed to keep his radio station going. He discovered that instead of targeting Nixon's silent majority he could teach his listeners to self-identify as the Moral Majority,[23] set them in opposition to liberals and secular humanists, and raise a ton of money. The Moral Majority demonized the humanitarian causes from the 1950s and 60s as secular humanism, ignoring the fact that their greatest support and leadership had come from religious humanists.[24] Falwell and the Moral Majority defined secular humanism as a threat to the Christian America that they believed, contrary to all historical evidence, Jesus intended America to be. Falwell proved that you can be intelligent and anti-intellectual, especially if it helps achieve your goals. You can have mature cognitive development coupled with immature moral development. This is not another example of a stupid commitment to ignorance. Rather, it's a cunning commitment to ignorance.

---

[23] A term Paul Weyrich helped him coin. We will visit Weyrich later.

[24] Humanism in grounded in both Judaic and Christian as well as secular traditions.

Jerry Falwell fell into political activity when he discovered that opposing secular humanism and the activist movements of the 1950s and 60s resonated with many of the folks who listened to him on his nationally syndicated radio show, Old Time Gospel Hour. Falwell was a Status Christian. He taught that only Jesus saves, and that once we're saved, we're saved forever with no social responsibility. Conveniently, Status Christians do not suffer "fear of the Lord." Their evil deeds do not threaten their eternal salvation.

Martin Luther King Jr. was the archetypal Christian humanist. He believed that every Christian must pursue salvation by working to bring the kingdom of God into this life. He supported the humanists movements of the 1950s and 60s through political action. Falwell used political action to spread the anti-humanism of Status Christianity. He fought for religious freedom that would allow religious schools to remain segregated. And that fight, for segregated religious schools, may have been the single greatest source of Falwell's success at rallying popular support among southern Status Christians.

In Green v. Kennedy, 1970, the U.S. District Court for the District of Columbia, found for plaintiffs who claimed that religious schools that were created to subvert the integration of public schools should not be allowed tax exempt status. The court granted a preliminary injunction that removed that status and also denied tax deductions for donations to those schools. Later that year, the Internal Revenue Service denied tax exempt status to all segregated schools in the United States. All this was based on 1954's Brown v Board of Education and the Civil Rights Act of 1964. Once again, southern Status Christians fought a racist battle, and this time, Jerry Falwell was their leader.

We can explain Falwell's interest in politics, the nature of his interest and how it came about. And we can understand how it grew in league with Pat Robertson and others. But how did it become such a major political force? How did southern Status Christians become politically powerful? Paul Weyrich and Barry Goldwater help tell that story.

The Political Alliance of Republicans and Status Christians

Barry Goldwater led a staggering political defeat in 1964, not just in his run for President but for the Republican party in Congress. Republicans had been out of power during the Presidency of FDR and beyond, from 1933 to 1953, and had lost again to John F. Kennedy in 1960 and Lyndon Johnson in 1964. They had to do something or they could be out of power for another generation, or more. Nixon had won in 1968, but by the narrowest of margins and even that victory was due far more to the chaos of the Democratic National Convention in Chicago than the country's approval of Nixon. And then there was Watergate and Nixon's impeachment and resignation. Jimmy Carter won in 1976 and was threatening to win a second election in 1980. From 1964 on, Republicans became increasingly desperate to do two things: First, they had to reject the humanism that had emerged in the 1950s and 60s. Politically, the humanism of the 1950s and 60 was an extension of FDR's humanism that had been enormously popular during and after the depression, especially throughout the south. Attacking the so called secular humanism of the 1950s and 60s provided Republicans with the opportunity, finally, to get Status Christians to reject the previously unassailable programs and policies of FDR. And second, they had to broaden the Republican political base. Barry Goldwater exposed the crisis. Paul Weyrich found the solutions.

Paul Weyrich was a pre-Vatican II Catholic. In other words, he rejected the liberal changes Pope John XXIII (1958-63) had brought to the Church during Vatican II. Weyrich rejected those changes and supported the reactionary policies of the popes between John the XXIII and Pope Francis. From 1963 to 2013, the Catholic Church was led by right wing popes who reversed much of the good of Vatican II. The most powerful anti-Vatican II figure of the time was Cardinal Ratzinger, later Pope Benedict XVI. In 1981, John Paul II appointed Ratzinger Prefect of the

Congregation of the Faith.[25] Ratzinger led the Vatican's fights against the ordination of women, birth control, abortion, gay rights, and even the punishment of Seattle's Archbishop Hunthausen for his opposition to nuclear weapons. He had a hand in making Catholic universities subject to the authority of local bishops in the teaching of theology in spite of the bishops' lack of academic qualifications. He suppressed democracy within the church in favor of papal authority. He participated in the cover-up of sex abuses within the church. Those were the guys Weyrich supported. To our point, pre-Vatican II Catholics like Weyrich are far more interested in using the authority of Rome to reject socialism and support radical capitalism than in bringing the kingdom of God into this world.

Weyrich helped lead the American Catholic Church's move to the political right and its opposition to Christian humanism. American Catholic universities, intimidated by the Vatican, did little to oppose the Vatican and Weyrich's anti-humanism. Their silence did much to support it.

But back to our story of the political alliance between Republicans and Status Christians.[26] In 1971, Weyrich went to Lynchburg and met with Falwell. He helped coin the term, Moral Majority, and begin that movement. He convinced Falwell to get political. Most important, he helped funnel money to Falwell's radio station and the Moral Majority. Their goal was to mobilize the discontent among southern white Status Christians against the religious and secular humanists' goals of the 1950s and 60s, and the desegregation of public schools. Christian schools became a huge wedge issue following the U. S. Supreme Court's decision in Coit v Green, 1971, that upheld Green v Kennedy's denial of tax exempt status to all-white schools. Status Christians were easy to organize and Republicans began to build their new base among them.

---

[25] Previously known as The Inquisition. Same offices in the Vatican, new name.
[26] Randall Balmer, "The Real Origins of the Religious Right," *Politico Magazine*, May 27, 2014.

But they also needed to do something about the intellectual and political foundations of humanism and America's tradition as a constitutional liberal democracy. Let's talk briefly about America as a liberal democracy. We know we have a Constitution, we're a Republic, and we're a democracy. All of that's in the Constitution. But is our democracy liberal? The American Revolution, Declaration of Independence, and U. S. Constitution rejected old world monarchies. The French Revolution was inspired by the American Revolution. Both the U.S. and France became models of liberal democracies. England limped along, maintaining its monarchy but evolving as a parliamentary government and qualifying as a liberal democracy, albeit without a constitution. But neither our Founding Fathers nor the French used the term liberal democracy, so where did the term come from?

John Stuart Mill (1806-1873) codified modern liberalism. Some readers may have to get used to thinking of the terms liberal and liberalism as good. Some may even have to fight a strongly held doctrine felt as fact that anything liberal is far left and headed for communism. Learning about Mill helps remove that doctrine felt as fact and more. It helps us recognize, understand, and care about our liberal democracy. Mill was born after the American and French revolutions and he benefitted from knowing what the leaders of those revolutions stood for. He set down in writing the political principles that others had worked out in practice. That's no mean contribution to political philosophy and political life because it helps societies educate their members on the basic principles of their government.

So what are the principles and goals that define a liberal democracy?

Liberty and equality
Freedom of speech, press, religion, and markets
Civil rights, secular government, gender equity
International cooperation and multilateralism[27].

---

[27] In international relations, multilateralism refers to an alliance of multiple countries pursuing a common goal.

Mill did not invent the goals. Jefferson and Madison get credit for their invention. But Mill invented the term Liberal Democracy and defined it the way Jefferson and Madison had defined the American form of government. Which means that we're talking about the definition of America's government: It's a Constitutional Liberal Democracy, or Liberal Democracy for short.

It's more than a political definition. It goes to the heart of whom we are as Americans. It forms an essential component of our identity, of our sense of who We the People are when we meet and argue about what laws and policies we should make.

Obviously, some of those principles support major Republican goals: Liberty, free markets, secular governments, international cooperation, and multilateralism. Others not so much. And it was the others that concerned Weyrich: Equality; freedom of speech, press, and religion; civil rights; and gender equity. And of course government taxation and regulation of business and finance.

In 1973, Weyrich convinced Joseph Coors of the Coors Brewing Company family to help fund the Heritage Foundation specifically to counter liberal views on taxation and regulation. The Heritage Foundation has become one of the world's largest public policy "research" institutes and, along with other conservative think tanks, has successfully advanced conservative policies in government, universities, and the media.

"Research." The goal of the Heritage Foundation has never been to conduct research, the dispassionate search for truth. It has always been to develop arguments that support the economic and political goals of radical capitalists and oppose the arguments that support liberal, humanistic goals. It's true that arguments for liberal, humanistic goals were often promoted in universities, the media, and most forcefully among 1950s and 60s activists. Frustrated by what they perceived as the liberal bias of universities and the media, Weyrich and Coors established the Heritage Foundation to wage a propaganda campaign that supports their special interests.

Let's talk about propaganda for a moment. Propaganda is misleading information (therefore it must be distinguished from information) used to promote or publicize a particular political cause or point of view. It's not based on dispassionate inquiry. It's grounded in the goals of a particular group that's sufficiently rich and powerful to wage both national and regional propaganda campaigns. It operates at Stage 3 moral reasoning. It's tribal. It seeks laws that create advantages for its group at the expense of everyone else. One can legitimately promote or publicize a particular political cause or point of view with information, but the information must be true and its sources transparent. That's not propaganda. Propaganda is misleading or downright false and it's political. It promotes or publicizes a particular political cause or point of view that favors a small but powerful group.

Propaganda supports privilege. Privilege is an interesting word. To be granted a privilege is to be granted a right, but looking deeper at the words meaning, we discover that privilege comes from two Latin words: *privus* "individual" and *lex* "law," meaning an advantage granted in law to an individual or group of individuals[28] to their benefit and the disadvantage of others not included in that group. Privilege is a legal and institutional application of Stage 3 Tribal moral reasoning. It's easy to see why those who are privileged fight to retain their privilege: Once lost, it's nearly impossible to regain. And it's easy to see why they employ propaganda to preserve their privilege. Political privilege by definition cannot survive rational scrutiny.

The goal of the Heritage Foundation and similar foundations that followed it isn't to aid discourse in the pursuit of the truth or of what is right and wrong in public policy. They exist to fortify within both the Democratic and Republican Party arguments aimed at promoting the political causes and points of view of radical capitalists. In order to accommodate these views and reap the political benefits they presented, the Republican Party changed. It abandoned many of its most strongly held political traditions. It gave in to radical capitalists. So did the Democratic Party, but not as much and some Democrats seem to be trying to bring the Party back to its roots.

Let's talk briefly about radical capitalists here. We will look at them extensively in Chapter 9, Economic Justice but I use the

---

[28] Online Etymology Dictionary.

term extensively and it demands some 'splainin'. Radical capitalists seek to create laws and policies that make them richer with no regard for the welfare of everyone else. Traditional capitalists believe that a rising tide lifts all boats and work toward that end. They promote laws and policies that help capitalists improve their lives and the lives of everyone else and the health of the nation. As we will see when we get deeper into this discussion in the Chapter 9, radical capitalism traces its history back to the economic theory that European monarchs employed from the 16th to the 18th century. It was called mercantilism. Our Founding Fathers did not just reject the monarchical form of government and replace it with what we call a liberal democracy. They rejected mercantilism and replaced it with capitalism. Today's radical capitalists seek a return to mercantilism by corrupting our liberal democracy to their advantage. They undermine both our traditional democracy and traditional capitalism.

Radical capitalists have taken over the Republican Party, destroyed the careers of traditional Republican politicians and traditional Republican values. They seek to undermine humanism and liberal democracy in America in pursuit of the long established goals of mercantilism. These radical capitalists set out to market their goals – marketing and advertising. That would be well and good if they adhered to fair marketing practices and truth in advertising principles. But they have gone far beyond presenting their views to the public. They have used psychological tools aimed at secreting their values in the minds of the public without rational discourse or scrutiny. These guys know what they want to do and how to do it. It's one thing when they're selling life style and materialism. It's another when they undermine the core values of our liberal democracy and traditional capitalism.

We talked earlier about entropy, the gradual decline of order in any system. Scientists discovered that natural entropy occurs with no expense of energy. That can also be true of social and political systems. They too can decline, without any application of energy, if energy is not applied to maintain them. But here we have a different and far more powerful kind of entropy. Here we witness radical capitalists applying enormous energy and resources to destroying the foundations of our liberal democracy because they stand in the way of their goal to retain the privileges of radical capitalists. The reader can refer below to A Formal Conceptual Framework for Economics located in Chapter 9. In it, I distinguish radical capitalism and radical capitalists from traditional American capitalism and capitalists.

Rev. Falwell and other Status Christian leaders were able to grow their communities among southern Status Christians with their long history of racism and demand for segregation. This group can be traced to the Dixiecrats who supported states rights and opposed any federal attempts to expand civil rights to minorities. It's the group President Johnson knew he lost when he signed the Civil Rights Act and the Voting Rights Act. These mostly southern voters' goals have nothing to do with their material needs. They seem addicted to the psychological rewards of feeling superior to people who often have vastly superior talent and intellect. The southern planter class started building this political base during Reconstruction, took it to a whole new level during Jim Crow, and handed it off to the emerging far right wing of the Republican Party after 1964. Think the John Birch Society and the far right organizations that have followed. They have rejected traditional Republican views and values.

But there was another group that forms an important part of the new Republican base. These are ordinary Americans who viewed the activist movements of the 1950s and 60s from the perspective of their pride and confidence in the country that had just defeated the Nazis and Imperial Japan. They were law abiding and patriotic and they were horrified by the violence and disorder in which the humanists of the 1950s and 60s were forced to play out their activism. They could not identify with the activists and found no excuse for the violence and disorder that they appeared to have caused.

These Americans still believed in that old time religion and law and order. Republicans expanded their base by appealing to these sincere people whose racism is best understood as doctrines felt as facts, unconscious habits of mind so unexamined and fixed that they're in total denial of them. They don't feel their hatred for African Americans (as long as African Americans behave). It's an inherited part of their culture, their persons and selves, of who they are. They deny the full humanity of African Americans as individuals, their biological natures, and what follows is complete ignorance and indifference to the full humanity of African Americans.

And they do not have sympathy for the demands of women and certainly not of the LGBT community.

The longevity of this political base depended on propaganda that told the story of the 1950s and 60s. To understand this source of our fractured body politic, we need to understand what happened in the 1950s and 60s. And to heal our body politic, we need to recapture the spirit and moral certitude of that time. We turn to that discussion now.

5
Religious Humanism and the Long Sixties

We have looked at the politicization of Status Christianity. Now we must turn to religious humanism and its impact on the American body politic.

Religious humanism opposed slavery. Religious humanism supported the Progressive movement of the late 19th and early 20th centuries that ended the dominance of the Robber Barons. Religious humanism supported FDR's policies that helped end the Great Depression and the suffering that attended it. Religious humanism supported the Allies in World War II. American Religious Humanism supported Civil Rights, Free Speech, Intellectual Freedom, Human Rights, and Anti-Vietnam War activists from the 1950s and into the 1970s.

So how in did Jerry Falwell successfully mount a Status Christian movement against secular humanism that took out American religious humanism and vitiated the concept and values of humanism? Why were Falwell and his followers not shamed into silence when they attacked humanism? Humanism with its Jewish, Christian, and secular roots. How could Falwell and his followers have turned on humanism with impunity?

To understand Falwell's dreadful achievements, we must understand the 1950s and 60s. We also need to understand the 1950s and 60s to understand how our body politic became fractured. Then maybe we can repair it. If we can repair it, we can reestablish activism and public moral certitude within our body politic.

The Amazing and Tragic 60s

It's disconcerting to see young people hold 60s parties and dress up all weird, their impression of hippies. Or reduce any civil rights protests to "Kumbaya," softness and delusion. They can have no idea about the 60s if they haven't put anything at risk. But their misguided view of the 60s is not their fault. A lot of money and effort have gone into the propaganda campaigns that make the 60s look un-American, weak, and ridiculous. We must understand the 60's so that we can recapture the spirit and humanism that will allow us to heal our fractured body politic.

The term "Long 60s" helps, for the 60s certainly began before the 60s and lasted probably until the election of Ronald Reagan. Even to begin to understand the early 60s, we must understand that humanism provided its core values. All activists of the period asserted humanistic values and humanistic ends. But we must be careful with the term humanism. Some define it as: "A focus on the importance of human concerns rather than divine or supernatural matters." But that's better understood as atheistic humanism.[29] It ignores the vast tradition of religious humanism and the historical fact that much of Western humanism would not exist without Jewish and Christian contributions. This is a better definition:

> Humanism is a cultural phenomenon that activates moral reasoning, the social sciences, literature, poetry, music and dance to celebrate the basic goodness of human beings, demands the recognition of the dignity and worth of all humans, and seeks rational solutions to the problems shared within the human family.[30]

---

[29] There is a genre of atheists I call "radical left wing evangelical atheists." They can better serve the public square by concentrating on Stage 5 moral reasoning and their commitment to the morally grounded purposes of our liberal democracy than trying to win their arguments for atheism which belongs in the religious square.

[30] I like this definition a lot, and I am not sure if I wrote it or if I got it from someone else. If I stole it I apologize. I may have paraphrased it from work by Kareem Abdul Jabbar.

Humanism requires a commitment to work for the full development of each human, as an individual, person, and self. And it works for the full development of society and the human race. Humanism recognizes not just the potential of humans; it recognizes the inherent dignity and worth of all humans and their unalienable rights. Humanists commit to a process of human improvement and development. Humanism has both religious and secular roots and the two are natural allies, if they allow themselves to be. This chapter focuses on religious humanism. We look at secular humanism extensively in Part III.

Stanley Hauerwas is part of a group of theologians, many but not all Lutheran, who have studied the rise of Nazism in Hitler's Germany and the role that Christians played in it. His insights help us see ourselves, slavery, and racism and the role white Americans played in its rise and endurance.

> For the complicity of Christians with Auschwitz did not begin with their failure to object to the first slightly anti-Semitic laws and actions. It rather began when Christians assumed that they could be the heirs and carriers of the symbols of faith without sacrifice and suffering.[31]

At its core, the Civil Rights movement was deeply religious and humanistic. It sought the recognition of the full humanity of African Americans. It aimed at ending racial segregation and discrimination against African Americans. It sought to recognize the full humanity of African Americans and to grant them the full protection of the United States Constitution and federal laws.

The Civil Rights movement committed to peaceful activism, peaceful strategies, and peaceful tactics. Its length and intensity and tragedy resulted from the legal, social, and institutional opposition waged against it, often with shocking violence. The Civil Rights activists did not assume that they could be the heirs and carriers of their symbols of faith without sacrifice and suffering.

---

[31] *Truthfulness and Tragedy.*

We need to stop and think about what we just read. The African Americans, and the white Jews and Christians who joined them, did what the German Christians did not do when the Jews of Germany needed them. They stood and marched and acted. They were the heirs and carriers of the symbols of their faith in the face of and without running away from sacrifice and suffering and even death. They were the great carriers of the symbols and truth of their faith, maybe the greatest in the history of our nation. What other private citizens in our history can stand with them in courage and sacrifice? And they were scorned then and have been scorned since. They stand as the great manifestation of their faith in our public square and shame the Status Christians who reviled, repressed, and rejected the religious humanism for which they sacrificed so much. And they shame the vast number of Americans who have remained indifferent to them, their goals, their struggle, and their achievements.

If we want to understand the 60s, we must face and accept the violence and institutional opposition that peaceful movements endured. Those victimized by violence were brave beyond imagination; those who perpetrated the violence were screaming cowards.

Origins of 1960's Activism

Again, the 60s did not start in the 60s. It's helpful to remember that the 50's were not just about African Americans' take on American society. The Beat Generation came out of the 1940s and flourished in the 1950s. It has been caricaturized with images of beatniks, hip guys with goatees and gals with straight long hair and black leotards speaking their own hip language. It was actually a serious literary movement that impacted social norms in the 50s and inspired social activists in the early 60's.

Far less sensational, and probably more widely influential on the 60s, were films from the period. A few examples will suffice. In 1954, Jane Wyman and Rock Hudson joined forces in *Magnificent Obsession*. It was a radical film. It rejected materialism for unselfish commitment to those in need. It was a secular humanist film that won the praise of religious humanists and the emerging body of Americans who were becoming less and less religious but sought to maintain the humanism of their religious roots.

The next year, Wyman and Hudson appeared together again in *All That Heaven Allows,* in which white upper middle class culture took a gently portrayed but brutal beating. It forced at least some men, women, and young adults to think about what they value most in themselves and each other as human beings and the potential they all have for full human development.

Young white rebels was not an invention of the 60s. In 1955, *Rebel Without a Cause,* featured high school kids who were alienated from their parents and confronted by brutal, judgmental police. In it, James Dean rebelled heroically, Sal Mineo tragically, and Natalie Wood with an important if only emerging role for women.

The next year, 1956, Hudson returned, this time with Elizabeth Taylor in *Giant,* which exposed the vacuous culture of rich Texas oilmen and the brutal treatment suffered by Mexican Americans in Texas. Brown v. Board of Education in 1954 and Giant in 1956.

The women's movement and the sexual revolution also has roots in the 50s. There was that little, seldom remembered 1959 film *A Summer Place.* It dealt with teenage sex, pregnancy, family disruption, parental betrayal contrasted with parental love. Just a couple years later, when The Pill became available, young women took control of their bodies and sexuality.

We should not leave the 50s without some discussion of popular music. Elvis Presley. Ya want a little rebellion? Well, shake rattle and roll. Ya got it. Parents, pundits, preachers, and politicians freaked out, but the kids kept dancing, right into the 60s when a quartet from Liverpool made things even more lively.

Also important, and less well remembered, is the enormous popularity of folk music. Anti-capitalism, pro labor, pro farmer, pro poor ordinary people. Woodie Guthrie, Pete Seeger, Cisco Houston, The Weavers, Harry Belafonte, Odetta, Joan Baez all resonated with the humanistic mood that was emerging on college campuses. Bob Dylan carried the movement forward into the 60s and transformed folk into folk rock. Folk music also sought peace. Made a big deal of peace, peacefully, even gently. Joan

Baez introduced "Just a Little Rain" by saying that it was a protest song, that "it sounds gentle but does not protest gently." Music from the long 60's supported, encouraged, and sometimes led the period's humanistic movements.

The early 60s clearly started in the 50s. The early 50s were about social change, and a fitting starting point is Brown v. Board of Education, the Supreme Court's 1954 decision that outlawed racial segregation in America's public schools. But Brown did not start in 1954. It's more useful to think of Brown as part of the Civil Rights movement and of the Civil Rights movement as a descendant of the Harlem Renaissance.[32]

The Harlem Renaissance started in the 1920s and was known at the time as the "New Negro Movement." The Harlem Renaissance's goal was to reverse the disdain and indifference of white Americans to blacks. That bears repeating. There was a major movement in Harlem that began in the 1920's that set out to "reverse the disdain and indifference of white Americans to blacks." The Harlem Renaissance was not just about Jim Crow. It spoke to all white Americans. To our disdain and indifference to Black Americans. To our denying their full humanity as individual, person, and self. It achieved a cultural, social, and artistic explosion by Black America, but it had little impact on White America.

It was a movement intended to lead the African American community into full citizenship and acceptance and respect in their own country. At the time, blacks in the south suffered such sever oppression that they could not imagine change. But the incredible output of music, dance, poetry, literature, and scholarly writing that came out of Harlem got the attention of blacks everywhere in America and stirred their hopes and dreams and aspirations. Martin Luther King, Jr. was inspired by the Harlem Renaissance. The Harlem Renaissance may not have reversed the disdain and indifference of White Americans to blacks, but it had a huge impact on how Black Americans thought of themselves. Eventually, a critical mass of young white Americans got the message.

---

[32] Kareem Abdul-Jabbar; *On the Shoulders of Giants: My Journey Through the Harlem Renaissance.*

The Civil Rights Movement

By 1960, young African Americans had their leaders and their goals, their strategies, and their moral certitude. They had already sat in lunch counters, sat in the front of the bus, marched, suffered, and died. Martin Luther King, Jr. led the Civil Rights movement. Malcolm X focused on black pride and called out white racism in terms that shocked white America. He was not wrong, but he shocked white Americans who thought of themselves as above reproach. The greatest generation had a chink in its armor.

1963. The March On Washington was held that summer, August 28. Martin Luther King Jr. not only gave his *I Have a Dream* speech, he also warned America that the protests represented "the whirlwinds of revolt." Everyone should read it. It's one of the great American speeches. It's poorly named. Yes, he described his dream, toward the end. But more chillingly, he explained that he and the other marchers came "here today to dramatize a shameful condition." He talked about the "promissory note" to which the signers of the Constitution obligated the country and to which "every American was to fall heir." They promised that all men, yes all men white and black, and all women, are guaranteed life, liberty, and the pursuit of happiness. He insisted that the Declaration of Independence and the United States Constitution mean what they say. If you haven't read that speech, please do.

On, September 15, 1963, a conspiracy of Ku Klux Klan members bombed the Sixteenth Street Baptist Church in Birmingham, Alabama, killing four young girls: Addie Mae Collins, 14; Denise McNair, 11; Carole Robertson, 14; and Cynthia Wesley, 14. Birmingham was just one of over a hundred cities, some in the North, that endured protests that summer. Five months before that tragic event, Martin Luther King Jr. had been jailed in Birmingham. There he wrote *Letter from Birmingham Jail.*[33] In it he responded to ministers from around the country who had written

---

[33] Both MLK's I Have a Dream speech and Letter from Birmingham Jail are easily accessible on line. They are required reading for all members of America's body politic.

to him supporting his goals but questioning the timing of his protests. With it he established himself as one of the world's great moral thinkers of the twentieth century. Its timing and eloquence makes the slaughter of those little girls so heartbreaking and humiliating to white America as to be almost unbearable.

The election of John F. Kennedy as the 35th President heightened optimism for change; his assassination on November 22, 1963, shattered that optimism. White America began its journey toward lost innocence.

Lyndon B. Johnson followed Kennedy and used his abundant political skills to pass the Civil Rights Act in 1964. The Civil Rights Act prohibited racial discrimination in employment and education and outlawed segregation in public places.

The Civil Rights Act was supposed to bring change, but because African Americans were denied the right to vote in southern states, they had no recourse to local abuses of the Civil Rights Act. Elected officials and judges perpetuated abuses by the police and public, and blacks had no capacity to use the democratic process to correct those abuses. So they marched for Voting Rights. The institutionalized cowardice and violence against the peaceful protesters, the institutionalized inhumanity of man to man, seen on national television, forced Johnson and Congress to pass the Voting Rights Act. The Voting Rights Act of 1965 set strict federal rules protecting the rights of African Americans to vote. Yes, Johnson gets and deserves credit, but courageous activists forced his hand. Progressive activists living their religious humanism experienced the kind of affirmation that encourages action.

The dreadful lesson that black activists had taught the nation in the 50s and especially the early 60s was that WASPs[34] will

---

[34] WASPs, White Anglo Saxon Protestants. They founded the country, created and condoned slavery, ran industry, the courts, and the government. And by the early 60s, they were still the dominant political, economic, and cultural force in America, in spite of the enormous numbers of Chinese, German, Irish, Italian and other immigrants who had found a place in the country. It was time for a change and young white people named their opponent: WASPs. Young white adults found solidarity with black Americans: they were all oppressed by WASPs. And for a brief time they stood united.

change but only after peaceful protesters are met with, endure and prevail against violence from white police and citizens. The fact that institutionalized violence must be endured was not lost on white activists who opposed the war in Vietnam. African American protesters had taught young white people a chilling lesson: you cannot be the heirs and carriers of the symbols of your faith without courage, sacrifice, suffering, and death. How could the 60's possibly remain peaceful when peaceful protesters knew the stakes? When they faced and confronted, however peacefully, violent institutions? How could peace prevail in the face of white leaders who violently rejected human rights for the rights of the establishment? WASPs who had one set of laws for whites, a different set for African Americans and anti-war protesters and the Vietnamese people. For all the good WASPs had brought to our country, they sank into brutal failure as they became more and more tribal, more and more committed to Stage 3 moral reasoning.

The Vietnam War Protests, 1964 – 1973

The Vietnam War was fought to stop the spread of Communism. The Communist International (1919–1943), advocated world communism. It pledged to overthrow international capitalism and establish an international communist republic. It collapsed during World War II when communist parties in the Allied countries committed to their counties' war goals. Nationalism trumped international communism. That should have been the end of the threat of international communism. But when China fell to the communists in 1949 and hooked up with the Soviet Union, fears of international communism swept the West. In the United States, vigorous arguments ensued among Republicans and Democrats assigning blame for the loss of China. Neither party wanted to be blamed for losing Vietnam to the communists.

By the time France pulled out of Vietnam, America had already made a substantial investment in the conflict. There was little argument in Congress or among the American people about the U.S. getting involved in Vietnam in those early years. China and the Soviet Union presented an existential threat to capitalism and democracy, or so it seemed during the 1950s and even into the Kennedy administration. That's a huge historical point. Both Russia and China were viewed in America as members of the Communist International, not as independent nations. Marx was seen as their intellectual and spiritual leader, Lenin as their political leader.

But the facts that supported this view did not hold up for long. The Chinese-Russian (Sino-Soviet) Alliance was short lived. The Sino-Soviet Split had begun in the 1950s over ideological issues exacerbated by Russia's refusal to give China nuclear weapons and had been completed by 1963, when Russia entered into "peaceful coexistence" with the West. The two great communist countries split over different ideologies and began to act on their own national interests. Marx, Lenin, and international communism were things of the past.

From that perspective, it became possible to see the struggles in Vietnam as twofold: a struggle against western (French and American) imperialism, and an internal struggle to re-unite their country. Vietnam has existed . . . let's put it this way. By the time of Christ, Vietnam was already as old as the U.S. is today. The north and south have interesting differences, as many regions in many countries do. But the division of Vietnam in 1954 between the communist north and the capitalist south resulted from a fight for independence from France, led by Ho Chi Minh, who clearly was Vietnamese first and communist second. In the early years of his fight for national unity, he was not an international communist. But he needed allies. He needed money and weapons and materiel. His requests in the West were rejected. Russia and China provided all three and North Vietnam became an ally of China and Russia.

Clearly, the U.S. was interfering in a civil war that had nothing to do with American security. That conclusion was difficult to defend in America at the time. Multiple arguments were presented that insisted that the fall of Vietnam to communism created a clear and present danger to the United States, in spite of the obvious and often repeated fact that Vietnam had neither an air force nor a navy. It was impossible to win an argument against the propaganda that claimed that Vietnam threatened

U.S. national security. Then. And it continues to be made today, even though it's now absurd.

How do we prove that the fall of Vietnam to communism did not present a clear and present danger to the United States? Easy, now. The U.S. lost the war. Vietnam united as a communist country. None of the security threats to the U.S. that we had fought the war to prevent occurred. None. We fought the damn war for nothing. Not only did it cost all those deaths, injuries, and shattered lives; it divided our country in ways from which we still suffer and which have only got worse. Even though it's obvious that the fate of Vietnam had nothing to do with the security of the United States.

Now, in fairness to those who supported the war, if one followed television and print news, one learned that the fate of the U.S. was tied to the fate of Vietnam. Furthermore, the U.S. military's heroic victories in World War II had saved the world from Nazi Germany and Imperial Japan. Most Americans believed in and trusted military leaders. When generals called Vietnam a threat, a whole lot of Americans did not need to hear anything more.

And there is always the impossible task of those who lost loved ones in a war admitting that those losses were made in vain. As more and more American lives were lost in Vietnam, support for the war grew among many of the families that had suffered those losses. They simply refused to believe that their sons and brothers, fathers and husbands had died for nothing. But they had died for nothing! They had died honorably even heroically, but they had died honorably and heroically for nothing. It's a painful thing to accept.

But many professors and students at our great universities knew far more about Vietnam than what was presented in the nightly news and what was felt in anguished families.

The Free Speech Movement

As a critical mass of college professors and students realized what was going on in Vietnam, protests against the war took shape. The famed Free Speech Movement had already been won at the

University of California at Berkeley by the time the Anti-Vietnam War protests began, but it forms such a critical part of the story that we must review it, albeit briefly. The Free Speech Movement opened the door to student protests against the war.

The Berkeley Free Speech Movement had begun in the 1950s when students showed interest in off campus political and cultural issues. The university's administration said that they could be as interested and active as they wanted, off campus. Students argued that academic freedom and free speech gave them the right to bring these issues onto campus. The disagreements persisted without notice outside of Berkeley until October 1, 1964, when police arrested Jack Weinberg, a former graduate student, who was sitting at a CORE (Commission on Racial Equality) table on campus and refused to produce his identification. Students spontaneously surrounded the police car in which Weinberg was placed and remained there for 32 hours until he was released. That event made national news.

But the issues of the right to protest on campus, academic freedom, and free speech had not been resolved. On December 2, 1964, a large group of students entered Berkeley's Sproul Hall to negotiate with the administration. They were orderly and peaceful, following the strategy that Martin Luther King, Jr. had taught in the fight for Civil Rights. They sat, were generally quiet, read, and sang songs, some led by a California girl named Joan Baez who was there to lend her support. They provided television news with great photo ops.

Now notice. These were highly privileged, mostly white students who attended the best public university in America and one of the great universities in the world. That's privileged. And they were working for the right to protest for Civil Rights and racial equality. That's an enlightened use of privilege. They asserted their right to academic freedom so that they could study and discuss these issues on campus. And the more the university's administration refused to grant these rights, the more the students began to see the university as part of the WASP establishment, an institution working for economic needs and goals with no regard for human goals. The humanism that had been growing on college campuses since the 50s was now confronted by the administration and police, just as African American humanism had been confronted by elected officials, judges, police, and civilians in the south. Mario Savio gave voice and context to student humanism in a speech delivered on the steps of Sproul Hall:

> . . . But we're a bunch of raw materials that don't mean to be – have any process upon us. Don't mean to be made into any product! Don't mean – Don't mean to end up being bought by some clients of the University, be they the government, be they industry, be they organized labor, be they anyone! We're human beings!

> . . . There's a time when the operation of the machine becomes so odious – makes you so sick at heart – that you can't take part. You can't even passively take part. And you've got to put your bodies upon the gears and upon the wheels, upon the levers, upon all the apparatus, and you've got to make it stop. And you've got to indicate to the people who run it, to the people who own it, that unless you're free, the machine will be prevented from working at all.

That's a voice of humanism fighting for the dignity and worth of all humans, in this case against the University of California and the institutions for which it appeared to be training its students. And as the Civil Rights marchers had taught these privileged young white students, they could not expect to stand up and fight for their rights if they did not have the courage to sacrifice, suffer, and die, put their bodies upon the gears . . . to make it stop. The Civil Rights movement had also bequeathed moral certitude to these students. That moral certitude formed a foundation of their moral courage. Moral certitude matters.

But sure enough, the administration participated in public discourse with the students the best way they knew how: The cowards called in the police. The administration operated with Stage 3 Tribal moral reasoning. They had one set of rules for the administration, another for faculty, and a third for students. That's why many members of the faculty supported the students and why the administration felt threatened. Shortly after 2 AM on December 4, 1964, police cordoned off the building, and at 3:30 AM began making arrests. Close to 800 students were arrested. Later, when the university brought charges against the students who had organized the sit-in, they caused an even larger student protest that all but shut down the university. It was on. Student rebels with a cause and a strategy, with moral courage and moral certitude took a stand.

University officials backed down, and allowed political activity on campus. Sproul Hall's front steps were designated an open discussion area (a real, physical public square) during certain hours of the day and tables were permitted. Such concessions seem ridiculous now, obvious. Like, the administration fought over that?! Kind of like the right to vote or sit anywhere on a bus or at a lunch counter, or drink from a water fountain, or look at a cute girl without fear of being lynched. Ah yes, how difficult is the obvious. How easy it is to reject humanism, no matter that such rejection offends reason and intelligence and one's own humanity.

The End Game – Victory and Defeat, Hope and Despair

Like African Americans, students had found their voice and in the spring of 1965 the Vietnam Day Committee took its place within the Free Speech Movement on the Berkeley campus providing substantial leadership in the student Anti-Vietnam War movement that spread across the country.

How do we understand the Vietnam War protests? That's an important question because it determines how we interpret the protests and what followed.

There was this critical mass of professors and students who started the protests on humanitarian grounds: the U.S. was using its military against a small Asian country that sought unity and independence. Independence from western imperialism and unity after a division that had been imposed on their country as a part of that fight. These professors and students knew that the Vietnam war for independence and unity had nothing to do with American security and believed that it was an unjust, immoral war. Again, moral certitude formed a foundation of their protests and courage. Their protests grew, although not in a way that attracted a lot of attention from Congress or the media or even university officials. Not at first.

From 1965 on, American participation in the war in Vietnam expanded. Johnson sent more troops and the generals ordered more bombs dropped, expanded their ground war tactics, and sent more American soldiers home in flagged draped caskets or transported them to American hospitals. Protests grew, not just among professors and students, but also among some parents and veterans. Americans who feared for their lives and the lives of their sons and loved ones in an unjust, useless war.

1967: Race Riots and Vietnam War Protests

In 1967, Martin Luther King Jr. went public with his opposition to the war bringing the Civil Rights movement and Black America into the fight. Muhammad Ali sacrificed his prime as the Heavy-weight Champion of the World. He refused to support the war effort by allowing himself to be drafted, even though he would never have seen a battle field. Rather, he would have been used to recruit black soldiers who, as Martin Luther King Jr. had pointed out, were already dying in disproportionate numbers to white soldiers.

Vietnam Veterans Against War (VVAW) began informally as part of the April 15, 1967 anti-war demonstration in New York City which attracted 400,000 protesters. Only about 20 Vietnam War veterans participated. Five members formed VVAW after the march and it became one of the most influential voices against the war.

On June 23, 1967, President Johnson, accompanied by his daughter Lynda Bird Johnson, attended a benefit at the Century Plaza Hotel in Los Angeles. At the time, 500 American soldiers were dying each month in Vietnam. Eighty anti-war groups had organized a protest march against the President's war and received permits. The police expected one to two thousand; 10,000 showed up, mostly middle class young adults, many of the men dressed in sport coats or suits with ties; many women in skirts or dresses.

They looked like a cross section of college kids and young professionals. They were peaceful, innocent, and courageous. And the city's leaders demonstrated that they were violent cowards, no different from in the South. They ordered the police to attack these peaceful, unarmed young people with billy clubs. They arrested 51 and injured scores. The Vietnam War protests had joined the Civil Rights movement: peaceful demonstrations met with police violence, courage with cowardice. Notably, it was Johnson's last public appearance outside safe locations such as military bases.

If the reader does not remember the Century Plaza Protest in Los Angeles or has never heard of it, that might be because on the same day, June 23, 1967, a race riot broke out in Detroit, Michigan. Let's look behind the popular historical take. Yes, the police raided an after hours bar in an all black neighborhood. But there was more. There were years of defacto segregation that caused poor housing, poor education, work place discrimination, low wage jobs. All that in one of America's richest cities. Detroit. The automobile boom town. Detroit with its elegant central business district and wide tree lined beautifully landscaped boulevards. Rich Detroit that abused its black citizens and children.

The June 23, 1967, Detroit riot was not about a bar raid. It was about years of segregation enforced by brutal police tactics. And this was not 1950's Alabama. This was 1967 Detroit. Blacks had seen on television and read in newspapers about institutional violence against peaceful black protesters in the south. They were having none of it. All hell broke out when the police raided that bar.

To regain control of the city, Governor Romney sent in the Michigan Army National Guard and President Johnson the 82nd and 101st Airborne Divisions. Numbers: 43 dead, 1,189 injured, over 7,200 arrested, more than 2,000 buildings destroyed. Only the 1863 draft riots in New York City and the 1992 Los Angeles riots exceed this riot in scale. It was witnessed by all America through live television coverage, extensive newspaper reporting, and featured stories in *Time* and *Life* magazines. *Life* has been gone for years, but those who grew up with it will never forget its photo journalism. But the year and the events were not over.

On October 21, 1967, nearly 100,000 protesters gathered at the Lincoln Memorial. That night, some 30,000 of them marched toward the Pentagon which is so well protected that they presented no real threat to people or facilities. But they were met and assaulted by soldiers and U.S. Marshals. Hundreds of demonstrators were arrested, among them the author Norman Mailer, who memorialized the night's events in his book *The Armies of the Night*.

Although Detroit's protest had erupted in violence, most of the 1967 protests began peacefully. Still, they were met with police and military violence. The violence matters, but more important to remember is that the President and Congress and the media rejected the activists' peaceful pleas for justice and peace. Instead, they vilified them. The country divided into doves and hawks.

What a dreadful time in American history. Peaceful protests against racial injustice and the unjustified war in Vietnam met by police violence, arrests and injuries; and police violence in Detroit waged against an angry, frustrated people. America had indeed lost its innocence, and unnoticed, but not by accident, American humanism was taking a huge hit. Things only got worse in 1968.

1968: National Tragedy

On January 31, 1968, 70,000 North Vietnamese and Viet Cong forces launched the Tet Offensive against more than 100 cities and towns in South Vietnam. Long before Daniel Ellsberg released the Pentagon Papers, Anti-Vietnam War activists knew that any thought that America could win the war was over. In order to win the war, America would have had to completely destroy both North and South Vietnam. Johnson announced that he would not seek re-election. The President who had brought America the Great Society, the Civil Rights Act, and the Voting Rights Act retired to Texas exhausted, heartbroken, and disgraced.

The campaign to replace Johnson as the Democratic nominee for President witnessed the meteoric rise of Robert F. Kennedy which ended with his assassination on June 6, 1968, just two months after the assassination of Dr. Martin Luther King Jr. The

Democratic Party did not recover from those tragedies as became evident at the Democratic National Convention.

It's easy to think of 1968 protests in terms of the assassination of Martin Luther King on April 4, 1968. But even before his death, the Orangeburg Massacre occurred on February 8 at South Carolina State University, Orangeburg, South Carolina. South Carolina Highway Patrol officers entered the South Carolina State University campus that evening and confronted approximately 200 protesters who earlier that night demonstrated against racial segregation at a local bowling alley. They shot and killed three African American male protestors and injured 27 others. Those killed were Samuel Hammond and Henry Smith, students at SCSU, and Delano Middleton, a student at Wilkinson High School in Orangeburg. It's a testament to white indifference and self-deception[35] that everyone knows about the four white Kent State University students who were killed by the Ohio National Guard on May 4, 1970, but few know about the three black students killed at South Carolina State on February 8, 1968.

The assassination of Martin Luther King caused demonstrations in 125 cities across the country, and in some, considerable rioting. Washington, D.C. endured five days of rioting from April 4–8. Chicago's West Side Riots ran April 5–7. Foreshadowing his disgraceful conduct in August, Mayor Daly brought in 12,000 Army troops, 6,000 National Guard and put half of the city's police on riot alert. Baltimore, Maryland, rioted April 6–12. Kansas City, Missouri's riot lasted just one day, April 9. Wilmington, Delaware's, April 9 and 10.

The Glenville Shootout was a gun battle between the radical Black Nationalist of New Libya and the Cleveland Police Department on July 23–28, 1968, in the Glenville section of Cleveland, Ohio. Seven people were killed: three policemen, three suspects, and a bystander. The gun fight sparked the Glenville Riots which continued through the evening of July 27.

---

[35] I learned the significance of white indifference from James Baldwin and Kareem Abdul Jabbar; of white self-deception from Stanley Hauerwas.

And then came the Democratic National Convention, August 1968, Chicago, Illinois. The entire event was viewed on national television. That was before CNN flooded events with cameras 24-7, but the American people saw enough.

The Democratic National Convention

Thousands of Americans who opposed the war in Vietnam showed up for the Democratic National Convention, both inside and outside the convention center. Democratic leaders like RFK and Eugene McCarthy had been working to provide young people with a clear view of politicians who opposed the war. They knew that anti-war activists needed evidence of political support to stem the growing tide of radicalism that had begun to take root even before the assassinations of Martin Luther King Jr. The activists were composed of McCarthy supporters who were famously tidy, Yippies who were incredibly mischievous (think street artists rather than violent radicals), a whole bunch of determined anti-war protesters who were becoming increasingly angry, and a few radicals.

This was the convention most politicians expected to select the nominee who would be the next President. After all, Johnson's margin of victory in 1964 had been enormous. But the convention, like the country, was divided. Orderly procedures gave way to fist fights in the aisles. After a chaotic, sometimes violent and obscenities loaded process, the anti-war delegates led by Senator Eugene McCarthy lost and Hubert Humphrey won the nomination. Political expediency bested moral certitude. Outside was even less orderly. The convention hurt Humphrey's chances against the less than popular Nixon. And the police riots outside the convention sealed the deal for Nixon. The long decline of moral certitude that TR and FDR had advanced, Martin Luther King expanded, and 1960s activists had depended upon began a downward spiral that has not been reversed. And it will not be reversed until We the People do it.

In response to the not so perfectly peaceful demonstrations outside the convention, Mayor Daly employed the same tactics he had used on Chicago's West Side in April. He brought in 23,000 police and National Guardsmen to deal with 10,000 demonstrators. Again, the police were the aggressors, beating and gassing protestors and others. Later that year, the Chicago Study Team[36] investigated the violent clashes between police and protesters, and its report, Rights in Conflict, published December 1, 1968, laid out their findings:

> There is no question but that many officers acted without restraint and exerted force beyond that necessary under the circumstances. The leadership at the point of conflict did little to prevent such conduct and the direct control of offices by first line supervisors was virtually non-existent.

The police action was viewed as:

> . . . unrestrained and indiscriminate police violence on many occasions, particularly at night. That violence was made all the more shocking by the fact that it was often inflicted upon persons who had broken no law, disobeyed no order, made no threat. These included peaceful demonstrators, onlookers, and large numbers of residents who were simply passing through, or happened to live in, the areas where confrontations were occurring.

Once again, peaceful demonstrators acting legally in a democratic society were met by violent cowards in authority. And they were stupid. The Chicago police inside the Convention assaulted network newsmen Mike Wallace, Dan Rather, and Edwin Newman. Afterward, there was nowhere the offending officers could hide. But that had not occurred to them as they played out their tribal furor.

---

[36] In June, 1968, after the assassinations of Martin Luther King Jr. and Robert Kennedy, President Johnson formed the National Commission on the Causes and Prevention of Violence. The Commission appointed the Chicago Study Team.

1968 ended with the election of Richard Nixon, a growing divide among hawks and doves, and increasing military and political propaganda that identified war protesters with hippies, yippies, love children, and radicals. And as the Black Power movement grew following the assassination of Dr. King, African American activism was identified more and more with selected interpretations of the writings of Malcolm X. All of the protesters, white and black, were said to be driven by communists. Tools of propaganda: Name calling and slander.

The humanism, both religious and secular, that had united black and white Americans in the 1950s and early 60s was crushed by police violence and the unfortunate but predictable reaction of young people to it. Most tragic and destructive was the bombing of the University of Wisconsin's Sterling Hall on August 24, 1970. The target was the Army Mathematics Research Center, but it killed Robert Fassnacht, a physics researcher and injured three others. It was a tragic and misguided event. But it was not perpetrated by terrorists. It was a desperate act by four frustrated and furious young adults who opposed the vast American military violence in Vietnam.

Dr. King had taught both black and white demonstrators the value and tactics of peaceful demonstrations. But those who watched the violence with which peaceful demonstrators were met had to wonder if some reaction was not justified. And as the useless violence and enormous harm done by the United State military in Vietnam grew, Malcolm X's call for armed defense of black people and black neighborhoods against police violence began to impact how black and white protesters began to think about their tactics. Black protesters met violence with rioting in their cities. White protesters began to throw rocks and a few, well educated white protesters, turned violent. The bombing of Sterling Hall stands out, but there were others. However, it must be noted that as a society we remember the violence of the protesters, the riots and bank robberies and bombings by a few radicals. But we have forgotten that they were driven to those tactics by the application of institutional violence against peaceful protesters and the enormous, incalculable and unjustified American military violence in Vietnam.

The Draft, Cambodia, Student Riots, and the End of the War

In 1965, the number of young men being drafted more than doubled, increasing from 17,000 per month to 35,000. It became a rallying point for students, regardless of deferments.

In 1969 the first draft lottery was conducted. No more deferments. College students could be drafted right out of school. Needless to say, student protests, which were already well organized throughout the country, grew after the lottery was installed and student deferments ended. And then, Cambodia.

On April 30, 1970, President Nixon made public the secret bombing campaign in Cambodia. He had authorized these bombings on March 18, 1969, but had publicly denied them. Some secret. The North Vietnamese and Cambodians knew that they were being bombed. Nixon kept the secret from the American people, not the enemy.

When the truth came out, the anti-war movement took on new intensity on college campuses. In the spring of 1970, university administrators faced so many striking students that they made class attendance and final exams optional. They allowed seniors and graduate students in their final semester to receive "Ps," passing grades, and graduate. It's a stark reminder of the vast opposition to the war and to President Nixon.

More chilling are the memories of the violence. Kent State. William Schroeder. Allison Kraause. Jefferey Miller. Sandra Lee Scheuer. Killed by the Ohio National Guard. 100,000 protesters in Washington, D.C. 150,000 protesters in San Francisco. 30 ROTC buildings set on fire.

"Another Mother for Peace" and other groups still worked peacefully for peace calling for the end of the Vietnam War and the creation of a cabinet level Peace Department. The overwhelming sentiment in the country called for the end of the war and the end of the draft.

Kumbaya. It's important to remember that these activists conducted peaceful protests and were confronted by institutional violence: The police and the National Guard and citizens whose violence was shielded by the police and National Guard. And in the face of that violence, they gathered together and sang Kumbaya, an incredibly gentle song that soothed their pain and fear. Later generations have mocked Kumbaya, use it as a metaphor for weakness. They have absolutely no understanding of the pain and sacrifice and courage that those who were comforted by it had endured while fighting for peace and justice. Courageous protests for peace met by violence. And Kumbaya has become a metaphor for weakness. Nice propaganda job. Courageous Americans forced our government to end an unjust war, and they're remembered as caricatures. One might reasonably ask, What has any generation of Americans since done that comes even close to the achievements of these young people and the adults who joined them? They stopped the Vietnam War. And yes, they sang Kumbaya.

On January 23, 1973, the U.S. signed the Paris Peace Accord, and President Nixon announced that the U.S. had achieved "peace with honor" replacing his earlier goal of "victorious peace." He declared victory and pulled the troops. The last American soldier left Vietnam on March 29, 1973. One month later, April 30, 1973, Saigon fell to North Vietnamese troops, the civil war ended, and Vietnam was re-united as a communist country. The dreaded events that threatened American security and justified the war happened with absolutely no threat to American security.

The Vietnam War Hangover

The U.S. had lost a war and the loss did not sit well with those Americans who still remembered our military for the incredible courage and sacrifice that had won victories against the Nazis and Imperial Japan in World War II. These Americans had never questioned their political and military leaders and resented the liberals who, as they saw it, had tied their generals' hands.

As these and other Americans stood back and pondered what had happened to their country, they did not mourn the loss of 1950s and 60s humanism. They saw burned out cities, angry mobs, and civil disorder. Civil Rights meant black anger. Women's Rights, burnt bras. Student Rights, closed universities. Social Justice, crime in the streets. Economic Justice, strikes.

The protesters had much to be proud of, but they had to return to their lives and they did so with considerable optimism about the direction of the country, the fulfillment of what it means to be humanists in a liberal democracy.

Brown v. Board of Education had ended legal segregation in public schools.

The Civil Rights Act assured equal protection under the law for all.

The Voting Rights Act established federal authority to assure the right to vote for all.

Free Speech and Intellectual Freedom had been institutionalized on college campuses.

Roe v. Wade gave women control over their bodies.

American citizens, largely young people, had ended the war in Vietnam.

However, by 1975, activists were exhausted and had to face the prospect of highly compromised professional lives in what remained corporate America. They turned their attention and energy to work and school, family and friends.

Radical capitalists knew that their goals had been challenged and were threatened. Even before the activists returned to normal lives, radical capitalists began to fight back. Their propaganda machines did not rest. They may have lost the 1960s, but the losers wrote the history. They manipulated the images of activists visually, culturally. They replaced images of humanistic social activism from the 1950's to the early 1970's with the highly visual and sensational images of sex, drugs, and rock 'n roll that prevailed in the 1970's. The moral certitude and humanism of the 50s and early 60s were marginalized by institutional violence and the eventual violent reactions against it, but in reality it was destroyed by the propaganda that has told its story. And while the radical capitalist propaganda machine reshaped the 60s in the minds of young Americans, the religious right emerged to discredit the moral certitude of religious and secular humanism.

Far more than entropy was at work. It was and continues to be a massively funded propaganda campaign by radical capitalists and Status Christians who threaten the institutions and body politic of our constitutional liberal democracy. We the People must be prepared to work together. We must reclaim and reassert the moral certitude of religious and secular humanism that advanced human rights in our liberal democracy from Teddy and Franklin Roosevelt to Martin Luther King Jr. and 1960s activists.

To do that, we must achieve our goal:

To conduct discourse in the public square that allows us to agree on what is right and what is wrong in public life so that we can make laws and develop public policies that support what is right and reject what is wrong.

We need:

A critical mass of Americans to show up in the public square and support our arguments. Religious humanists who believe that social responsibility is a prerequisite to redemption. Secular humanists who believe that a good life requires that they help others. Americans who believe that they're members of and responsible for our community and our liberal democracy.

Pat's Notes

We begin to understand our fractured public body politic. We're a liberal democracy, but we can't complete the sentence: We hold these truths . . . We admit that we have never acted on what we claim to believe: That all men are created equal. From the beginning, we have tolerated Stage 3 Tribal moral reasoning in our laws, policies, and personal actions. We permitted slavery, eventually defeated it, but then allowed racism to flourish. We thought the black and white activists of the 1950s and 60s had finally claimed the moral high ground for our nation. They helped us institutionalize Civil Rights and Voting Rights for all Americans and established free speech and academic freedom in our universities. They stopped an unjust war. Everything was in place for our liberal democracy's core values to flourish. Satisfied but exhausted, the activists went back to school and work.

It was not to be. Up rose the great purveyors of Stage 3 Tribal moral reasoning: the radical capitalists whose financial, economic, and political privileges appeared to be slipping into history. They needed help: numbers to vote with them and intellectuals to promote their propaganda. Paul Weyrich emerged as their front man, Joseph Coors as their first financier. Jerry Falwell delivered Status Christians who turned out and voted in throngs to maintain their racist doctrines felt as fact, memorials, and institutions. Status Christians gave radical capitalists their base.

Traditional Americans joined the moral majority. They had never accepted the humanism of the 1950s and 60s activists. What they sought was the preservation of good old WASP America. They too operated at Stage 3 Tribal moral reasoning. And as we have seen, Stage 3 is so immature, so irrational, that it can't be supported by mature rational arguments. By imposing their Stage 3 moral goals on the public square, radical capitalists and their minions destroyed our body politic's capacity for mature moral reasoning and discourse. They fractured our body politic through their rejection of reason.

PART III

CHALLENGES IN MORAL PHILOSOPHY AND SOCIAL SCIENCE

Pat's Notes

Philosophy. We're going to talk about philosophy? Are you kidding me? What's next? Math? First, get over the math thing. Math is practical and all that most of us need to know is easy to learn. It's just badly taught, often by teachers who do not understand it. The philosophy we need to know has been known for a long time, some for thousands of years, other for hundreds. Some really smart dudes figured it out. All we have to do is learn it. And what we have to learn is easy and pretty dang cool. However, the last thing radical capitalists and status Christians want us to do is learn moral philosophy. It allows us to gut their self serving, Stage 3 Tribal moral arguments.

For example, we bring back the golden rule: Do unto others as you would have them do unto you. We all know and respect that. And it goes to the heart of Stage 5 We the People moral reasoning.

But the larger problem We the People face is that our moral philosophers and social scientists have lost the golden rule and any capacity for clear moral reasoning. They have lost their moral compass and as a result We the People find ourselves arguing in the public square with no moral certitude, no basis for moral agreement. So Part III does a lot of work with intellectuals. Some readers will find this whole story and our solutions incredibly interesting. Others may wish to skip the work and go straight to the summary of Part III. But no doubt, this is important stuff.

Many of us rely on religion to provide our moral compass. That's great when it gets us to Stage 5 moral reasoning. But if we do not have mature religious moral reasoning to guide us, we need public moral philosophy. Reject both religion and moral philosophy, and we're headed for the wilderness. Even if we're really smart, we're vulnerable to stupid, persistent ignorance.

6
Early Western Moral Philosophy and Social Science

The reader may want to take a break before starting this chapter. We shift our focus, both in time and subject. We go back to the High Middle Ages briefly for essential context, context that matters enormously today but is unknown, overlooked. And then we move into the birth of science, which is familiar to virtually every educated American. But we have a new take on the period. We're more interested in what happened to moral philosophy during the 16th and 17th Centuries than to the achievements in science. So take a break and let your mind prepare for a totally new story, new setting, new characters, and a new plot. It's a cool and important story.

Religious moral philosophers look beyond scripture to know what is right and what is wrong. They do not abandon scripture, but they look beyond it. They use reason. Religious moral philosophy was invented during the High Middle Ages (1050 – 1300), a period of enormous change for the good in Europe. Peace. The Germanic tribal migrations and Viking invasions had ceased. Growth. All of Europe's great cities that would exist before 1700 were founded by 1300, as were Europe's great universities. Those alone are such fascinating facts that they justify our interest in the period. Many cities grew into city states that rivaled the power of monarchs and the pope. Economies flourished, generating food, materials, and wealth that would not be matched from 1300 to 1700. It was an astounding period of peace and prosperity and growth. For our purposes, the most important changes occurred due to the expansion of trade with the Arab world. Trade ended Europe's nearly absolute isolation.

All that change and growth created a new vastly more complex society. Leading theologians encountered moral questions whose answers could not be found in scripture. Arabs had taught them to use the works of Aristotle and Plato to answer moral questions. They used reason. Thus religious moral philosophy has a secular component to it. It uses reason, not just scripture. Western Christianity figured this out during the High Middle Ages. Status Christians still don't get it.

Thomas Aquinas (1225-1274) is a major figure from this period and is best understood as a theologian who used moral philosophy to assist his work. He did traditional theology that was bound to religious text and he used reason. With a significant amount of luck, he made the West safe for reason. The reader needs to hang with me on all of this.

Aquinas accommodated the major works of Aristotle with Christian theology. From Aquinas on, it was safe to study the philosophy of Aristotle and Plato and all of the knowledge preserved and developed in the Arab world. All that knowledge had been studied earlier, but Aquinas made it safe after it finally threatened Western Christianity. We will talk about that threat soon, but Aquinas's achievement deserves special attention. Aquinas's success which was accomplished in the 13th century was so great that by the late 16th century, 300 years later, the place of reason was so secure in the West that Copernicus, Galileo, Bacon, Newton, Leibniz et al were able to lead the Copernican revolution and prevail even in the face of the massive opposition from Rome that included the house arrest of Galileo. Because of Aquinas and the development of reason that followed his achievements, the West could not turn its back on reason.

But what was the luck involved? Two significant intellectual phenomena dominated the Early Middle (Dark) Ages. One was the complete isolation of Western Europe from the Arab world. While the West suffered an astonishingly long period of political chaos and economic degradation, the Arab world thrived politically, economically, intellectually, and culturally. Western Europe knew nothing of those achievements. Europe was isolated, alone, and dark.

Second, what intellectual life that did exist was located in monasteries guided by Church teachings. In that context, theology was the dominant discipline. Western theologians suffered no challenges to their claim that theology is the queen of the sciences, that theology holds the ultimate answer to all questions. That all knowledge can be improved by theology because theology understands the ultimate significance of all knowledge. The study of what we call the social sciences was included in theology. Crafts advanced through trial and error, but, as Francis Bacon[37] pointed out, no science was done at all.

Because Western Christianity had been isolated since the Fall of Rome, Western Christianity's leaders in Rome had developed unquestioned confidence about theology and its place in the hierarchy of knowledge. When Arab and Greek knowledge flooded Western Christendom,[38] the Church felt so secure that Rome did not question any of it. Church leaders and Christian intellectuals treated this new, secular knowledge as just human knowledge. They assumed that all of it would be improved by Christian theology, the queen of the sciences. Western universities gathered, catalogued, and began to study Eastern knowledge with no interference from Rome. Principles of academic freedom did not secure eastern knowledge in the West. Blind luck did.

And then the luck ran out. Averroes (1126 – 1198), was an Arab scholar who lived in Spain and wrote on philosophy, theology, medicine, astronomy, physics, Islamic jurisprudence and law, and linguistics. His brilliant writings on all these topics demanded the attention of Western scholars but the more they studied his work, the more they realized that it presented fundamental conflicts with Christian teachings. Christian scholars at the University of Paris were the first to feel the impact of the conflict

---

[37] *Essays, Advancement of Learning.*

[38] Europe was officially given the title Europe in 1824. It was known as Western Christianity from the fall of Rome and the divide with Eastern Christianity until the Protestant Reformation and religious wars resulted divided the continent. The Holy Roman Empire, etc. prevailed. No longer Western Christendom, but not yet Europe.

between Eastern and Western knowledge, specifically between the works of Aristotle and Christian theology. But remember, a ton of this Eastern knowledge had already taken hold in Western universities.

Rome was caught between a rock and a hard place. If the Church suppressed Eastern knowledge, it would admit that theology could not accommodate it to say nothing of improve it. But if they let it just run free, it would undermine the intellectual foundations of Christianity. Something had to be done.

Rome sent Thomas Aquinas from Bologna to Paris to sort things out. And he did. He demonstrated the compatibility of Aristotlean and Christian teachings and in doing that, he made the West safe for reason.

We must know that the accommodation of religion and reason in the West has its roots in Aquinas during the Middle Ages and has been indispensable to the advancement of Western humanism, culture, and our intellectual and political traditions. All of this matters today because the attempts by anti-intellectual Status Christians to reject reason in preference of their doctrines felt as facts put a great deal at risk. Without knowing it, of course. That's the problem with being anti-intellectual: you can cause huge problems without understanding them. To understand what is at risk, consider the consequences that the rejection of reason had on Islam.

The Rejection of Reason in Islam

The history of Islam helps us appreciate and fear the damage that Status Christianity brings to America's public square. At virtually the same time that Aquinas made the West safe for reason, Islam went in the opposite direction. Reason took a distant back seat to fundamentalist religious teachings. Islamic political authority had always been in the hands of religious leaders, but it now passed into the hands of fundamentalist, anti-intellectual religious leaders. We need to appreciate what the Arab world had achieved and learn from what they did to destroy their culture. Actually, those achievements are so vast that books have been written to describe them. We can only glimpse them.

The golden age of Islamic learning lasted from the 8th to the 13th century. They advanced learning in medicine, mathematics, and science. We owe them for the decimal system including the Zero and the fundamental operations connected with it: addition, subtraction, multiplication, division, exponentiation, and extracting the root. Their trigonometry was algebraic rather than geometric.

One does not have to be a mathematician or scientist to appreciate the enormous achievements of the Arab world. In the West, at the same time that Arabs were making huge advancements in mathematics, Western "scholars" were studying numerology, the occult significance of numbers.

The Arab world was vast. Arabs had conquered many countries, absorbed many cultures. And they proved quite tolerant. Muslims had advantages in Islamic countries, but non-Muslims lived quite well and enjoyed considerable rights and security.

But the Arab world collapsed because fundamentalist, anti-intellectual religious leaders took control of their government and rejected reason for their religious doctrines, their doctrines felt as facts. Islamic religious leaders used their hostility to reason to seize political and military power and control all facets of Islamic life with their fundamentalist religious views. Intellectual progress stopped and regressed throughout Islam. It was not entropy that destroyed Islam. It was the domination of religion and government by anti-intellectual religious fundamentalists. Sound familiar?

Islam has not yet overcome the influence of religion over reason in governance and public discourse and has not yet recovered the political, economic, intellectual, and cultural status of its distant past. Sunnis and Shiites continue, today, to wage war, destroying nations and lives, fighting over religious differences that have no place in government or the public square. But they can't get over their ancient irrational religious differences.

It was no small thing that Aquinas made the west safe for reason, a safety that we must protect. And of course, it was no small thing that the Copernican Revolution, acting within that blanket of security provided by Aquinas, invented natural science and redefined mathematics in the West. And what a revolution it was.

The Ascendance of Natural Science

Now, let's jump forward from the 13th century to the 16th and 17th Centuries. And let's jump into both familiar intellectual history, and intellectual history the reader has probably never thought about.

Copernicus, Galileo, Newton et al rejected and replaced Aristotle's whole theory of knowledge.[39] That change represents one of the great intellectual revolutions in human history. It rejected and replaced an entire way of thinking. Most of us are familiar with the change from the geocentric (earth is the center) to the heliocentric (sun is the center) views in astronomy. But most of us aren't aware that Newton invented more than the scientific method. He also invented a new theory of knowledge. Aristotle used the same theory of knowledge to conduct both natural philosophy (science) and moral philosophy which includes what we call social science. Newton's rejection of Aristotle's theory of knowledge helped create the problems moral philosophers have faced since the 17th century.

A useful example of the difference between how Aristotle and Newton thought deals with gravity. We start with Aristotle. How he thought about what we call science is not difficult to understand, and from our perspective it's funny. Aristotle did not even think about the physical forces that cause objects to fall. He knew that one of the ultimate goals of all objects, its purpose or *telos* (thus the term *teleological* reasoning) is to be on the ground. If an object that belongs on the ground is not on the ground, its

---

[39] I use the term "theory of knowledge" rather than the word used by philosophers, "epistemology" so that the reader can become used to the concept without dealing with a strange word. Epistemology is the area of philosophy that studies the conditions under which we can claim to know something. It's the study of theories of knowledge, and it can be used to name a specific discipline's theory of knowledge. I use the more familiar term as long as seems practical.

goal is to get to the ground. So Aristotle's explanation for why objects fall was essentially moral: They fall because it's in their nature to fall so that they can achieve their ultimate goal, to be on the ground. They fall because they "should be" on the ground. "Should." Moral. Falling to the ground helps it achieve it purpose, so falling to the ground is like a virtue. Virtues help us achieve our moral goals, vices prohibit us from achieving our moral goals. Cute, isn't it? But that's how Aristotle thought, both about moral philosophy and natural philosophy (science). And because Aristotle and Aquinas and Christian theology and philosophy dominated Western inquiry, natural science made no progress in the West for over two thousand years.

Newton treated nature as the source of knowledge in natural science. Nature exists and is there to be studied. He studied and thought about natural phenomena as he was able to observe them. From the 17th century on, natural scientists have added mathematics and all kinds of concepts and tools and technology to aid their observations of nature, their inquiry into the nature of what is in nature. They no longer concern themselves with what natural objects ought to do or not do, as Aristotle thought.

When Newton published *Mathematical Principles of Natural Philosophy* (1687), he did not just set forth the foundations of the scientific method, he rejected Aristotle's teleological reasoning in natural science. He described scientific reasoning, the scientific method, and the mathematically structured hypothesis. The mathematically structured hypothesis gave entirely new intellectual power to scientific research and made mathematics indispensable to science. *Mathematical Principles of Natural Philosophy* stands as a huge achievement both in changing the theory of knowledge in natural science and in making mathematics indispensable to natural science. What followed Newton has been a period of continuous advancement in both natural science and mathematics. Natural science has thrived. But what about moral philosophy?

Like Aristotle, moral philosophers used metaphysical and teleological reasoning. A brief definition of each is helpful. As I use it, metaphysical reasoning begins with *a priori* assumptions, assumptions known or accepted as true, and proceeds through rigorous logical arguments to conclusions. Teleological reasoning begins with goals, what I call morally grounded purposes, which are used both as goals and as criteria for evaluating moral and social claims. Should we do this? It depends. Does it help us achieve our goals or does it frustrate our attempts to achieve our goals. Teleological reasoning has three components:

The Telos or ultimate purpose of a thing.
Virtues, behaviors that achieve that Purpose.
Vices, behaviors that prevent the achievement of that Purpose,

Philosophers assumed that they held a superior place in Western universities until they confronted problems they could not solve. But it was not just that they failed to solve moral problems. Their failure accompanied the emergence of the incredible success of natural science. Natural science humiliated moral philosophy. The enormous failure of moral philosophy to meet the challenges of the day stood in stark contrast to the enormous achievements being made in natural science.

Here we go. Saddle up. Another big break in our subject matter. New plot, setting, and characters. What were the problems that moral philosophers could not solve?

Religious Wars and Religious Moral Philosophy

Let's recall the times, the 16th and 17th Centuries, and of course, the people. Martin Luther published his 95 Theses on October 31, 1517, and in effect founded the Lutheran Church. Henry VIII declared himself the Supreme Head of the Church of England, rejected the Pope's authority, and created the Church of England in 1534. In 1536, John Calvin published his work, *Institutes of the Christian Religion* and created Calvinism. 1517-1536. In merely 20 years, the three major branches of Protestantism were founded, and the Roman Catholic Church lost its domination of Western Christianity. Indeed, with the Protestant Reformation, Western Christianity ceased to exist as a meaningful geographical term.

For the first time, Western monarchs committed to different religions. And they fought wars over their differences. Do I need to mention Stage 3 Tribal moral reasoning? Or are you with me by now? European monarchs returned to their tribal past. We need to mention just two of the religious wars: The Thirty Years War ravaged German states from 1618 to 1648. The French Wars of Religion caused havoc in France from 1562 to 1685.

1648. The Treaty of Westphalia ended the Thirty Years War and removed the Pope from political prominence in the West.

1685. The end of the French Wars of Religion marked the end of the Protestant Reformation. Western religions (plural, religions), thrived in ever increasing denominations. Many were persecuted or repressed, but no more wars were fought over them.

Galileo (1564-1642) lived his entire life during the Protestant Reformation and the religious wars that attended it. Newton's great work was published just two years after the French Wars of Religion ended. Natural science was born and thrived during a time of religious, social, and political upheaval.

What about moral theology and moral philosophy during the same time. They encountered problems they could not solve. Indeed, they made them worse. Michel de Montaigne's description of how moral philosophy was practiced in France at this time is instructive:[40]

> See the horrible impudence with which we toss back and forth arguments concerning God's will, and how irreligiously we have both rejected them and re-adopted them as fortune has changed sides in these public storms.

In religious moral philosophy, and all moral philosophy at that time was religious moral philosophy, the essential question is, What is God's will? Scholars discerned God's will from scripture and tradition and reason. But of course, with the Protestant Reformation, different scholars interpreted scripture differently. Moral philosophers invented new and rejected old traditions. They waged new arguments regarding what exactly is God's will. But to Montaigne's point: Moral philosophers changed their

---

[40] *In Defense of Raymond Sebond.*

arguments "as fortune . . . changed." First they chose the conclusion they wanted, then they constructed the argument for it. When fortunes changed, they needed new conclusions so they changed their arguments. Montaigne continues.

> This most solemn proposition: "Whether it is permissible for the subject to rebel and take up arms against a prince for the defense of religion," remember in what mouths this past year the affirmative was the buttress of one party, the negative the buttress of what other party? . . .

How moral philosophers answered the question: Is it right to kill the king to protect your religion? depended entirely on the religion of the moral philosopher, the king, and those who would kill the king. If the subjects were Catholic, the philosopher was Catholic, and the king was Protestant; it was permissible to kill the king. But if the subjects were Protestant, and the philosopher and king were Catholic, then it was not permissible to kill the king. Protestant moral philosophers, with similar impudence, tossed back and forth the same arguments concerning God's will. Montaigne seethed:

> And we burn people who say that one must subject truth to the yoke of our expediency. And how much worse is France in doing it rather than merely saying it.

Philosophers were burned for claiming that truth is not absolute, that it depends on context or expediency, that it does not come from God. Yet there they were, French moral philosophers, not just saying that truth depends on one's point of view. French moral philosophers were doing just that to justify regicide and religious wars.

Religious moral philosophy contributed to violence and unrest at a time of enormous crisis all across Europe. Instead of lighting paths to peace, religious moral philosophers, on all sides, opened wide the paths to war. And while moral philosophy failed to do what it must do, natural science did what it must do better than ever anticipated in the history of the human race. Science emerged as the most productive, explanatory discipline in Western universities. It began to dominate Western culture and thought. Religious moral philosophy began its long decline.

To understand the importance of moral philosophy, we had to visit the 13th century. To understand the cause of the decline of moral philosophy, we had to visit the 16th and 17th Centuries. All that background helps us understand moral philosophy today, why we need it, why we fail to use it, and how we can use it to help us heal our fractured body politic. We turn to that discussion and in doing so, we turn to both moral philosophy and social science.

7
Modern Western Moral Philosophy and Social Science

It's helpful to understand what I am trying to do in this section. I am reviewing the history of moral philosophy and social science, the challenges they faced and what they did in responding to those challenges. As we will see, what they did to their theory of knowledge undermined social science, did not help philosophy in general, and destroyed moral philosophy. Some mention of what happened to moral philosophy and social science seems necessary so that the reader can appreciate their longstanding relationship. Their history explains their inability today to lead discourse within the public square. And as we will see, their inability to contribute intellectual leadership in the public square has led to the fracturing of our body politic and chaos in the public square. Again, it was nothing as benign and indifferent as entropy that has fractured our body politic. Our intellectual leaders did it, albeit without meaning to.

The Divorce of Moral Philosophy and Social Science

The Copernican Revolution, the Protestant Reformation, and the religious wars of the 16th and 17th Centuries had a huge impact on moral philosophy and those areas of moral philosophy that came to be known as the social sciences. From being the big brother in the university, religious moral philosophy (remember, all moral philosophy was religious moral philosophy) became the little brother to natural science. Philosophers did not sit still for such humiliation. They felt it and they did something about it. Philosophers abandoned theology.

But many philosophers did not just abandon theology. Moral philosophers studied society (law, economics, politics, etc.). But in the face of moral philosophy's failures, some philosophers began to distance themselves not just from theology but also from moral philosophy. They became just philosophers. How did they do that?

Partly by how they selected their objects of inquiry.

But these scholars also abandoned moral philosophy's theory of knowledge which was grounded in metaphysics and teleological reasoning, and adopted the theory of knowledge that Newton had invented for natural science. Eventually (and here I am collapsing centuries of history) philosophers changed their name to social scientists who study society as it is and adopted the scientific theory of knowledge, the scientific method, and mathematics. By the time they became social scientists in roughly the first decade of the 20th century, philosophy had become the philosophy of science (analytical philosophy and positivism). Philosophers totally abandoned moral philosophy.[41] The more philosophers used the scientific method, the less they remained philosophers at all. But at least they were no longer embarrassed to be around natural scientists in the university.

But here is the kicker. By abandoning moral philosophy, these philosophers abandoned the pursuit of full moral development, the pursuit of mature moral reasoning. They did not know that intellectual development depends upon both cognitive development and moral development. Because they did not advance moral reasoning from Stage 3 to Stage 5, they could not continue to practice moral philosophy. They could not apply anything they

---

[41] Today, the history of moral philosophy is taught. Virtually no one is doing moral philosophy. And no one in any field of study walks across campus to get help from moral philosophers in addressing current challenges, current research.

figured out to anyone but themselves. How could anyone build an academic career out of that?

A major issue that we must address, then, is not just the demise of Western moral philosophy. We must address the consequences that have confronted the social sciences because they split from moral philosophy. The reader won't find any discussion of these issues and their consequences in the social science literature. They don't see it. That's not a problem for us. In fact, it encourages us to believe that we're onto something because we're trying to solve problems that the social sciences created and don't even think about. Obviously, we must think differently from how they think.

I have to admit, I did not expect this line of thought to emerge as so important when I started writing this book, but it turns out to be unavoidable. It's obvious that natural science needs mathematics and mathematics needs natural science. We will also see that social science needs moral philosophy and that moral philosophy needs social science. They need each other to reach their full development. That interdependence becomes unarguable in Part IV when we solve what seem to be intractable public problems by integrating moral philosophy and social science. For now, we can only talk about their relationships and discuss their need for each other. But it's important for the reader to know that we don't just talk. We solve problems. We make complex, intractable problems simple and highly susceptible to solutions. But now, let's finish this discussion of philosophy and philosophers. Let's look at what all of this means to us today. We gain a whole new insight into our fractured body politic and why We the People haven't been able to mount the powerful opposition to the forces that have sought to dis-empower our constitutional liberal democracy's institutions.

Moral Philosophy Today

So what happened to the philosophers who were left doing moral philosophy when the social scientists abandoned them? Collapsing 300 years of history, move into the 20th century when philosophers reached the conclusion that the only valid moral statement anyone can make is one that applies only to one's self. Further, any moral norm upon which one acts is acceptable as long as it does not hurt someone else or break valid laws. In other words, by the 20th century, moral philosophers were no longer doing philosophy at all. That may sound rash but consider Quine.

Willard Van Orman Quine (1908 – 2000, Van to his friends,) spent his entire college and adult life in or associated with Harvard University. He was an analytic philosopher[42] and is recognized as one of the most influential American philosophers of the twentieth century. He famously stated that the philosophy of science is the only philosophy worth studying. He compared philosophy to mathematics, justifying the study of mathematics because it's indispensable to inquiry in science and dismissing philosophy because it's useless. Moral philosophy in particular does not contribute to inquiry in any other discipline. That's an important point. Indeed, a fact regarding the state of moral philosophy.

But it is not the truth about the nature of moral philosophy. Moral philosophy can and must become indispensable to inquiry in the social sciences if the social sciences are to reach full development.

I have used Quine's observation about the nature of mathematics and the uselessness of moral philosophy to focus our attention on making moral philosophy indispensable to social science. I owe Quine quite a bit for his focusing our attention, but I reject his conclusion that moral philosophy as such is useless. ("Moral philosophy qua moral philosophy" as philosophers once said.)

Quine was right when he pointed out that moral philosophy was useless. It is currently useless when We the People try to decide in the public square what we should do and not do, what is right and wrong, in public life. Moral philosophy gives us no help at all.

The greatest achievement of 20th century moral philosophy is the endorsement of solipsism, philosophy's ancient name for individualism. I use the ancient name to emphasize the fact that

---

[42] I discuss analytic philosophy in *Intellectual Leadership in Education*, p 142-7, and can't give it additional space here.

there is nothing new with individualism and to point out that moral philosophers rejected it for centuries. Newman called it assent, the individual's right and practice of deciding for one's self what is right and what is wrong. But Newman is clear. Assent is great for individuals making decisions for themselves about how to live, how to activate their freedom. But it's useless in public discourse. It can't guide how We the People think because it shuts itself up in its own standard. It is the accident of the person who uses it.

Assent belongs with the individual in his or her private life. Assent is useless in the public square. Thus modern moral philosophy has rendered itself comforting, even invigorating, to individuals who want to live their lives "my way," but it has made itself useless both in the university and the public square. That bears repeating. Modern philosophy is invigorating and comforting to individuals. To living my life my way. It therefore wins the support of a vast number of individuals. But still, it's useless as a guide to We the People in the public square.

However, not all individualism is so benign as to be just useless. Nietzsche advanced the notion of the superman, not just the individual. He called for the heroic individual and his work remains attractive to inexperienced youth who know nothing of his contribution to the corruption of Nazi Germany.

We're no longer We the People. Rather we're individual members of our body politic who get to pick the model of individualism we will follow: Nietzschy's autonomous super-hero, Sartre and Camus's authentic individual, Ayn Rand's selfish, self promoting radical capitalists, Status Christianity's socially indifferent but politically active zealots, or the casual preference for individual assent. None of these philosophical views provides indispensable intellectual tools to We the People trying to conduct discourse in the public square. Quine was right in his assessment of the uselessness of moral philosophy. He was wrong in being satisfied with that conclusion. He should have worked to fix it.

Not all that gradually, moral philosophy became isolated in the university, so much so that no other disciplines require moral philosophy to guide or even contribute to their development. The social sciences used to be considered moral philosophy. Since these disciplines moved to social science, they haven't depended on, or even thought about, moral philosophy. That has had important consequences for the theory of knowledge in the social sciences, for the social sciences can't reach full intellectual development without the aid of mature moral reasoning.

If the social sciences need mature moral philosophy to provide them with mature moral reasoning so that they can reach full development, then how well moral philosophy serves the social sciences becomes the criteria for the evaluation of moral philosophy. Yes, the first thing that must happen is that social scientists must seek help from moral philosophy, but moral philosophers must answer the bell. Moral philosophy and the social sciences must reconnect with each other. That claim needs some support.

A quick reminder. In order to re-form, re-congregate, as We the People, we must attend to full cognitive and moral development. But it's silly to talk about our doing that by ourselves. Moral philosophers and social scientists have created the intellectual barriers to our uniting. Our intellectuals have helped divide us at a time when radical capitalists and Status Christians have worked to undermine the institutions that preserve and protect our liberal democracy. Our intellectuals have passively contributed to the entropy that undermines our liberal democracy. We need our intellectuals to re-order their theory of knowledge, and re-unite their intellectual communities.

Social Science and the Interface of Moral Philosophy and Science

Let's stop and work on our comparison/contrast of natural science and social science. Mathematics did not make itself indispensable to science. Natural scientists developed a scientific method that made mathematics indispensable to science. These scientists were also mathematicians and they developed mathematical solutions that solved problems. Out of necessity, mathematics emerged during the 17th and 18th Centuries in ways that had been unimaginable in the West prior to the Copernican Revolution. Descartes did important work in optics and invented analytical geometry. Newton and Leibniz invented calculus. But my favorite story is of Pascal. He invented probability theory in mathematics in order to help a friend who was an inveterate and failing gambler.

Similarly, moral philosophy can't make itself indispensable to the social sciences. Social scientists must learn to think about how they think and change how they think. They must identify their source of knowledge, and that's really interesting. Social scientists study what is in society, which means that social scientists seem to have the same source of knowledge as natural scientists, what is.

Emile Durkheim (1858-1917), the architect of modern sociology,[43] listed two rules for the sociological method:

First, sociology must have specific objects (in society)
to study; it must study facts; and
Second, it must apply a recognized scientific method.

There you go: Study what is using the scientific method. Natural science applied to society. Social science did not just wander into positivism;[44] it made a concerted effort to get there. But of course, there is more to social science than the use of the scientific method.

What is in nature is a bit more stable than what is in society. Some of what is in society is the result of someone saying, "Come on dammit, quit talking. We have got to make a decision! Here is what we're going to do." Often, the results of those urgent, expedient decisions don't work well. (There are more reasons why "what is in society" is messed up, but that example suffices for our purposes.) The point is: Social scientists can't take what is in society as their source of knowledge. Clearly, it is their object of inquiry, what they study and evaluate so that they can decide what

---

[43] Durkheim was aided by Karl Marx, 1818-1883; Friedrich Engels, 1820-1896; and Max Weber, 1864-1920; all of whom were influenced by Auguste Comte, 1798-1857.
[44] Noted early Positivist philosophers include G.E. Moore, 1873-1958; Bertrand Russell, 1872-1970; L. Wittgenstein, 1889-1951. I include Positivism in Analytical Philosophy.

must be preserved and protected, and what must be abandoned, eliminated. But society is not their source of knowledge.

What Durkheim demanded and what social scientists have done is not wrong, but it's insufficient. Durkheim didn't even consider the "ought" question. What ought to exist in society? What ought we, what should we, do? Those are moral questions, and Durkheim did nothing in designing the social science method to help social scientists answer moral questions such as, What should society be like? What is a just war? What must we do to achieve economic justice? What is social justice? The social sciences must be able to answer various "ought" questions. But because they have abandoned moral philosophy's theory of knowledge, they have no capacity to ask or answer ought questions. They have none of the intellectual tools needed to answer those kinds of questions. They need moral philosophy. We will improve upon Durkheim's social science method in the next chapter.

Moral philosophy also has work to do. It must show up with the intellectual tools needed to solve moral problems, answer moral questions that the social sciences encounter when they accept the fact that they aren't just studying what is in society.

Moral philosophers must figure out what ought to be in society and social scientists must figure out what currently is in society, what needs to be fixed, and what we can do to fix it.

It's up to social scientists to figure out how to achieve what ought to be, but they need mature moral philosophy to figure out what ought to be. The social sciences don't have the tools to answer "what ought to be" questions. However, social science challenges lie deeper than connecting with and using mature moral philosophy. They have their own internal problems. We will get to them below, but first we need to pay attention to 20th century moral philosophers who have been ignored for too long.

Understanding Today's Moral Philosophers

It's important to understand why 20th century moral philosophers and social scientists haven't been able to address the moral and political challenges that we know face them. Remember Hemingway and Fitzgerald and the Lost Generation? Why were they lost?

Because all of the confidence and hope that thrilled and inspired their generation in the last half of the 19th century and early years of the 20th century were destroyed by the horrors of The Great War. Who caused it? Aristocrats and politicians. All of the optimism that created the dreams of young people at the turn of the 20th Century came crashing down as inept leaders caused vast, unimaginable suffering and death. Oh yes, they had intellectual authority. They claimed it. And the people bought into it. But what did they do with it?

The Great War (WWI): Leaders on both sides used Stage 3 moral authority to take the world into a stupid, greedy, horrendous world war.

The Great Depression: Radical capitalists used Stage 3 Tribal moral reasoning to create economic theory, laws, and practice that caused world wide financial ruin.

WWII: Hitler's Stage 3 moral reasoning created a politics of greed and hate that took the world into war and attempted to exterminate an entire people and others disdained as inferior.

From the second half of the 20th century into the present, moral philosophers and social scientists tried to cure the ills created by corrupt institutionalized moral authority by permanently removing moral authority from powerful institutions, governments, and the body politic.

And what about the courageous activists from the '60's? Why did they not work to develop powerful, purposeful moral reasoning and social science that could provide the intellectual agreement and authority that's indispensable to productive discourse in the public square? Recall! They had already made powerful moral arguments in the public square for Civil Rights and freedom of speech and against an unjust war. And they had been met by institutionalized moral authority that protected powerful cowards who beat, imprisoned, murdered, and assassinated them, their friends, and their leaders. When those activists joined departments of philosophy and social science, they brought with them ingrained distrust of institutionalized moral authority that matched that of the older faculty who greeted them.

Generations of moral philosophers and social scientists thought that they were doing the right thing, limiting and controlling institutionalized moral authority. But they failed in their goal. I think because they did not understand the enemy. They did nothing to confront the power and stature of the moral authority that radical capitalists and Status Christians have bestowed upon themselves.

Unfortunately, their research, writing, and teaching have undermined any attempt to think about how to bring mature moral reasoning to the public square and our institutions. In abhorring the evils of institutionalized tribal moral authority, moral philosophers and social scientists have failed to predict the harm that the complete absence of mature moral authority would do to the public square and our body politic. Since intellectual development consists of both cognitive and moral development, intellectual authority depends upon both cognitive development and moral development. Generations of moral philosophers and social scientists have lost the capacity to exert intellectual authority because they have made no attempt to establish moral authority, moral certitude.

Having taken this stand against institutionalized moral authority, these philosophers found existentialism and phenomenology attractive. Existentialism is interesting but not needed in our work other than to say that it's an interesting alternative to answering questions about the meaning of life in the face of death. It's a religion for atheists if they have the courage it requires. Phenomenology, on the other hand, is useful in Part IV.

Phenomenology

Phenomenology came out of the work of Husserl, Heidegger, Sartre, and others. Phenomenology is important because it teaches us to think about others as they think of themselves. Phenomenology is highly individualistic for it focuses on the unique experiences that each of us has which define our understanding of things, their meaning to us, our selves. Luigi Pirandello expressed the concern of phenomenology in *Six Characters In Search of an Author*:

Each one of us has within us a whole world of things, each one of us, our own special world. And how can we ever come to an understanding, if I put in the words I utter the sense and value of things as I see them; while you who listen to me, must inevitably, translate them according to the . . . things . . . you see? . . . We think we understand each other, but we never really do.[45]

It's not just the inadequacy of words that prevents us from understanding each other, it's the vast differences in our experiences and specifically our individual interpretations of experience: I put in the words I utter the sense and value of things as I see them; while you who listen to me must inevitably translate them according to the way you see them.

Not surprisingly, philosophers used phenomenology as one more belief system to advance moral individualism and undermine the whole premise of institutionalized moral authority. Newman taught us that individuals have the right to their own views, to form their own opinions on how to live their lives. We get that. But We the People need to rise above our individual opinions and our casual ways of forming them, to build agreement in the public square. These philosophers have ignored Murray's warning that productive political discourse depends upon agreement.

Many politicians tell us that we're entitled to our own opinion but not to our own facts. Actually the challenge runs much deeper than agreeing on facts. We the People need to agree on our core values and what we believe is right and wrong in public life. We need to reestablish our identity, our moral certitude, as Americans and protect and preserve our liberal democracy.

Moral philosophers were able to abandon any attempt to build agreement in the public square and to contribute to legitimate public moral authority because nothing was at stake for moral philosophy. Twentieth and 21st century moral philosophers

---

[45] I changed this quotation to provide gender neutral language and added a few commas to make it easier to read.

have operated in a vacuum, much as European mathematicians did during the Middle Ages.

Because the social sciences divorced themselves from moral philosophy, moral philosophy has not been challenged to grow, to solve moral problems in society that are identified by the social sciences. Not only do the social sciences require mature moral reasoning to reach their full development, moral philosophy requires the social sciences to reach its full development. And there is more.

Because the social sciences divorced moral philosophy, social scientists haven't noticed, haven't even been able to think about, how moral reasoning relates to and impacts social science. They haven't been able to think about their full cognitive and moral development. Full intellectual development of the social sciences and society depends upon both cognitive development and moral development. But social scientists do not think about moral development, except as individuals and as an individual issue.

And all of this started when the Copernican Revolution, the Reformation, and religious wars led natural scientists to abandon moral philosophy and its theory of knowledge and replace it with Newton's theory of knowledge and the scientific method. When natural scientists made their theoretical and methodological change, they quickly achieved enormous success. But when moral philosophy became isolated, when the social sciences abandoned moral philosophy, both became failed disciplines that are incapable of full development. As Quine would say, they're both irrelevant because they're both useless.

Since that's where the problems began, that's where we must start to fix the problem, with the theoretical challenges that moral philosophy and the social sciences faced but did not solve. We must work and solve it.

8
Integrating Moral Philosophy and Social Science

This chapter makes all the work we have done up until now worthwhile, and it will make all of the work we do in Part IV possible. We have been using the term "theory of knowledge" because it's immediately familiar. However, the reader has had a chance to get used to thinking about "theory of knowledge" as a topic that's interesting and important. Now we might as well start using the technical term: Epistemology. Epistemology is the branch of philosophy that studies knowledge, what is required to claim we know something and the method, source, organization, structure, and standards of knowledge in a discipline. An Epistemology unites knowledge in its discipline. An epistemology does not "shut itself up in its own standard" or conflicting standards. It unites knowledge in a common, unified standard. In this chapter we work on the epistemology of public moral philosophy and the epistemology of social science. Public moral philosophy. Not religious moral philosophy or personal moral philosophy . . . moral philosophy. With that said, we will . . . use the term moral philosophy.

But why epistemology? Because nothing helps us think about how we think as much as learning about different epistemologies. And nothing helps us think about how we think in different disciplines as much as a sound epistemology. Learning about and developing the epistemologies of moral philosophy and social science is indispensable to our full intellectual development, to both how we reason and how we reason morally. In this discussion, we demonstrate what we have been assuming since the beginning of the book: Full intellectual development depends upon both mature cognitive and moral development.

We're going to study and solve epistemological problems in these two disciplines. We're going to study and do epistemology. To develop an epistemology, we need to identify the sources of knowledge in each discipline as well as the organization, structure, and standards of knowledge in each discipline. This whole discussion is necessary and it holds some very cool surprises.

First we develop an epistemology for moral philosophy. We discover that only moral philosophy's source of knowledge works independent of social sciences. The structure, standards, and methods of moral philosophy cannot be developed and used in just the work that moral philosophy does. The structure, standards, and methods of moral philosophy have no use without the social sciences. They cannot do anything on their own. They must be used in the social sciences. Moral philosophy can only get its own jobs started. Social science is necessary to get those jobs done. Needless to say, that's an important discovery. The structure, standards, and methods of moral reasoning in moral philosophy are incomplete without the contributions that only the social sciences can make to them.

Then we turn to the epistemology of social science and discover that it has the same epistemology as is used in science, kind of. We use the scientific method in social science, but we also add to it. We bring moral philosophy into social science's epistemology. So while we maintain a clear distinction between moral philosophy and social science, we also integrate them.

When we have completed our discussion of the epistemologies of moral philosophy and social science, we have integrated them and we have accounted for the source of knowledge in each, their methods, structure, and standards. We put off the discussion of their organization of knowledge because that discussion deals with paradigms. We save it for the chapter on Education Justice because there we get to learn from my Education Paradigms: CP 1.0 and CP 2.0, the only fully articulated paradigms that exist in any of the social sciences. My work on CP 1.0 started when I was writing *Intellectual Leadership in Education.* I expanded it to CP 2.0 between that book and this one.

Finally we talk about how natural science, moral philosophy, and social science can work together in the public square and the powerful leadership they can provide We the People when we work together and when we work with them. That discussion calls for significant cognitive modification as a prerequisite to our behavior modification.

The Epistemology of Moral Philosophy

Immanuel Kant (1724 – 1804) cleared the air regarding the fundamental difference between inquiry in the natural sciences and inquiry in moral philosophy. He also explains the difference between inquiry in the natural sciences and the social sciences. We have referred to this distinction earlier, we have just assumed it, now we explain it, and give Kant his due.

In the *Metaphysics of Morals*, Kant taught us that natural science inquires into the nature of what is, into "laws according to which everything does happen." On the other hand, he wrote, moral philosophy inquires into the nature of what ought to be, "laws according to which everything ought to happen." The natural sciences are perfectly suited to studying the nature of what is, but they don't have the tools needed to inquire into what ought to be. What is exists in the physical world and is there to be studied, weighed, measured, observed, calculated, manipulated, and restructured. That's what scientists do.

But "what ought to be" does not exist in the physical world. "What ought to be" is a way of thinking about the social world, how we think we should design it, structure it. "What ought to be" tells us what our laws, policies, and programs ought to achieve. "What ought to be" provides us with the **standard of knowledge** in social science, the criteria for evaluating what is in society, and the criteria for evaluating the efficacy of the laws, policies, and programs we create to maintain and improve society. What ought to be guides our arguments in the public square about laws, policies, and programs that are supposed to make our society become what it ought to be.

So how do we inquire into the nature of What ought to be? We must use tools developed in moral philosophy. We will use two methods of moral reasoning: metaphysical moral reasoning and teleological moral reasoning, and one intellectual tool from moral philosophy, the Golden Mean.

Metaphysical moral reasoning is deductive. It starts with *a priori* assumptions and works toward specific conclusions about what ought to be. We only use it when we discuss women's reproductive rights and will save our discussion about it until then.

We use teleological moral reasoning extensively. If it is a new term for you, just hang with me a moment. I describe it at length below.

I mention the Golden Mean because it proved essential when I was thinking about economic justice, trying to figure out how we think about it and how we should think about it. Most young readers have probably never heard of it, and many older readers probably remember their most interesting friends disparaging it. Generations of young people have dismissed the Golden Mean, associated it with the Greeks' call for "all things in moderation." Moderation? You don't pursue excellence by seeking moderation. You don't do extreme skate boarding by seeking moderation. Fair enough. But as we will see, it can be a powerful tool in public moral reasoning. It can force us to look for concepts that are not immediately obvious. We will have that discussion when talking about economic justice.

The bulk of our work will employ teleological reasoning. The reader may recall that we made fun of Aristotle's use of teleological reasoning when he applied it to natural science. Further, we celebrated Newton's rejection of it. But we must take it seriously when we apply it to moral reasoning. And it turns out to be compatible with the social science method. It does not change the scientific method used by social sciences, it adds to it. We use teleological reasoning to establish our list of what ought to be in society, what we should do. Statements that describe what we should do are moral statements. We call them our morally grounded purposes. Aristotle called them *teloi. Telos* is the singular form, *teloi*, the plural. *Teloi* rhymes with Malloy. We get teleological reasoning from Aristotle, but we limit it to moral philosophy and the social sciences, and we vastly improve it by applying the power of the social sciences to it.

The Teleological Structure and Standards of Moral Reasoning

In teleological reasoning, we establish our *telos,* our goal, our morally grounded purpose, and then we identify the actions that help us achieve our purpose. That's our structure, and it includes our standards. Aristotle called the actions that help achieve one's *telos* virtues, and he called the actions that undermine or prevent us from achieving our *telos* vices. There you go. Classic moral language. Virtues and vices. And we see that they provide the standards, the criteria, we use to judge actions as good or bad. We evaluate what we do by asking, Does it help or hurt our attempts to achieve our goals? Aristotle's language of the teleological structure and standards of moral reasoning are easily translated into language that fits public moral reasoning:

Teloi: The morally grounded purposes we establish for our society.

Virtues: Good Laws, programs, and policies that help us achieve our morally grounded purposes.

Vices: Bad laws, programs and policies that prevent us from achieving our morally grounded purposes.

Our morally grounded purposes tell us what we want to achieve, the ultimate goals that We the People seek in the public square. Not in our private lives. In our public lives.

Importantly, we are not talking about being good little girls and boys. We are talking about We the People being able to evaluate laws and public policies. They are good laws and policies if they help us achieve our goals, our morally grounded purposes. They are bad laws and policies if they prevent us from achieving our goals, our morally grounded purposes.

But notice, moral philosophy can't identify what laws, policies, and programs help us achieve our morally grounded purposes and what laws, policies, and programs prevent us from achieving those morally grounded purposes. Moral philosophy does not have the tools required to do that job. That's the job of the social sciences. Teleological moral reasoning can't function, can't get the whole job done, without the social sciences. That means that our epistemology of moral philosophy must be integrated with social science.[46]

We achieve that structure and use those standards in both moral philosophy and the social sciences or they don't exist at all. What we **do** with "what ought to be" must be done in society, and only the social sciences can conduct the research and development needed to tell us what is in society, how it measures up against our morally grounded purposes, what we can and should do, and what we must not do to achieve our morally grounded purposes.

We improve upon Aristotle's structure. For one, we're doing stuff and we're paying attention to the results. That's consistent with the scientific method, and in philosophy it's called being pragmatic. That's what it means to be pragmatic: set a goal, do stuff, and pay attention to results. But pragmatism has a huge weakness. Pragmatism is related to analytic philosophy and positivism both of which attempted to fix philosophy by making it scientific. And as we have seen, science does not have the tools required to investigate what ought to be. Similarly, pragmatism reminds us to focus on our goals and on our results, but it does not provide the criteria for selecting our goals, what we ought to achieve. We fix that weakness in pragmatism when we identify our morally grounded purposes, what we ought to achieve.

We're in the public square and we're interested in what works and what does not work. But something only works if it does what it ought to do, if it achieves what ought to be. We have put what works in the context of morally grounded purposes. We have united pragmatism with moral philosophy to establish our criteria regarding what works and what does not work. We have been doing this all along, but now we can name what we're

---

[46] One might be tempted to re-integrate moral philosophy and social science as they were in the High Middle Ages. But that would ignore the significant advances social science has made by being scientific.

doing: When we do public moral philosophy, we do Morally Grounded Pragmatism. Not pragmatic morality. Morally Grounded Pragmatism. As we will see, morally grounded pragmatism is wonderfully compatible with the scientific method used by social scientists.

We establish our morally grounded purposes and we use them as criteria (standards) to evaluate what is in society. We're doing moral philosophy and social science. We have certainly talked a lot about our morally grounded purposes. It's time we find out what they are.

The Morally Grounded Purposes of America's Liberal Democracy

The American Constitution established the United States as a Constitutional Democratic Republic. It was also founded and has been preserved as a liberal democracy. We have already described the role that John Stuart Mill (1806-1873) played in defining the core principles of the United States as a liberal democracy. Protecting core principles is essential to fighting and reversing entropy.

What are the core principles of our liberal democracy? In identifying our morally grounded purposes, we don't have to start with a blank slate. This is America. We have had national goals and values since the signing of the Declaration of Independence which stated:

> We hold these truths to be self-evident, that all men are created equal, that they are endowed by their Creator with certain unalienable Rights, that among these are Life, Liberty and the pursuit of Happiness.

Our morally grounded purposes then can start with all humans being created equal and with the unalienable right to life, liberty, and the pursuit of happiness. But those are only "among" our unalienable rights. Even before those ends, we must declare our goal of freedom and how we will protect it while making laws. The Declaration of Independence, in justifying the American

Revolution, lists the offenses the King of England committed against the people of the American colonies and ended that list with this assertion: "A Prince, whose character is thus marked by every act which may define a Tyrant, is unfit to be the ruler of a free people." We're first of all "a free people." We must start with freedom. Anytime we suggest a law, we suggest that in some manner or other, we will impact someone's freedom. In this country, we have chosen:

> . . . civil freedom of the citizen under a government whose powers are limited, and under a rule of law whose reach is likewise limited, chiefly by the axiom that the constraints of law must serve the cause of essential social freedom.[47]

As we think and talk about creating public laws and policies, we must be able to argue that our laws serve the cause of essential social freedom. Public laws preserve personal and social freedom. Essential social freedom is one of our morally grounded purposes.

We begin with the assumption that all of our citizens enjoy complete social freedom: how they act with others in any social setting, in their home, with their family, what churches and clubs they join, and how they act in those churches and clubs; what they say and write; and so on. In every facet of their lives, all citizens in a liberal democracy are free. The laws that the government of a liberal democracy makes always impact, reduce in some way, essential social freedom. So even though arguments for laws and policies are intended to clarify and protect our social freedom, they must protect personal and civil freedom. If laws destroy the

---

[47] John Courtney Murray, *We Hold These Truths*, p. 164. Murray was an Irish American, born in New York City in 1920, a Jesuit priest, and an internationally renowned theologian who played a key role in persuading the Catholic bishops assembled at the Second Vatican Council to adopt the Council's ground-breaking Declaration on Religious Liberty, *Dignitatis Humanae*. It established in Church doctrine the ". . . inviolable rights of the human person and the constitutional order of society." It acknowledged that there is salvation outside the Catholic Church. He infuriated traditional, authoritarian Catholics.

personal or civil freedom of some of our citizens, telling them that if they don't like it they can leave the country is not just a stupid statement, it violates a moral axiom of our liberal democracy. It operates at Stage 3 Tribal moral reasoning. It violates the rights of some citizens while giving advantages to others. It undermines and threatens our liberal democracy.

Life and liberty are rights that have received considerable attention in the public square. We could treat safety as a separate responsibility, but I think that it's obviously included in "life." Rather than write life/safety, I will ask the reader to assume that safety is included in "life." Our laws and policies can't serve the cause of essential social freedom if they don't provide life and liberty. Using Kant's insight, a law that undermines life and liberty for some but not for others "destroys itself in practice."

We're building our list of morally grounded purposes:

> Essential social freedom,
> Life and liberty.

I should clarify what I mean by freedom and liberty. Dictionaries may treat them as synonymous. I think it's useful to think of freedom as social freedom, freedom in one's personal life and in one's relationships with others. Liberty relates to one's political life. Our commitment to liberty means that rulers can't conduct themselves as if they're above the law or impose their authority on individuals. In a liberal democracy, rulers rule through the power given to them in the Constitution and are affirmed or replaced through elections. Rulers, in America's case, the executive, legislative, and judicial branches of government, must exercise their authority in a way that preserves the Constitution and the liberty of everyone who lives in our country. We exercise our freedom independent of the law. The law protects our political liberty and our social freedom.

Next, we can strengthen our morally grounded purposes by adopting an axiom that's ubiquitous in the Eastern Intellectual Tradition: One's happiness can't cause pain in others. That's a nifty commitment to Stage 5 moral reasoning.

What else?

As a nation we haven't been so clear regarding peace. We haven't adequately linked peace with justice. That's just weird. The Declaration of Independence cited the violation of justice as grounds for the people to declare their ruler a tyrant who is unfit to rule and for their right to overthrow him, even to take up arms against him. In brief: No Justice, No Peace! It's right there in the Declaration of Independence. And yet our government and institutional leaders haven't hesitated to use violence to suppress activists who have used peaceful demonstrations to demand their Constitutional rights. We must include peace and justice among our morally grounded purposes.

The pursuit of happiness has been largely ignored as a public responsibility and treated as a private matter, a personal respon-sibility. The pursuit of happiness is not a new claim. Jefferson put it in the Declaration of Independence. Our Founding Fathers risked their lives when they signed off on the document that includes it. It deserves a lot more intellectual attention in the public square so that we understand which areas of happiness and fulfillment are best thought of as personal and which are impossible to pursue alone, can only be achieved with the support of our community. We may not know what to do about the pursuit of happiness, but we know that it must be included in the morally grounded purposes of our liberal democracy. It's a goal, not an achievement. We give this topic more attention in the chapter Social Justice.

We might also acknowledge that public policy must deal with the just distribution of wealth. But as communist countries have taught us, the distribution of wealth is not an interesting topic if there is no wealth. Our economic system must both generate wealth and distribute wealth. Economic justice is better understood as a set of economic laws and policies that either help or frustrate our attempts to achieve our morally grounded purposes. So we have developed another insight. Our morally grounded purposes stand alone. They provide the standards by which we evaluate what is in society and the laws, policies and programs we adopt to achieve those purposes. The areas of our lives that require laws and policies can be described as areas of public responsibility, not morally grounded purposes. The just distribution of wealth is achieved through laws, policies, and programs that are evaluated in terms of their ability to achieve our morally grounded purposes.

What morally grounded purposes do we have so far?

Preserve and protect essential social freedom.

Provide for life, liberty, and the pursuit of happiness.

Guarantee justice and peace.

Make no laws that give happiness or benefit to some at the cost of doing harm to others.

That list looks pretty good, but it lacks clarity on one essential issue we studied in moral development. Stage 5 moral reasoning treats everyone the same. Our moral statements must apply to all, equally. Just like it says in the Declaration of Independence ("All men are created equal") and the Pledge of Allegiance ("With liberty and justice for all"). And as we have seen, to treat everyone equally, we must acknowledge and protect the full humanity of all of our people: All races, all religions, all genders, all sexual orientations. We acknowledge that full humanity includes the domains of the individual, person, and self. Now we're getting at our morally grounded purposes, our core American values.

Recognize, preserve, and promote the dignity and worth of all humans.

Preserve and protect essential social freedom of all humans.

Provide for life, liberty, and the pursuit of happiness for all humans.

Guarantee peace and safety for all humans.

Make no laws that give happiness or benefit to some at the cost of doing harm to any other humans.

Murray's insistence that agreement does not end argument but that useful argument begins with agreement applies to how we work to achieve our morally grounded purposes. Yes, we must agree about what we're trying to accomplish, our morally grounded purposes. And when we have agreed, we treat them as axioms: Unquestioned core values that stand on their own, that everyone agrees to, and guide inquiry, practice, and most of all arguments in the public square.

Obviously, because the *teloi* or morally grounded purposes of a teleological argument or teleological reasoning play a defining role in the argument, in the reasoning that supports the argument, they must be unarguably true. They must be accepted by everyone participating in the argument. A false *telos* produces a fallacious argument. Unaccepted *teloi* produces the kind of disagreement that makes productive argument impossible. I have not made arguments for our morally grounded purposes. I did not have to. First, I took them from our founding documents and added one that's ubiquitous in eastern philosophy and seems useful here. Second, once we committed to mature moral reasoning, our morally grounded purposes became self-evident, as Jefferson said they were. One might be able to "just disagree" but as we have seen, that's fine in private life but childish conduct in the public square. One must present a rational argument to support one's rejection of any of our morally grounded purposes, and to do so one must advance the philosophy of a different form of government than ours or one grounded in Stage 3 moral reasoning. On the other hand, it is quite possible that we could add new morally grounded purposes to our list, like to protect the earth and our environment. But to do so would require our developing whole arguments to defend them which would be easy, but is not the job of this book. This book is designed to help We the People conduct all public arguments productively, not to carry them out. These morally grounded purposes suffice for now, and are unarguable, but they may not be exhaustive. There may be more.

Once we agree on our morally grounded purposes, there is enormous room for argument about how to achieve them. The important point to remember is that it's impossible even to begin rational discourse on what **we ought to *do* in society**, if we haven't agreed on what **we ought to achieve**. This list of morally grounded purposes provides a solid foundation upon which to conduct moral discourse in the social sciences and in the public square. It supports the full development of the social sciences, our body politic, and our political mind.

Checking back in on what we have done and what we must do, we recall that we're working on how we think about how we think. Epistemology consists of the source, organization, structure, and standards of knowledge in a discipline. Aristotle helped us think about our structure and standards. But what is our source? This is where mathematics helps us think.

The Source of Knowledge in Moral Philosophy

It's helpful to think of moral philosophy as similar to mathematics and social science as similar to natural science. Mathematics and natural science are indispensable to each other, and develop knowledge differently. Moral philosophy and social science are indispensable to each other, and develop knowledge differently.

When mathematicians[48] develop knowledge they identify mathematical axioms and conduct rational arguments based on the best mathematical knowledge and deductive reason. What is their source of knowledge? In a nut shell: The mathematics community, working together with shared rules is the source of knowledge in mathematics. But we have also seen that mathematics was not able to reach full development on its own. Only when mathematics became indispensable to science, only when

---

[48] See Simon Singh, *Fermat's Last Theorem* for a fascinating story of Andrew Wiles' quest to solve this theorem. The problem had existed in mathematics since 1637 and was not solved until 1994, published in 1995, 358 years later. But why could Wiles solve it? Because of the knowledge that had grown in the mathematics community, and because he worked heroically to solve it. He knew he had solved it when the mathematics community confirmed his solution.

mathematics was forced to solve problems within the scientific method, did it begin to reach full development.

Moral philosophy has a lot in common with mathematics. Working together, moral philosophers correct and contribute to each other when they operate with mature cognitive development and mature moral reasoning. The moral philosophy community working together with shared rules of logic is the source of knowledge in moral philosophy. But the work of moral philosophers can't reach full development unless it becomes indispensable to social science. And to become indispensable to social science, it must engage and confront and solve moral questions for the social sciences. The source of knowledge in moral philosophy is the moral philosophy community. The tests or standards of knowledge in moral philosophy occur in the social sciences which confirms or rejects the capacity of the assertions of moral philosophy to aid the full development of the social sciences.

So our work on epistemology in moral philosophy has produced our source of knowledge, the moral philosophy community. It has also provided our structure of moral reasoning, Aristotle's teleological structure of goals, virtues and vices; and standards of knowledge, our morally grounded purposes. But these standards only become real when operating in the social sciences. And we can't even think about the organization of knowledge in moral philosophy because that organization occurs in the organization of knowledge in the social sciences. That discussion takes place entirely within our discussion of social science.

Is there a moral philosophy method? Yes, but it's like the mathematical method, not the scientific method. The mathematical method establishes mathematical axioms and uses strict rules of logic. Its proofs are entirely mathematical. Its applications occur in science. Moral philosophy must establish morally grounded purposes and moral axioms, but ultimately, the truth, the standards used to evaluate moral philosophy's conclusions, must be established in society by the social sciences acting within the public square and government.

As we will see, everything we think about how we think in moral philosophy, our entire epistemology of moral philosophy, makes more sense when combined with social science. So let's get to that conversation.

Social Science Method and Epistemology

There was something to be said for treating the social sciences as branches of moral philosophy. They're that connected. But the social science method goes way beyond what moral philosophy is capable of. It really is an advancement in thinking and learning to treat them as interdependent but different. But from an epistemological point of view, they make little sense except as integrated fields of study: Moral philosophy provides answers to the question What ought to be? And the social sciences use What Ought to Be in so many ways that a list is helpful.

The social sciences learn What Ought to Be from moral philosophy and use it:

As the criteria for evaluating What Is in society.
To decide what to change and what to keep in society.
To develop new laws, policies, and programs to aid society.
To evaluate those laws, policies, and programs.

We need to look more closely at social science. As we have seen, Durkheim taught social scientists to study objects in society and to use the scientific method in that study, but the social sciences do more than just use the scientific method when testing results. They aren't just interested in being able to describe what is happening or predict what will happen, they must prove that what will happen when public laws, policies, and programs are implemented will be what ought to happen.

The social science method must commit to achieving both predictability and morality. Social scientists must strive to say with an acceptable level of confidence that if we do A we will get B and B is good. That gets us close to the social science method. Social scientists have developed the statistical methods that measure predictability. Now we turn to the social science epistemology. Again, an Epistemology tells us the source, organization, structure, and standards of knowledge in a discipline.

The Source of Knowledge in Social Science

The most obvious source of knowledge in social science is society. That's what the social sciences study. That's what defines social science as a science: It studies what is. The fact that it studies what is in society defines it as a social science. But the social sciences must also study what ought to be. That's what defines social science as social science, not natural science. So the social sciences have two sources of knowledge: What Is in Society and What Ought to Be in Society, or the morally grounded purposes of our society as established by moral philosophy. At the source of knowledge level, social science integrates science and moral philosophy. We will come back to that.

The Structure and Standards of Knowledge in Social Science

Social science has both moral structure/standards and scientific structure/standards.[49] Social science must structure the study of what is in the context of what ought to be. Social science must evaluate what is in society against what ought to be. Studying what is against what ought to be is one of the structures of social science and studying what ought to be is one of the standards. Using that structure and those standards, social science acts with moral philosophy.

But social science is also science. Social science constructs best guesses about what ought to be done to make society better and translates those suppositions into mathematically structured hypotheses.

That's exactly what scientists do and it's exactly what social scientists do: They design mathematically structured hypotheses, experiments that accommodate the collection of data in a form that can be subjected to mathematical analysis, with the standard of a prescribed level of predictability. Social science uses the structure and standards inherent in the scientific method. That's

---

[49] When I read this chapter, it feels like I am stating the obvious. It's obvious now, but it took a ton of work to get here.

the scientific structure and the scientific standards in the social science method. But in the design of its research, the social sciences must also design research that pays attention to what they're trying to predict: That it works and is good. All social science research, in sociology and management and economics and education, all of it can be vastly improved, made more useful, by focusing on both mathematical predictability and morality.

When social scientists design their experiments, design what data they collect and how they analyze it, they must account for both predictability and morality. Predictability is required in science. Morality is required because the social sciences are useless if they can't help us achieve what ought to be. Again, the epistemology of social science integrates social science with moral philosophy. It integrates the structure and standards of science and moral philosophy. In a nut shell: scientific/mathematical predictability and morality.

As we will see when we investigate Feuerstein in Chapter 10, Education Justice, we're talking about changing how social scientists think and what they do. We're not talking about behavior modification, although behavior does change. We're talking about structural cognitive modification, changing the structure of how social scientists think. How they design research is what they do, but to fix how they do it, they must change how they think about it. Cognitive modification. Then they can help We the People change how we think, modify our cognition, so that we can change how we behave, how we talk in the public square.

The Organization of Knowledge in Social Science

We have talked about the source, method, structure, and standards of knowledge in social science. What about organization? This is where Thomas Kuhn is useful, and when combined with Piaget, is a game changer. Kuhn helps us expand our understanding of formal operations; he describes paradigms, the organization of knowledge that unites both knowledge in a discipline and the members that make up the discipline's community.

As we have seen, formal reasoning consists of syllogisms, formal conceptual frameworks, and paradigms. However, the development of paradigms has the greatest impact on how social scientists think and what they do, what unites them as a community. In our discussion of Education Justice we will discuss paradigms, their power and structure and impact on disciplines that have one. It's not enough to talk about paradigms. We must see how one works and its impact on a discipline that gets one.

Natural Science, Social Science, and Moral Philosophy

We have seen that moral philosophy and social science cannot reach full development without each other. They're useless without each other. But what about natural science? How does it relate to moral philosophy and social science? In an important way, it does not. Science reaches its full development when it does what it does free of interference from moral philosophy and social science. But that does not mean that science does not have a role to play in the public square.

A vast percentage of the research in natural science is morally neutral. It has no need for moral philosophy. But some scientific research begs social solutions. And we must listen to what scientists tell us when they come to the public square and say:

> Hey, we found this out, and We the People (yes, scientists too are members of the body politic when they enter the public square) must do something about it.

But scientists have no way of studying what We the People "ought" to do to fix a social problem. They can discover problems that impact society by using scientific research, but they cannot fix problems that require social solutions. All scientists can do is tell We the People what the problem is and give some technical advice on how to fix it. But We the People must decide what we will do to fix social problems.

Now that scientists have proven scientifically that global climate change threatens all life on earth, both natural scientists and the rest of us must ask, What should we do? Natural science is not capable of answering an "ought" question. Immediately, social science and moral philosophy enter the scene. Social science and moral philosophy have roles to play and must play them well as our body politic, as We the People, respond to what natural science tells us about global climate change. Natural science has given us unarguable scientific facts. These facts are unarguable using scientific reasoning. Of course, anyone stuck on stupid, stupidly committed to ignorance, can argue with them. But as we have seen, they cannot participate in arguments being conducted in the public square because they cannot participate in rational arguments. One cannot rationally participate in scientific arguments, accept or reject scientific evidence, unless one uses scientific knowledge and methods of reasoning. We the People must decide what we ought to do and how to do it. But we can't deny the facts. We the People can't ignore the truth of natural science regarding global climate change, and We the People must decide what to do about it.

Similarly, natural science is capable of developing artificial intelligence that rivals a kind of human intelligence. How should it be developed? How should it be allowed to impact society? How should it be restrained? Again, natural science can't answer those questions. Social science and moral philosophy have central roles to play and they must play them well. Indeed, what social science and moral philosophy bring to the challenge is at least arguably more crucial to the fate of humanity than what natural science brings.

It's no small matter that today social science and moral philosophy play minor roles in the university compared to natural science and that all three have virtually no voice in the public square. Part of the problem is that moral philosophers and social scientists have been silent in the public square. They have abandoned their role of establishing intellectual leadership and moral certitude in the public square. They have left a vacuum that radical capitalists and Status Christians have filled with doctrines felt as facts.

When Aquinas made the West safe for reason, he allowed reason to trump religion in the public square. That success was evident when Rome could not stop the Copernican Revolution and during other public battles waged between religion and reason over the years. But right now, reason is taking a back seat to radical capitalists supported by Status Christians. Social scientists and moral philosophers face enormous intellectual and political challenges to set things straight in the public square. They cannot do it alone. We the People must work with them. But first, they have to show up.

Pat's Notes

In Part III we reviewed the emergence of Christian moral philosophy during the High Middle Ages, its challenge from the teaching of Aristotle, and Aquinas's successful integration of the two. Aquinas made the West safe for reason, and moral philosophy became the dominant area of inquiry in Western universities. And then along came the Protestant Reformation, the religious wars than ensued, and the utter failure of Catholic and Protestant moral philosophers to advance the cause of peace. Rather, they opened wide the paths to war.

At the same time moral philosophy suffered these dreadful failures, natural science took off. By the eighteenth century, moral philosophy had divorced religion, and disciplines that we now recognize as the social sciences had begun to distance themselves from moral philosophy. By the early 20th century, positivism and analytical philosophy had come to dominate philosophy in general and moral philosophy became increasingly a topic in the study of the history of philosophy, not a branch of philosophy that was actually practiced. Moral philosophy was no longer a seat of inquiry.

Also in the twentieth century, the social sciences became increasingly well defined as science with no relationship at all to moral philosophy.

The major achievement of Part III has been to demonstrate the utter failure of both moral philosophy and social science to reach full intellectual development. The problem? They need each other. Neither can reach full development without the other. But the past does not contain the solution. Social science cannot return to being a branch of moral philosophy. What it has learned by being scientific is indispensable to its success. But it must rely on moral philosophy just as natural science must rely on mathematics. They're different, but the need each other.

Moral philosophy provides natural science with the knowledge of what society ought to be, what it must achieve, its ultimate goals. What we call the morally grounded purposes of society.

But only social science has the tools to study society and evaluate what is against the criteria, the standards, established by these morally grounded purposes. Equally important, only social science can conduct the research and development needed to develop programs and policies that work, that when implemented, help society achieve its morally grounded purposes.

Moral philosophy must bring to We the People clear statements of society's morally grounded purposes.

Social science must bring to We the People a clear description of what is in society, what is working and what is not working. And social science must bring to We the People public laws, programs, and policies that can be implemented to help achieve our morally grounded purposes. And those solutions must have been tested scientifically and morally. Social scientists must be able to tell We the People with an accepted level of predictability that: If you do A, you will get B, and B is good.

At the core of public moral philosophy and social science is teleological reasoning that's as old as Aristotle.

Identify what you want to achieve, your morally grounded purposes.

Identify what exists in society that helps achieve those purposes and keep them.

Identify what exists in society that undermines or destroys the ability to achieve those purposes and eliminate them.

Develop new laws, programs, and policies that will help achieve those purposes.

The social sciences need the research tools they received from natural science and they need the moral clarity and certitude they can only gain from public moral philosophy.

And we need them to achieve our goal:

To conduct discourse in the public square that allows us to agree on what is right and what is wrong in public life so that we can make laws and develop public policies that support what is right and reject what is wrong

We need:

A critical mass of Americans to show up in the public square and support our arguments. Religious humanists who believe that social responsibility is a prerequisite to redemption. Secular humanists who believe that a good life requires that they help others. Americans who believe that they're members of and responsible for our community and our liberal democracy.

PART IV

USING MORAL PHILOSOPHY AND SOCIAL SCIENCE

Pat's Notes

We have done a lot of work to get to Part IV. I know I have. I have worked through concepts from different disciplines, constructed some new ones, and tied them all together. And I have gone over and over my text trying to make it as easy to read as possible. But still, any reader who has stayed with me this far has worked. It has not been a beach read. Now I want to take a minute and reassure the reader that all this work has been purposeful and we're about to put it to use.

Cognitive Development: First, we're committed to formal reasoning. We want to be able to think about how we think and think in formal conceptual frameworks at a minimum and paradigms when possible. I have chosen Economic Justice as the chapter to lead off Part IV because it employs a formal conceptual framework that kind of jumped out at me when I was writing an early draft and it has proved invaluable. Maybe a game changer. The reader will decide. And I share my education paradigms, CP 1.0 and CP 2.0, when we deal with education justice. Obviously, we use formal operations to get out of Stage 3 and 4 moral reason and into Stage 5. Formal reason is a big deal.

Moral Development: Reject Stage 3 Tribal moral reasoning. Just flat reject it. It's a major cause of harm within and between nations. Understand the strengths and limits of Stage 4 moral reasoning and use it appropriately. It's fine within organizations and institutions, but totally inadequate in the Public Square. Stage 5 moral reasoning. That's the key to success when We the People conduct discourse in the Public Square. Stage 5 moral reasoning is the therapy we use to heal our fractured body politic. It's the *sine qua non* to healing the wounds of racism, America's Original Sin, and it allows us to discuss economic, education, and social justice like grownups.

Religion in the Public Square: Aquinas made the West safe for reason. Aquinas demonstrated that reason trumps religion in the public square. Entropy and greed have worked to undermine Aquinas's achievement. We must work to bring reason back to prominence in the public square. We don't reject religion. But we challenge religious leaders to meet in what we call the Religious Square and build agreement there. If they can't agree on various moral assertions, it will be for an obvious reason: They're working from incompatible religious texts or traditions. If they can't agree on moral assertions, there is no way that the body politic will be able to agree regarding them. They can't bring moral assertions to the public square that will divide rather than unite We the People. Further, if they're able to agree, it will be because their moral assertions enjoy universal acceptance (don't steal or kill or do harm to others for one's own benefit, etc.) or because they used mature moral reasoning (rather than religious texts or traditions) in constructing their agreement. Anti-intellectual, anti-social religious leaders listen up. Ain't no place for you or yours in conducting discourse in the public square.

Moral Philosophy and Social Science: Thanks a lot. These academics have caused us the most difficult work. But we did it because they are indispensable to the capacity of We the People to conduct rational discourse and to establish intellectual authority and moral certitude in the public square. We need them so that we know what we ought to do, what will work and what will not work as we address major social and political issues. We have integrated their epistemologies and methods. We will use those intellectual tools when we discuss our topics in Part IV, but we also need these intellectuals to follow up. We need them to support us and we need them to provide us with better research and more highly developed solutions. We need them to work together so that they present us with complete solutions. We can't do the R&D they ignore. That's not our job and it is their job. By the way, this includes economists and educators, not just sociologists, social workers, etc. In the chapter, Education Justice, I spend a lot of time describing how education's most prominent intellectual leaders have failed to lead education and assure that it is an effective and efficient socialist enterprise. The purpose of that discussion is not just to challenge intellectual leaders in education. It challenges intellectual leaders in all of the social sciences. They all can either help our socialist enterprises succeed or they will help them fail.

That's a brief summary of the work we have done and of some of the tools that we developed and will use. Tools, they make jobs easier. They also make work more precise. We will use our intellectual tools to both ends: to make our work easier and more precise.

But again, we're dealing with forces that radical capitalists and Status Christians have brought to the public square in pursuit of their ends, to destroy or limit the capacity of our liberal democracy to advance its morally grounded purposes. We must limit the capacity of these negative forces in the public square. We can't be casual in our approach. We too must work. We must bring energy to the forces we apply to heal our fractured body politic and invigorate our public square.

9
Economic Justice

It's always helpful to get our morally grounded purposes out front when be begin a discussion of a social science. They remind us that we're dealing with moral issues and must evaluate everything we think and do with these moral goals in mind. And we remind ourselves that our full intellectual development depends upon full cognitive and moral development.

The Morally Grounded Purposes of America's Liberal Democracy

Recognize, preserve, and promote the dignity and worth of all humans.

Preserve and protect essential social freedoms of all humans.

Provide for life, liberty, and the pursuit of happiness for all humans.

Guarantee justice and peace for all humans.

Make no laws that give happiness or benefit to some at the cost of doing harm to any other humans.

This chapter begins by looking at economic theories, what they are, how we evaluate them, and how we use them to think about economic issues. And by using our morally grounded purposes as criteria for evaluating what we think and do in economics, we use the work we did in moral philosophy. But two additional tools emerge. First, we use the Golden Mean. It helps us investigate and evaluate economic theories. It makes our analysis of economic theories easier and more precise. And second, what we discover in our analysis of economic theories allows us to expand one of our major intellectual tools. Morally Grounded Pragmatism becomes Morally Grounded Pragmatic Dialectic. As we do moral philosophy and we do social science, we improve both and we improve what we do.

Economic systems have two major jobs that impact economic justice: They generate wealth and they distribute wealth. It's obvious that American capitalism generates wealth but fails to distribute it justly. A lot has been written about U.S. wealth inequality, but noting is being done about it. How do we discuss what is right and what is wrong in the pursuit of economic justice?

Economics is a highly developed social science. And yet it can't meet its most glaring challenge: To distribute wealth justly. We the People and our government have failed to meet this challenge because radical capitalists have exerted enormous influence over economic theory and economic laws, policies and programs. Other countries have done a far better job distributing wealth, but We the People of the United States cannot even have productive arguments about how to do it.

Here is the key to this whole issue. Radical capitalists have used their money, power, and influence to wage a massive propaganda campaign in think tanks, universities, the media, and government to convince Americans that the purpose of economics is the full development of capitalism. They use teleological reasoning. They insist that whatever is good for capitalism is good for America and Americans. We have established that the goals of a teleological argument must be valid, accepted. Just as the *a priori* assumptions of a metaphysical argument must be valid. Otherwise, the entire argument must be rejected. The morally grounded purposes of a teleological argument must be valid. We reject the radical capitalist's claim that the purpose of the American economic system is to achieve the full development of capitalism. To make our argument, we study economic theories. And to account for all of the hypotheses around economic theories, we must use formal reasoning. We must invent a formal conceptual framework for economics.

A Formal Conceptual Framework for Economics

First, we select our fundamental assumptions about economics from economic theory. Our decisions regarding which theories to accept will be guided by a fairly obvious criterion. Which theories help us achieve the two major goals of economics: First to generate wealth[50] and second, to distribute wealth justly? Then, within those theories we ask: Which achieve the morally grounded purposes of our liberal democracy and which undermine them? If the theory achieves all of our goals, we accept it. If it does not, we reject it. If two theories contribute, we use the one that's most effective and efficient: Effective, does the job best. Efficient, does the job with the fewest resources. But if no theory is able to achieve all of our goals, but two theories can if they work together, we use them together. But if we want two theories to work together, we must figure out how to do that. This chapter takes on and solves a very interesting puzzle.

When I was writing this chapter, I encountered a big time problem that was made evident to me because I grew up under-standing the power and importance of the Golden Mean when thinking about personal and public morals. I have referred to the Golden Mean, but put off discussing it until now when I am about to use it. The Golden Mean is an intellectual tool. It helps us think better. It makes our thinking easier and more precise.

---

[50] Obviously, the generation of wealth has a moral component to it. Our enterprises that generate wealth must do so without harming life and the planet. That conversation would require another chapter. Suffice it to say that we have developed the intellectual tools that will allow We the People to address environmental justice.

An obvious example is courage. It's an important virtue.[51] But how do we understand it. I want my children to be courageous, but I don't want them to put themselves in danger. But there can be no courage without danger. So we teach them to seek the Golden Mean between recklessness and timidity. We must act, and we must be smart. Careful, but not timid. Assertive, but not reckless. The key to using the Golden Mean is to identify the extremes that must be avoided. They help us understand what we must do and not do. One could write books describing the content of the continuum between recklessness and timidity for it reveals all of the hypotheses around courage. And thinking about that kind of continuum, the extremes and the middle or Golden Mean, helps us think about economic theories. It accounts for all of the hypotheses around economic justice.

There are three obvious economic theories: capitalism, socialism, and communism. And we all know that communism is bad and that we cannot trust socialism because it puts us on the slippery slope to communism. But that just leaves capitalism as our economic theory. And we all know that capitalism can be taken to extremes. We saw it with the Robber Barrons and we feel it today with the vast inequality in wealth. But we do not have a name for what I call radical capitalism. Further, radical capitalism is not an economic theory. It has no history or context that helps us understand it as a theory. Notice, I assumed that capitalism is good, but radical capitalism is not. But we don't even have a name for a theory that accounts for the extreme form of capitalism.

The Golden Mean is an intellectual tool that tells us that our thinking is incomplete. If we cannot identify the extremes, we cannot identify the Golden Mean. And that means that our formal conceptual framework is incomplete: We have not accounted for all of the hypotheses at play in economic theory.

My inability to identify the theory that represents the extreme of capitalism drove me to research the history of economics.

---

[51] There are seven widely recognized virtues in Western civilization. Four come from the Greeks: Prudence, Justice, Temperance, and Courage. Three from Christianity: Faith, Hope, and Charity.

Voila! Mercantilism. It's a well established theory with a long history and we know a lot about its relationship with capitalism. We can use mercantilism to help us locate the Golden Mean of economics and economic justice.

Here we go then, our four major theories of economics: mercantilism, capitalism, socialism, and communism. They all have political assumptions and are associated with political systems.

Mercantilism

Mercantilism is the oldest of our four theories, but it also exists today. Mercantilism was the economic system that replaced feudalism. It was employed by monarchs in parts of Europe from the 16th to the 18th century. Mercantilism emerged as monarchs realized that they could garner enormous wealth if they took control of their economic systems, controlled them as they did their political systems and foreign policy. It's helpful to recall that European monarchies grew out of feudalism and that monarchs retained the ownership of all their nations' wealth and resources (lands, mines, forests, rivers, lakes, etc.) in the person of the monarch. Monarchs distributed such wealth to nobles and reclaimed them as they saw fit, mainly as a means of controlling those with whom they shared wealth and power.

It isn't an accident that mercantilism flourished in authoritarian political systems. Mercantilism was controlled either by a monarch or by the monarch and a group of nobles. The latter system is called an oligarchy: Rule by the very few who are both rich and powerful and use their political power to run their economic and political systems in a way that makes them richer and more powerful. We're not talking ancient history here. The Russia of Vladimir Putin is a political oligarchy with mercantilism as its economic system. It has made Putin (by some estimates) the richest man in the world, his henchmen enormously wealthy, and has impoverished Russia. Donald Trump may be best understood when viewed through the lens of mercantilism. Trump wants to be an oligarch.[52] That also helps explain his weird affection for authoritarian rulers in Russia, Saudi Arabia, Turkey, North Korea, etc. More on Trump and economics later.

Mercantilism's goal was to maximize the nation's wealth as measured in the accumulation of gold and silver by the monarch. Today, wealth includes precious metals but much more. Still the goal of mercantilism is clear, accumulate wealth for the oligarchs.

Mercantilism promotes governmental regulation of a nation's economy for the purpose of augmenting state power at the expense of rival national powers. With the establishment of overseas colonies in the 17th century, mercantilism became both nationalistic and imperialistic. Americans can quickly acquaint themselves with this system by recalling the economic abuses heaped upon the American colonies by the British crown:

> High tariffs imposed in England on goods imported from the colonies.

> Forbidding the colonies to trade with any nation but England.

> Forbidding goods to be carried in ships that weren't English, the Navigation Acts.

Policies applied in England that aided that nation's trade and the monarch's accumulation of wealth included:

> Subsidies on exports.

> Banning the export of gold and silver, even for payments.

---

[52] The fact that Judge T.S. Ellis equated oligarchs with just wealthy individuals and prohibited prosecutors in the Manafort trial from using it as a pejorative in his court highlights the need to expand our understanding of mercantilism, oligarchs, and oligarchys.

Promoting manufacturing and industry through research or direct subsidies but mainly for the enrichment of the monarch.

Limiting wages.

Maximizing the use of domestic resources as opposed to free trade.

Some of these activities seem to make sense for any nation. But we must focus on the fact that any good, any profits that resulted from these policies, accrued mostly to the benefit of the monarch or oligarchs. Building wealth was understood as a zero-sum game: if someone gains wealth someone else must lose wealth. As Americans, we can recall the abuses of mercantilism to the colonies. But a quick review of it also allows us to realize that when the major goal of an economic system is the accumulation of wealth in the hands of the monarch or oligarchs, no attention is paid to the distribution of wealth. Putting a premium on low wages actually promotes both of mercantilism's major goals. It accumulates wealth in the hands of a few and increases their power. But it also creates widespread poverty. Mercantilism is grounded in Stage 3 Tribal moral reasoning. We think of Stage 3 as typical of junior high children, but it has dominated the moral reasoning of many monarchs and all oligarchs[53] for centuries and continues to support the goals of today's radical capitalists.

Mercantilism operates at Stage 3 moral reasoning. In Russia, it creates laws and policies that benefit the oligarchs and impoverishes a vast majority of the Russian people. It can only be sustained by a totalitarian form of government, which Putin with his abundant skills learned while in the KGB and has mastered. If

---

[53] China could be considered an oligarchy, but I think we need to bring sophisticated social science research to that question. China's historical connection to socialism requires it to attend to the needs of all of its people. China's economy is growing but its population is so huge that it will be easy to identify millions of people who are being left out while millions of others are benefitting. What do we look at? Big surprise. China is complex and inscrutable.

an economic system can only be sustained with a totalitarian form of government, it must be rejected. At its core, it is evil.

Adam Smith (1723–1790) published *The Wealth of Nations* in 1776 and with it launched a vigorous attack against mercantilism and for free trade and capitalism. That's a huge point. Capitalism was invented as an argument against mercantilism and as an economic system to replace it. A goal of capitalism is to extinguish and replace mercantilism. And yet, radical capitalists put capitalism on the slippery slope to mercantilism.

Capitalism

Capitalism can feel like The American Economic System because it and the nation were born in the same year: Capitalism in March, 1776, America in July. Further, our Founding Fathers specifically rejected mercantilism and promoted capitalism and free trade. That timing can create a sense that capitalism is the morally grounded purpose of the American economic system, that what is good for capitalism is good for our country; what is bad for capitalism is bad for our country.

Capitalism rejected mercantilism. Capitalism is a system that's grounded in free trade and private ownership of resources and production with the goal of achieving private profit and private wealth. Capitalism and our liberal democracy grew up together. Together, they rejected and replaced both mercantilism and monarchies with their aristocracy and oligarchs. Capitalism seems to be the American Way.

It's helpful for We the People to step back and look at what has happened to capitalism and our economy since the founding of our nation. The capitalism of our Founding Fathers was different from what our capitalism has grown into. The early United States economy consisted of privately owned farms and privately owned and operated manufacturing and service companies. Natural resources and the means of production were owned by a huge number of private individuals. Farmers owned and worked their land. Manufacturers owned and directly ran and often worked in their factories. Adam Smith taught us that because the owners brought both labor and capital to their ventures, they deserve greater return than those who only labor without any capital investment. That's a critical fundamental assumption of capitalism:

$$Labor + capital > Labor$$

Capital has special value because it's combined with labor.

Capitalism typically includes such economic features as: private property, capital accumulation by private individuals not a monarch or oligarchs, wage labor, exchange by a willing buyer and willing seller, and competitive national and international markets. The owners of capital and production and financial markets make all the important decisions, not the monarch. Competition in the marketplace determines prices and the distribution of goods. That's the way capitalism works in theory and the way it worked during roughly the first century of operation in the United States.

But of course, capitalism does not operate at the theoretical level. It operates in the real world and has evolved over time. And with time capitalism changed. Capitalists competed against each other for the private accumulation of wealth. And over time, some won and others lost. The winners took control of larger and larger businesses, more and more wealth. As corporations grew, resources and production accumulated in the hands of fewer and fewer capitalists. Turns out that over time, capitalism is great at generating wealth and accumulating wealth, but it's not so good at distributing wealth. And that inefficiency led, in the late 19th century, to a massive gap in wealth between the very few, very rich Robber Barons; and the very many, very poor rest of America. Our Founding Fathers helped create a capitalistic system that made Stage 5 moral reasoning possible. But radical capitalists want an economic system that can only be supported by Stage 3 Tribal moral reasoning. The obvious threat to radical capitalists is We the People operating with mature moral reasoning. They need to control the political system. They need to control We the People so that they can control the economic system. We the People need to understand the major economic theories so that we can win arguments with radical capitalists and radical socialists.

The massive economic injustice that developed during the 19th century inspired new and sometimes revolutionary economic theories. We need to understand them, especially their differences and why their differences have been lost to We the People.

Communism

Communism is an economic system that identifies with the political and economic theories of Karl Marx whose description of the weaknesses of capitalism have influenced economic thinking in every generation since he first published *Das Kapital*. Alas, although his criticisms of radical capitalism are spot on, his solutions are deeply flawed.

Politically, Marx was revolutionary. He advocated class war designed to eliminate capitalism and capitalists (the bourgeoisies). Communism creates political definitions of winners and losers and eliminates not just free markets but also freedom. It can only be implemented via a totalitarian form of government. It advocates a kind of monarchy of the people, but of course since it can't be sustained through democracy and free elections, the political system degenerates into a tyranny of a political party and bureaucrats.

Economically, Marx called for public ownership of all resources, means of production, and property. Each person was to work and be paid according to their abilities and needs. It proves to be quite efficient at distributing wealth, but it's so inefficient at generating wealth that it leaves too little wealth to distribute and starves its people and itself to death. As Kant would say, communism destroys itself in practice.

Clearly, Marx's communism would have died its own death, proved its unique ineptitude, disappeared leaving no trace. But Marx made two unfortunate mistakes that have persisted and made a mess of economic discourse. Marx (ironically, aided by radical capitalists) undermined the capacity of our body politic to conduct rational discourse on economics for generations.

First, he claimed that socialism (see below) is a transitional economic system that's best understood as a brief stop on the journey to communism. Of course, that was just rhetoric Marx used to undermine socialism which he viewed as a threat to communism because it was too cozy with capitalism. But as capitalism evolved and the very rich got richer and richer and greedier and greedier, they used Marx's claim that socialism is a brief stop on the inevitable path to communism to reduce socialism to a form of communism and a threat to freedom as well as prosperity. Radical capitalists made Marx's argument against socialism their own. Ya gotta love that irony. To serve their selfish interests, they insisted that any move toward socialism, however small, was a gigantic step on the slippery slope to communism. And they continue to use that argument today, doing vast harm to economic discourse, the American economy, and the American people.

Marx's second mistake was not just to notice that religion tends to sooth the people and remove from them the will to fight for economic justice, but to insist on replacing religion with atheism in communist countries. This second, totally unnecessary revolution made an enemy of all religions, religious leaders, and especially the Pope. The Pope bought into Marx's argument against socialism and treated it as a slippery slope to communism. As a result of these two unfortunate arguments about capitalism and socialism on the one hand, and religion on the other; radical capitalists have enjoyed the passive support of many secular moral philosophers, and the active support of conservatives who have developed doctrines felt as facts that side with the rich and powerful. And the Pope and fundamentalist religious leaders who hate atheism and have always equivocated on social and economic justice, have sided with radical capitalists. It's necessary, therefore that we take a careful look at socialism and see it through the eyes of both mature moral reasoning and objective analysis of economic theory, not through the eyes of Marx, self serving radical capitalists, or terrified religious leaders.

Socialism

Socialism can't be understood as a single economic system. There are different versions of it that make quite a bit of difference. However, some generalities are useful.

First, as it relates to political systems, socialism can thrive in a democracy. It does not require a totalitarian government to sustain it.

Second, socialism distributes wealth through the collection of taxes that are used to pay for products and services delivered by the state, and through laws that require fair wages and benefits. (Capitalism rejects taxes and suppresses wages.)

Third, socialism does not require the destruction of capitalism. Indeed, all successful applications of socialism are accomplished alongside capitalism. Both systems seem to work best in concert with each other. Various arrangements between capitalism and socialism in different countries account for the many varieties of socialism.

Socialism calls for social ownership and democratic control of some areas of the economy.

Economists and governments and people have figured out that those segments of the economy that don't involve a willing buyer and a willing seller require socialist economic laws, policies, and programs. In other words, where sole private ownership does not work, social ownership is required.

Education, for example. Complete private ownership of education could certainly generate profits, and perhaps efficiencies, but at what cost? Liberal democracies need an educated population and capitalism needs educated workers and everyone needs an education to have a reasonable shot at maintaining their dignity, achieving freedom, enjoying liberty, and pursuing happiness. Education provides the foundation of full human development. Education can't be commoditized, subjected to market forces. There is no problem if members of our community are priced out of an Audi. They can purchase a less expensive car. But education, by its nature, can't be subjected to the forces of the market place. Education must be affordable, to everyone.

Most countries recognize that medicine and health care don't involve a willing buyer and a willing seller. If I need a drug to save my life or my child's life, I can't enter into equal negotiations with a pharmaceutical company, drug store, or hospital that's only interested in profits. The key term is "equal negotiations." In equal negotiations, the willing buyer and the willing seller have equal ability to execute the transaction or walk away from it. A buyer can walk away from an Audi because it costs too much. A buyer can't walk away from medicine and health care in a life threatening situation, regardless of the cost. Socialized medicine makes as much sense as public schools. If the term "socialized medicine" makes the reader shudder; or worse, seems revolting, it's not your fault, and it's not a legitimate emotion. Americans have been taught to emotionally reject socialism by radical capitalists through vast, self-serving propaganda campaigns that have exploited Marx's claim that socialism is a mere step in an inevitable move toward communism. We will reject that view below and relieve the reader's discomfort.

Analyzing and Evaluating Economic Theories

Understanding these four economic theories allows us to develop our formal conceptual framework for economics. Most notable is that we have not found one economic system as our Golden Mean. Rather capitalism and socialism combine to do that. This framework allows us to begin our analysis of our four economic theories.

Economic Justice Formal Conceptual Framework		
Fatal Extreme	**Golden Mean**	**Fatal Extreme**
Mercantilism <-------->	Capitalism vs Socialism	<--------> Communism

When we think about our four economic theories and place them in a formal conceptual framework, we identify mercantilism and communism as the fatal extremes required to identify the Golden Mean. Both Mercantilism and Communism are excessive, unsustainable economic systems that are also exclusive opposites. They can't tolerate each other or any other systems. They require totalitarian governments to sustain them. They can't survive in a liberal democracy.

But neither capitalism nor socialism can be listed as our Golden Mean. Capitalism is flawed because it does not distribute wealth. Socialism is flawed because it does not generate wealth. By definition, socialist enterprises are cost centers. Socialism collects wealth from capitalists and capitalist enterprises and distributes it. Fortunately, capitalism and socialism are compatible. Capitalism is great at generating wealth, but not at distributing it justly. Socialism is great at distributing wealth but not at generating wealth. All socialist enterprises operate as cost centers in our economy and capitalist enterprises as profit centers or they cease to exist. Every business has both cost centers and profit centers, and so does our economy.

The more capitalism moves toward mercantilism, the more corrupt, the more radical it becomes. Let's look at that more carefully. As capitalism moves toward mercantilism it reduces its capacity to distribute wealth. It does not just cease to be capitalism, it under funds and destroys all socialist enterprises.

The more capitalism moves toward socialism, without becoming socialist, the more effective it becomes. The better it generates and distributes wealth and the better it funds socialist enterprises. It serves all of the people, not just the wealthy.

Similarly, the more socialism moves toward communism, the more corrupt, the more radical it becomes. As socialism moves toward communism, it reduces the capacity of capitalism to generate wealth and thereby destroys its sources of revenue. The closer socialism moves toward communism, it destroys both itself and capitalism in practice.

The more socialism moves toward capitalism, without becoming capitalist, the more efficient it becomes. The better it uses the resources it is given.

Both capitalism and socialism risk getting on a slippery slope: capitalism toward mercantilism, socialism toward communism. The more they engage each other and work together, the safer and better each is.

It is worth noticing that by using the Golden Mean for economics and economic justice we have accounted for all of the hypotheses in this topic. It takes a complex topic and makes our understanding of it both easy and precise. But in this case, we have not created a continuum. The mean breaks the continuum. It creates two continua, one on each side of the mean. And how we locate our two major concepts, capitalism and socialism, on their continua reveals the extent to which they support or undermine each other. That's pretty cool and it warns us not to get too far from the Mean, but it does not tell us which laws and policies help or hurt. We need social science to do that, but still, it is a very cool conceptual framework, if you like conceptual frameworks.

The Morally Grounded Pragmatic Dialectic of Capitalism and Socialism

But how do we think of the unity of capitalism and socialism so that we establish a Golden Mean? We cannot merge them because they have different jobs to do and must preserve their separate identities to do them. Here we get to introduce a new concept, a new dynamic that has ancient roots: the dialectic. Aristotle used the term in describing conversations, the back and forth we have that enhances our thinking and allows us to reach a better conclusion than we started with. Hegal described it as a thesis confronted by an antithesis. The confrontation or argument can go on for some time, but if all goes well, it results in a new view that uses both the thesis and antithesis and is better than either, a synthesis. The concept of a dialectic provides a practical and efficient solution to how we think about and construct the relationship between capitalism and socialism in our economic arguments.

When We the People talk about economics and ponder what laws and policies we need, a major question we must ask is: Which areas of our lives operate best as capitalist enterprises with private ownership, private control, private profits, and free markets? And which areas of our lives operate best with socialist enterprises with social ownership, social control, tax revenue, and socially controlled services? But perfect answers do not exist. The social sciences working with capitalist and socialist leaders use their best efforts to answer those questions and create appropriate enterprises. And they probably can't come up with perfect solutions. We must recognize that we're dealing with a work in progress, a process (as Nick Saban would say).

The best economic system constructs a balance between capitalism and socialism. Economic arguments in the public square aim at developing economic laws and policies that establish and maintain this balance. We the People make laws and evaluate them in terms of their ability to achieve our morally grounded purposes. I call this process Morally Grounded Pragmatism. But we have added not just a new concept in dialectic, but a new form of action. We create a new term: Morally Grounded Pragmatic Dialectic. Sometimes we will use Morally Grounded Pragmatism, most obviously when we have established a Golden Mean with just one term. At other times we will need our Morally Grounded Pragmatic Dialectic, most obviously when our Golden Mean produces two terms that must operate together but remain separate.

We elaborate that approach and make it more concrete in economics by acknowledging that it requires an ongoing attempt to find a balance between capitalism and socialism. Two different approaches to pursuing our morally grounded purposes and solving problems in that pursuit. We have got to make decisions, and it is impossible to make perfect decisions when we are trying to figure things out, in the social sciences, the public square, and government. So we make decisions, we create laws and policies, and we evaluate their results. Did they help us achieve our morally grounded purposes or other goals we set for them or did they create unexpected problems, unintended consequences? That's what we do when we use a pragmatic dialectic process. We set goals, do stuff, pay attention to results, and fix what needs to be fixed.

We keep developing new intellectual tools in moral philosophy and social science. As well we should. Mathematics and natural science certainly do.

With our Formal Conceptual Framework for Economics and our Morally Grounded Pragmatic Dialectic, we can now look at major issues that belong to capitalism. How do we think about

them when we keep in mind America's morally grounded purposes, our formal conceptual frame work for economics, and our
Golden Mean that's constructed as a dialectic.

We will provide a model for analyzing and evaluating
socialist enterprises in our chapter Education Justice. Education is
America's oldest and largest socialist enterprise. In the chapter
Social Justice we acknowledge that by definition individuals and
communities pursue their ends independent of the government
and yet there are some areas of individual and community life that
cannot reach full development without the support of the government in either capitalist and/or socialist enterprises. But now let's
look at some major economic issues that confront us in the public
square.

Capitalist Issues that Confront We the People

It's possible to simplify the discussion of these topics because we
have already eliminated the goals of radical capitalists and their
move to mercantilism and radical socialists and their move
toward communism. Rather we discuss each topic in the context
of its helping us achieve our morally grounded purposes. Of
course, the real discussions must be conducted by We the People.
I just give examples of how our Formal Conceptual Framework
and Morally Grounded Purposes frame each issue and support
calm, rational, mutually respectful discourse.

Competition

Capitalists compete to win which eliminates competition. Mo
money. But they insist that everyone else must compete to make
radical capitalism as productive as possible. That is a powerful
expression of Stage 3 Tribal moral reasoning, and We the People
reject it without apology. We the People regulate capitalism when
capitalists have eliminated competition either in their business or
in their relationship with their communities or employees. But We
the People must be careful. It is always better if capitalists regulate themselves, strive for profits and justice. We the people must
be careful not to over-regulate. Capitalists, socialists, and We the

People can undermine attempts to achieve our goals. We all must pay attention to results.

Employment and Unemployment

Employment costs money. Low unemployment was traditionally the enemy of capitalists because it forced them to compete for employees. Mo costs. But the goals of our economic system are not limited to generating wealth for capitalists. They also seek to create wealth for the entire nation, and that requires the just distribution of wealth. The more capitalist enterprises recognize and pursue our morally grounded purposes as well as profits, the healthier they are and the better they serve our nation and our people. But capitalism cannot distribute wealth as efficiently and effectively as it generates wealth. And the primary goal of capitalist enterprises must be to generate wealth. Without wealth, there is nothing for us to talk about.

We the People must step in to assure that wealth is distributed justly. And that work can begin with employment. One way to regulate capitalists and provide for the distribution of wealth is to make sure that employees have "equal negotiating" power with management. Equal negotiating power is at the heart of the principal of the willing buyer and the willing seller, a core principle of capitalism. But again, We the People must be careful. Power corrupts. Powerful labor unions have waged their power with Stage 3 Tribal moral reasoning. We the People cannot support the combination of power and Stage 3 moral reasoning anywhere in our economy. Unions and management must be regulated so that their negotiations are effective and efficient and assure the continued success of the enterprise.

We the People can take a lot of pressure off of unions and management. We can support laws that: Raise minimum wages, provide universal health care (which saves corporations a lot of money), require paid leave and much longer maternity leave, and strengthen social security. We the People can also provide paid retraining for displaced workers to help them develop the skills needed by more demanding work. And we can expand education to include German style apprenticeship programs. These programs retrain lower skill workers so that they can do the higher skill jobs that are in demand in capitalist enterprises. All of these programs cost money. We can provide tax incentives for companies that distribute wealth in these ways or we can collect taxes that are needed to pay for them. But again, none of these efforts can work if there is no wealth to distribute. We the People must be smart and pay attention to the results we get, our intended and unintended consequences.

And we need to stop providing tax incentives to American corporations that send jobs overseas. Enough said.

Artificial intelligence (AI) and robots present huge challenges. AI and robots eliminate jobs and create new, often better jobs. Someone must build and service robots. Someone has to write and maintain robots' and AI software. These are high paying jobs. That's all good. But we also cannot ignore what appears to be a fact. More jobs will be lost than created, and the jobs that are created will require higher skills than the jobs that were eliminated.

We the People must figure out how to assure full employment. Good work and the ability to support oneself and one's family is a fundamental human need. It is a prerequisite to the health of the individual and the development of the person and the self. To the extent that our capitalist enterprises cannot provide jobs and stay competitive, We the People must find socialist solutions. But we must find efficient ways to fund new socialist programs. When robots eliminate jobs and increase profits, those profits do not belong solely to investors. Those profits, that new wealth, need to be distributed justly. Valued added taxes (VATs) on every robot could be used to replace the income tax revenue that was lost when robots replaced human workers.

What interesting challenges We the People face. What must we do to make sure that we do no harm to our capitalist enterprises? That's where our bread is buttered. And what socialist programs can we create? Programs that justify the revenue collected to fund them and provide interesting, rewarding work for our people, and serve our nation well? Any socialist program we create must be effective and efficient. It must be well led and well managed.

Rights of Inheritance

Many wealthy capitalists insist that work and competition are the paths to happiness for everyone else but want to make sure that their children don't face the risks of open competition. They know what the Chinese have known for a couple thousand years: One generation makes the wealth, the next generation spends it, the third loses it and returns to the crowd. Wealthy families should be able to inherit privately held companies in which they work and property in which they live. Work on it, We the People. We must be reasonable and just, not punitive. But we can't afford an oligarchy to emerge in our country and unregulated inheritance will do just that. Adam Smith and our Founding Fathers worked to defeat and replace the monarchy, aristocracy, oligarchy, and mercantilism. We must keep up that fight while treating wealthy people justly.

Just Taxes and the Distribution of Wealth

Simple. The more people that organizations employ and the better the wages they pay, the fewer taxes must be collected to distribute wealth. On the other hand, when capitalist enterprises use their power to pay less than a living wage, We the People must step in and tax those enterprises and use that revenue to enhance the living standard of those employees, make up for what their wages do not provide. This topic forces We the People to decide what we mean by fair wages and a good and just standard of living. The arguments are aided by our attention to the morally grounded purposes of our liberal democracy. What income must families earn to realize those goals? Later we will talk about the support only communities can give and the socialist enterprises that must be in place to assure that those goals are real for all of our families. Capitalists must be free to make decisions, and We the People must help capitalists when they cannot help themselves. This discussion becomes more focused when we think about the distribution of profits.

Controlling the Distribution of Profits

This topic requires careful intellectual attention because it goes to the heart of capitalism. We the People and investors must become very smart about the financial markets because healthy financial markets are indispensable to capitalist enterprises and a healthy capitalist economy. Investors must become smarter because they cause their own problems and no regulations can fix the harm they do through their own stupidity.

Let's talk briefly about investors. Smart investors pay close attention to the economic fundamentals of the companies and markets they invest in. From the tulip madness that hit Holland in the 17th century (whether true or mostly myth) to the dot com bubble of the late 1990s to the housing bubble that almost resulted in the complete destruction of our monetary system in 2008, investors have ignored fundamentals and fallen into the trap of chasing profits. They have ignored the fact that markets that get out of whack inevitably correct themselves. Often painfully so. And typically the further a market is out of whack, the more painful the correction. As I write, investors have lost common sense about the profits that a healthy economy and market pro-duce and what should be a reasonable risk adjusted rate of return. Instead of a realistic range of 10 to 12% per year with moderate risk, in crazy markets, investors, both private and institutional, make rash decisions if profits fail to reach 25% in six months. This was particularly true during the dotcom bubble and the subsequent real estate bubble that followed.

Few regulations can help when investors become irrational, but increasing the length of time stocks must be held to qualify as long term investments in the tax code would help. If We the People are going to provide tax breaks for long term investments, an obvious good for companies and markets, the rewards should be attached to genuinely long term investments and not short term speculation.

But what do We the People need to know about financial markets? There are three major categories of financial markets: commodity/futures exchanges, and Stock Markets. Most people think of stocks as the publicly traded stocks that are listed on exchanges like the NYSE and NASDAQ. But there are also privately held stocks, and one area of critical importance to a healthy capitalist economy is Venture Capital. Venture capitalist buy privately held stock in early stage companies long before they are publicly listed. We will discuss the critical importance of these investors as well.

It is helpful if we get rid of misconceptions and focus on the strengths of each, the contributions each makes to capitalist enterprises, and the problems that We the People can help solve.

Commodities and futures exchanges were invented to allow producers (farmers) and consumers (food companies that buy a lot of corn) of commodities to hedge their bets on the price they will receive or pay for their commodities. There are futures on lumber, metals, financial instruments, weather and all sorts of other categories. They are very risky for novice investors but they exist to provide the opportunity to reduce risk for sophisticated investors. There is a popular belief that futures markets are great to hedge price fluctuations, but that speculators ruin these markets and take advantage of the folks who actually produce or consume the goods. The problem with that view is that without the speculators, there would be such a limited market for these futures that the parties interested in hedging their risk would not be able to afford them. The transaction cost and execution would be too uncertain. Speculators actually create the liquidity that makes it possible for producers and consumers to efficiently hedge their bets. But farmers, other producers, and consumers better know what they are doing if they decide to use commodity markets to hedge their bets. They are willing buyers and are responsible for their decisions.

We will discuss stock markets but first we need to talk about the Venture Capital. Venture capitalists invest in early stage start ups and companies that show rapid growth but do not yet have the revenues and profits that would make them attractive as acquisitions or initial public offerings (IPOs), or able to cope with the risks of debt financing to fund future growth. Venture capitalists invest directly in companies and acquire ownership of those companies in the form of stock. They often take a seat on the companies boards of directors and try to help with expertise and connections to help the company grow. Venture capitalists receive large percentages of stock for their investment, because without their money, the company would have no chance of starting or surviving. Furthermore, the share of a company's stock held by venture capitalists may increase with future rounds of venture financing if the venture capitalists choose to fund later rounds. The sooner a company becomes profitable and can finance itself out of profits, the more stock the company founders retain.

Venture capital is indispensable in any capitalist economy. It funds new companies, new jobs, and economic growth. It is the lifeblood of entrepreneurial spirit that the U.S. has long been known for. It is called "venture" capital because there is a lot of adventure in funding start ups and young companies, just as there is a lot of risk assumed by founders and early stage employees. Most of these companies do not survive and investors often lose their entire investment when a company fails. On the other hand, those that do survive often become enormously successful and have grown into many of the large companies that are household names today. When venture capital investing is done well, the profits of a few successful companies more than make up for the losses in the others, but it takes time. The average venture capital investment can often be held for 5-7 years or even as long as ten years. Venture capital investors deserve reasonable tax breaks on their profits so that they are incented to participate in this essential market which truly qualifies as long term investing.

Start ups and new companies typically have three goals. Some are in it for the long haul. The founders and early employees want to build a great company and retain control of their private stock so that they can control how they operate the company. There are all kinds of rewards for them if they are successful. Others want to build a profitable company and cash out by either having a large company buy their stock or by issuing an IPO in which a percentage of the company's stock is sold to the public. IPOs provide capital to fuel further growth while allowing early investors the chance to cash in on their investment. All three goals depend upon public and/or private equity markets.

When start ups are acquired or go public, someone buys their stock. The founders might cash out some of their equity, their insiders stock, or they may be required to hold it for 1-2 years following the IPO. Early employees in start ups can earn shares of stock, or typically receive options on shares over time, because they work harder for longer hours and with lower wages than they would have experienced in more mature companies. They also take on greater career risk. Unfortunately the latest tax changes passed by the Republican Congress and Trump Administration cause those share options to be taxed before the employee exercises and sells them. That is patently unfair to these employees. It creates an immediate tax burden which of course requires cash to meet but it hits before those taxed have received the cash they need to pay the taxes. This seemed to be largely targeted at the state of California because of its recent, rather astonishing move to the left and support of Democratic candidates for Congress and President. But it also hurts startup companies and employees in enclaves all over the country. Putting financial strain on entrepreneurial founders and employees that are trying to build the next great American companies is foolish and clearly exhibits Stage 3 Tribal moral reasoning. These preemptive taxes should be rolled back and appropriate taxes should be paid when options are exercised and the shares are sold. These taxes should recognize the long terms and commitment that these investments required.

Established companies that acquire new companies provide liquidity to venture capital investors and entrepreneurs. Liquidity is huge. Without it, no one can sell what they want to sell. Without trusting that their assets will be liquid, no one would participate in venture capital.

When a company issues an IPO, it works with an Investment Banker to develop the terms of the issue, write the prospectus that lays out the fundamentals of the company, and justifies the cost of the offering and the risks investors face in purchasing the stock. IPO funds, less investment banking fees, go directly to the company to fund future growth or in some cases, as described in the prospectus, may be used to purchase shares from early stage investors or founders. All subsequent trades in the company's stock occur on the public stock exchange where it is listed. These trades are made between those who own the stock currently and would like to sell and those who want to purchase the stock at the current price. So a fair question is: What the hell good does all the activity in a stock market do for companies or the country after the IPO is complete?

Stock markets provide a valuable description of a company's value, its financial condition. All companies whose stock is publicly traded are required by law to publish quarterly and annual financials that allow current shareholders and analysts to assess their value and predict the risk adjusted rate of return they can expect if they purchase their stock. When investors buy stock that is trading on an exchange, they demonstrate their confidence in that company. When rational investors make rational decisions regarding the purchase of stocks, they help establish the fundamental value of the company. That's a big deal. As an aside, when economists and pundits promote irrational investing, treat it like it is the great reality of stock market participation, they undermine rational investing. They promote irrationality. They attack reason in the public mind.

Companies use the health of their company as described in the value of their stock as one of the most obvious ways they have of informing their current and future employees that things are going well and of gaining favorable terms from banks when they seek either short or long term debt financing. The existence of major corporate bond markets provides ample evidence of the importance of debt financing to capitalist enterprises. Debt financing is important because it allows owners and shareholders to retain ownership without diluting the value of their stock.

This is just a glimpse into the complex arena of financial markets. Hopefully it is sufficient to alert all of us when we enter the public square that We the People must be smart when we argue about how to regulate capitalism. Capitalism requires a lot of freedom for capitalists or it simply will not work. Over regulation moves capitalism too close to socialism and as we have noticed, socialist enterprises do not generate wealth. We need our capitalist enterprises to succeed. Capitalist enterprises create our national wealth. But, as we have seen, if capitalism is not regulated at all it has this troubling tendency to get on the slippery slope to mercantilism. So what needs to be regulated?

Because we have set capitalism and socialism in a morally grounded pragmatic dialectic, by definition we expect to learn from experience, learn from the consequences of our decisions. And what we learn is that some decisions produce desired results and must be maintained, and some decisions produce negative results that must be fixed. What are some things that need to be fixed?

Long term investment is an obvious good for companies and the economy, but both individual and institutional investors have abandoned this strategy and been rewarded in the tax code. The current holding time for a long term capital gain is only one year. It used to be six months. That is not a long term investment. Long term investments must be redefined in the tax code for a three year holding period or at least two years at a minimum.

Chief Executive compensation has gone off the rails. CEOs are paid too much and their compensation has too often lost any relationship to their long term success on the job. CEO compensation is typically made up of a combination of salary, bonus, and stock options. It is the latter two that do not align with the goals of the organization or its stakeholders. In almost all cases, CEO bonuses depend on annual results. Annual results cause the CEO and executive team to make decisions that will produce quarterly and annual results while undermining the company's long term growth. This practice violates Stage 4 moral reason. It creates Stage 3 Tribal norms among the CEO, executive team, and Board of Directors.

Allowing CEOs to vest in share options of their company's stock is actually a sensible way of compensating them. It rewards them for working hard to make the company better. But the way Boards allow CEOs to vest is almost always counterproductive. Boards typically allow CEOs to vest a large amount of their share options too early, they reward the CEO before they have had time to evaluate the CEO's contributions to the company. Boards should implement options vesting plans where the bulk of the options vest after the CEO has been in place for five years. This will help ensure that a CEO earns this form of compensation from the value added to the company and its stakeholders. Boards must be smart, and it is appropriate for We the People to pay attention to what Boards do regarding CEO compensation and the overall use of profits. Vesting schedules should be back loaded and tied to performance metrics and bonuses should be tied to both near term and long-term performance. If Boards cannot do it, We the People will have to regulate them.

Golden parachutes have become a scandal. There is no way that they can withstand rational scrutiny. Of course, capitalist enterprises must be able to attract talented CEOs, and to do that they have to pay up front for them. Severance packages are an important part of those contracts. But We the People need to step in and limit severance agreements for CEOs to no more than two years' salary and limit immediate option vesting clauses and golden parachute bonuses.

Decisions regarding chief executive salaries are made by the Boards of Directors of companies. Membership on these boards consists almost entirely of the CEOs of other companies or retired CEOs. This club of CEOs is generous to the extreme with each other. Stage 3 tribal moral reasoning. We the People must be interested in the decisions Boards make regarding CEO salaries. We must support salaries that are fair and effective, salaries that allow companies to attract talented executives. But we also must think through what it means for salaries to be excessive and either regulate Boards or tax the excesses. Companies find better ways to spend money than on excessive CEO salaries if most of those excesses go to federal income tax. Rather, they will spend that money on R&D, capital improvements, increased salaries and benefits for employees. A lot of good can come from Boards of Directors and CEOs committing to the goals of the organization and the interests of all of the company's stakeholders.

Fiduciary Responsibility and the Distribution of Profits

"Fiduciary Responsibility" is often used by corporate boards and chief executives to justify their excessive commitment to shareholders. As we have seen, financial markets are essential to the life of capitalist enterprises, but shareholders are not the only important stakeholders in a company. Labor matters, and we have already discussed the importance of fair wages and the duty of We the People to assure that fair wages exist.

Corporations exist in communities. Their largest benefit to communities is that they provide employment and benefit other companies and employees in the community. We should not underestimate the value of large corporations to a community. But they also create direct and hidden costs to communities. Communities must provide roads and utilities, police and fire protection, and other services to companies. (Most local taxes are great buys for companies and families.) It is appropriate that companies pay fair local taxes. But the major issues that interest We the People are the hidden costs of corporations. Do they pollute air or water? How do they get rid of harmful waste? And who pays for the restoration of their site if they move?

A simple formula for profit is: Income − Costs = Profits. But who gets to decide what the costs are? Just the CEO and Board who maximize profits by minimizing costs? Mercantilism. Pollute the air and water? Not our problem. Not our cost. Contribute to global climate change and the vast harm it causes? Not our problem. Not our cost.

We the People have a role to play in defining the fiduciary responsibilities of CEOs and Boards. We must identify the costs incurred by companies and who is responsible to pay them, the company or the community. We cannot leave the law so vague that it allows CEOs to ignore real costs or shareholders successfully to sue Boards or fire CEOs if they demonstrate fiduciary responsibility to all of their stakeholders.

Capitalism and Free International Trade

This topic provides important insights into what Donald Trump seems to be about. International Capitalism, like national capitalism, must be regulated. But only international institutions with significant legal authority can regulate international capitalism. Trump has undermined all international legal authority: The European Union, the Paris Climate Agreement, NAFTA, the Trans Pacific Partnership (TPP), NATO, the Joint Comprehensive Plan of Action better known as the Iran Nuclear Deal. He even supported Brexit which was created in a scandalous election and was none of his business. What have I missed? Why would Trump be interested in messing with these international multilateral treaties and agreements? IMHO, simple. He wants to become an international oligarch and that requires the elimination of international legal authority capable of regulating international business and trade so that they benefit everyone not just oligarchs.

It also explains why he has alienated America's traditional allies and aligned himself with authoritarian leaders around the world: These authoritarian leaders are oligarchs who seek to maximize their authority and wealth. There is ample evidence that they want to establish an Oligarch International. In half a century, Russia has gone from the seat of International Communism to an aspiring liberal democracy to the center of International Oligarchy. Amazing. In less than two decades, Putin has abandoned any attempt to establish a liberal democracy and free economy in Russia and has returned Russia to the authoritarianism of the Tsars, created mercantilism as Russia's economic system, and established a dictatorship run by oligarchs. And Trump can find nothing in Putin to criticize, nothing that conflicts with his role as President of the United States. Indeed, Trump is working to undermine the capacity of the United States government to regulate business and trade at home. It seems that his goal is to become an oligarch and he has the complete support of radical capitalists in the U.S. who share his goals. Any Americans who don't fear what Trump is doing need only look closely at what Putin has done to the Russian economy and to freedom in Russia. We the People must fight to expand the capacity of international organizations to regulate international trade.

That's a needed negative view of things. I should add that Adam Smith established the value that free trade creates for an economy and also for all of a nation's people. Again, our Founding Fathers rejected monarchs, the aristocracy, and oligarchs, and replaced them with our liberal democracy. They also rejected mercantilism and established laws that enabled capitalism and free trade to flourish. The American economy has flourished under capitalism and free trade. We must preserve and protect both our liberal democracy and capitalism and free trade.

These snap shots of major issues that confront capitalism demonstrate the efficacy of our way of thinking about economics and economic justice. Agreement on our morally grounded purposes and the addition of thinking in a morally grounded pragmatic dialectic both simplifies and strengthens arguments for capitalism and socialism, and totally rejects mercantilism, communism and authoritarian government.

We can leave our discussion of economic justice knowing how to think about it and confident that it's a topic We the People can address rationally, calmly, and effectively. But we also know that We the People will put everything that radical capitalists care about at risk. That's not true of traditional American capitalists, but it's true of radical capitalists. We the People must stand strong in order to protect our democratic institutions and develop socialist tax policies, regulations of capital, and institutions needed to bring balance back to the dialectic between capitalism and socialism. And we know how to keep an eye on socialists. As we support bringing radical capitalism into check, we can prevent socialism from becoming radical.

We can achieve our goal:

To conduct discourse in the public square that allows us to agree on what is right and what is wrong in public life so that we can make laws and develop public policies that support what is right and reject what is wrong.

We need:

A critical mass of Americans to show up in the public square and support our arguments. Religious humanists who believe that social responsibility is a prerequisite to redemption. Secular humanists who believe that a good life requires that they help others. Americans who believe that they're members of and responsible for our community and our liberal democracy.

10
Education Justice

We begin by noticing that this chapter is titled "Education Justice," not "Equal Education." Equal Education is too easily interpreted to mean that everyone learns the same things at the same levels. That is just silly. Different children and young adults want and need different things from education. They don't need the same education, but they all need good educations, educations that prepare them for the futures that are available to them and the futures they want. They all need to learn, and they all need to learn to learn, and they all need to become better learners, better at learning, every year. They need to learn to read better, every year. They need to learn to do more math, every year. And they need to become better learners, every year. Schools that provide that kind of learning provide education justice.

Obviously, American schools do not provide education justice. There is an education gap in the U.S. that is similar to the economic gap. There's no 1% of Americans who are vastly better educated than the rest of us. But there are vast differences in education based on wealth. Education is a good predictor of income and income is a good predictor of education. And we have known about this relationship for over 50 years.

In 1966 James Coleman published *Equality of Educational Opportunity*, (The Coleman Report). It was by far the most important book on education published in his generation. Coleman studied American schools to find out what was working and what was not working. As we have seen, that is what social science is good at. Studying what is in society. But what he found out was disturbing. Coleman demonstrated that the greatest predictor of student achievement was not the education or training of teachers or the quality of facilities or discipline practices. None of the variables that educators might want to point to as making a big difference in the education of children mattered. By far the greatest predictor of student achievement was the socio-economic background of the students in a school. If there were enough students from high income families in schools to assure that their culture dominated the student culture, the students in those schools outperformed students from schools with student cultures that did not reflect that level of commitment to education. School and student achievement is all about the socio-economic background of the students, not about the facilities or the teachers. So for over 50 years, we have known that public schools cannot provide education justice.

Coleman was correct in describing the correlation between socioeconomic background and student achievement, but he could not explain what caused the relationship and how to change education so that teachers could help all students achieve at high levels, regardless of their socio-economic background. That is the question we must answer. How do we impact learning?

But before we get into the meat of this chapter, let me remind the reader that not only is American education our greatest and oldest socialist program, it is one of the greatest in the world.

The United States not only has the greatest capitalist economic system in the world, it has the greatest education infrastructure in the world and many of the most talented educators. No other nation can even come close to our graduate schools of education. Harvard's Graduate School of Education, Columbia's Teachers College, Stanford's Graduate School of Education. The University of Texas school of education has more endowed professorships that most schools of education have tenured professors. And our public schools! Are you kidding me? They are everywhere and most are fabulous facilities with dedicated, talented teachers and administrators.

But American education is a fractured community, just like our public square. American educators cannot complete the sentence: This is what we know works and what we must do, and this is what we know does not work and what we must not do. They are fractured, just like our public square.

But imagine what they could become, all these potentially fabulous institutions and all these dedicated and talented teachers, if American educators could work together. Remember the human genome project? Unbelievably complex. It was going to take decades to complete. It was completed in a heartbeat. Why? Because biologists from all over the world worked within the same paradigm, worked together. They brought astonishing human resources to the project and got it done in no time at all.

Imagine all American educators working within the same paradigm, working together to develop new knowledge and skills, to improve the education and training of teachers, and to educate all of our children. Education's total body of knowledge would totally change. First, educators would distinguish good from bad research, get rid of the bad and expand the good. Education knowledge would be unified and would grow every year. Teacher education would improve every year. Teacher training would improve every year. Teaching would improve every year. Students would increase their ability to learn every year. Students would increase what they know and are able to do every year.

The tragedy being played out in American education cannot be grasped by thinking about what it does not do. The tragedy in American education can only be grasped if we understand what it could do. But education needs a paradigm, an intellectual achievement that unifies knowledge in education and unites the entire community of educators into a professional community.

We need to understand why American education is not united, why it is fractured. And we need to fix it. When we sought the sources of our fractured public square, we discovered that radical capitalists and Status Christians have worked to undermine our core beliefs, our ability to say, together, We hold these truths to be self-evident. But we did not find our solution in thinking about them. They helped us understand the problem. We found our solutions by showing intellectual leaders in our universities how to reassert their intellectual leadership and moral certitude among themselves and in the public square.

Similarly, we must understand the failure of the intellectual leaders in education to lead and we must provide them with solutions.

Professional Leadership in Education

In 1999 the National Academy of Education published *Issues in Education Research*. At least for our purposes, it is the most important book published in American education since the Coleman Report. But the book is not important for what it does as much as for what it does not do. One paragraph frames the issues we need to analyze. Without realizing it, in one paragraph the authors explain why education's leaders can't lead. They wrote:

> Early in the twentieth century, the National Society of College Teachers of Education (NSCTE) aspired to become an umbrella organization for all university-based scholars of education. Trying to distinguish it members from teachers, including normal school teachers who might claim to be engaged in research, the NSCTE was not able to generate a lasting sense of community among its briefly united members. The differences that divided them proved stronger than their common identification as professors of education, the result being a steady proliferation of less broad, or specialized associations, each with its own purposes and membership requirements. Even within the American Educational Research Association, there is little sense of community and few common standards to distinguish good from bad research, or significant from trivial.

First, you don't get more established and influential intellectual leaders in American education than the National Academy of Education which published this book. Just think about their title: the National Academy of Education. It is education's version of the National Academy of Science. Or the French Academy of Science. Or the Royal Academy of Science. And they mention the American Educational Research Association. That is the premier research association in American education. What these people say and write matters.

Let's start with our goal: to unite the education profession. How did the National Academy of Education address that topic? They described the attempt made by the National Society of College Teachers of Education's to become the umbrella organization for "university-based scholars of education."

But the attempt failed because "the differences that divided them proved stronger than the common identification as professors of education."

The Academy did not miss the grave consequences: ". . . the result being a steady proliferation of less broad or specialized associations, each with its own purposes and membership requirements."

In other words, after an attempt to unify the community of university-based scholars of education, that community fractured into more and more little groups. Something went terribly wrong. But let's go back to the beginning of their efforts.

The Academy's authors note, with no further reflection, that NSCTE sought to become an umbrella organization for all "university-based scholars of education." They wanted ". . . to distinguish their members from teachers, including normal school teachers who might claim to be engaged in research." So NSCTE started by fracturing the education community in the way they defined the membership in their umbrella organization. That was a mistake early in the 20th century. But for the National Academy of Education not to notice the mistake at the very end of the 20th century was neglect. It demonstrated a stupid commitment to ignorance. For by then, the incredible power of our united communities in natural science had been observed and documented. It was a major feature of the universities where these scholars were based.

This discussion points out the tragedy in American education because of the failure of educations' leaders to lead. I do not want to beat a dead horse, but we must notice one more astonishing reality that these authors pointed out.

The authors wrote that The National Academy of Education and the American Education Research Association have ". . . few common standards to distinguish good from bad research, or significant from trivial." Combine that with ". . . the result being a steady proliferation of less broad, or specialized associations, each with its own purposes . . ."

"Each with its own purposes . . ." We have seen in our study of teleological reasoning that establishing agreed upon purposes is a prerequisite to developing the criteria for the evaluation of what we do. Does what we do help us achieve our purposes? Does it hurt? Our purposes provide our criteria for evaluating what we do, our standards.

The National Academy of Education wrote in 1999 that educators have no common standards that allow them to distinguish good from bad research. Really? One might reasonably ask, If the National Academy of Education cannot distinguish good from bad research, significant from trivial, upon what basis is anyone selected to be a member of the Academy? And why was the Academy founded. I am sure that the Academy could give answers to those questions, but it is at least interesting to ask.

We might expect that everything that followed that paragraph would have been aimed at fixing the problems that keep the intellectual leaders of American education from being able to agree on the purposes and standards that would allow them to distinguish good from bad, significant from trivial research in education. But they said nothing further about it.

The Academy promised to address the problems later, in another book, and they did. They published a pamphlet titled: *Reflections on Education Research and Ways the National Academy of Education Might Help to Further Strengthen It.*

I got the report, read it, and shared my insights with the Academy. I did not hear back from them. Later, when a friend requested a copy of the pamphlet, staff at the Academy told him that it was no longer being distributed.

I have described how the failure of education's intellectual leaders to lead has fractured the education community. But why does it matter? What is the impact of all this on school teachers? A little story is instructive.

In the late 1990s, I was a member of a North Central Association team that visited an excellent high school. North Central

Association of Colleges and Schools is a voluntary association. It has a process its members use to accredit member colleges and schools. By the time a visiting team arrives at the school, the faculty has completed an extensive self-study. It's a powerful, purposeful, and helpful process if the principal and teachers are interested in improving.

The visit ends with a general meeting that includes all of the members of the visiting team and the school's administration and department chairs. Members of the visiting team get to ask questions of the school's leaders, and they get to ask the team questions. In my question, I acknowledged that it would be hard to imagine a school in which more current education research was being used than in this school. But, I noted, different departments use different research, and sometimes, different teachers in the same department use different research. I then asked, how is it possible that as a faculty you have accessed the best research in the country but you haven't been able to agree on which to use as a faculty?

Their answer was telling. Oh, we tried, they told me. We had faculty meetings, and we argued. And we had more meetings, and we argued. But then it started getting mean and it started to break up car pools. So then we met and said, Enough! And we agreed that we would each do what we thought best, and if there was someone we could work with, that would be great. But if not. No problem. But we were not going to tear our faculty apart, destroy old friendships, and certainly not risk car pools by trying to conduct arguments that we had no ability to resolve.

I said it was a great school and it is. It is also located in one of the most affluent communities in Colorado. As Coleman taught us, it doesn't really matter what those teachers do. Odds are, the students will do well. But, the same realities about education research and education epistemology that made it impossible for the teachers in that school to agree about how children learn and how best to teach their students, plague schools where student success depends on their teachers agreeing and getting it right. High needs students in high needs schools need highly competent teachers who work together.

The failure of education's intellectual leaders to solve major intellectual problems, to integrate knowledge in education, creates fractured faculties in schools, just as the failure of social scientists to solve major intellectual problems, establish intellectual leadership and moral certitude among We the People, has fractured our body politic. It turns out that I have been working on the same problem, at its core, for around 25 years.

It's important to blame these educational leaders for the state of American education. Education's leaders must be blamed for not providing the leadership their professional community needs. But we must blame without blaming. We can assign blame where it belongs without getting mean about it. They too deserve our understanding as human beings. But what is there to understand? We can identify three sources of empathy for education's intellectual leaders.

First, most of them have no background in philosophy, either epistemology or moral philosophy. Second, remember how I kind of made fun of the idea of professors of education creating a National Academy of Education? The truth is, it's not ironic and it's not funny. University-based scholars of education are among the least respected faculty in any university. They seek legitimacy from psychology and history and sociology and even business schools. Worst of all, from behavioral scientists (behaviorists).

I did not understand the social-intellectual challenges professors of education faced when I wrote *ILE*. They do not have the prestige they would need to take on the intellectual challenges that face them and other social scientists. However, this book has identified the challenges education professors face as tied in with the challenges that all social scientists and moral philosophers face. Together, they can meet these challenges and solve them.

And we are going to talk about a very big solution. As promised, we are going to understand paradigms and their power to unify knowledge in an intellectual community and the professionals who work in that community.

Conroy's Education Paradigms CP 1.0 and CP 2.0

In *Intellectual Leadership in Education,* I set out to remove the intellectual barriers to:

The integration of education research,

The integration of education research and teacher education and training,

The capacity of educators to conduct arguments that lead to the kind of agreement and commitment that can be sustained through program and personnel evaluations.

At the time, I did not think of education as a fractured community, even though I set out to make it possible for education researchers to integrate their work. That goal makes it pretty clear that education's researchers were fractured. And I wanted to make it possible for education researchers to integrate their work with the work of teacher educators and trainers. Obviously, I was dealing with a highly fractured community. So I actually set out to remove the intellectual barriers to forming a unified community of educators.

I addressed different sources of these barriers. In the end, the most productive work turned out to focus on the intellectual barriers. The goal that motivated me was to help principals conduct faculty meetings in which they and their faculty argue productively and reach agreement on how their students learn and the best ways to aid that learning with all of their students.

Teachers will agree to anything to bring an end to faculty meetings, but that kind of agreement has no staying power. I am talking about the kind of agreement and commitment that drives teachers and administrators to accept challenges, work hard, and even change in order to achieve agreed upon goals. Change how they teach. Change their curriculum. Change how they think about teaching and how they think about our students.

I don't need or care to repeat the content of that book in this one. But I do need briefly to outline the mini paradigm I developed and explain how it not only allows us to distinguish good from bad research, but also allows us to think about how we think, to think about how children learn, and to figure out how best to teach different children. And returning to the context of this book, I will show how this paradigm fits with our morally grounded purposes and epistemology, how it provides a model for the organization of knowledge in the social sciences. Let's start at the beginning, with my mini paradigm. But before we get into that discussion, let me clarify what Khun meant by paradigms as compared to theoretical models.

Paradigms vs. Theoretical Models

Kuhn used both terms, paradigms and theoretical models in important ways. They're constructed of identical components.

The difference: If a discipline has not accepted and committed to a paradigm, it's probably dealing with competing theoretical models. Once one theoretical model wins, once the community commits to one theoretical model, it becomes the discipline's paradigm and unites all knowledge within the discipline and it unites the members of the discipline into one intellectual community. So a theoretical model is a paradigm that has not yet been accepted by the community and is in competition with at least one other theoretical model.

A theoretical model becomes a paradigm only if a community accepts it as its paradigm. A theoretical model does not change when it becomes a paradigm. But the knowledge in the discipline is changed and the community is changed.

Originally I referred, ever so humbly, to Conroy's Complete Coherent Theoretical Model. I expected education researchers to develop theoretical models to compete with mine and each others. But since the education community has had nearly twenty years to come up with competing theoretical models but has not, the hell with them. I did an enormous amount of work on CP 2.0, and now refer to it and CP 1.0 as my paradigms. But CP 2.0 really is not a paradigm because the education community has not committed to it. It unites knowledge in education and accounts for all hypotheses, but it has not united the education community. But it could do both if the education community would pay attention. Of course, if the education community paid attention, it would probably develop theoretical models to compete with CP 2.0. That would create a great kind of competition. When one wins, no one really loses. Everyone wins.

The Story Behind Conroy's Paradigm 1.0

When I taught graduate students in education, I spent a lot of time at the beginning of courses talking with and getting to know them. Inevitably, I learned what they thought about how children learn and how best to teach. I learned what they thought before they began my classes.

Knowing what they thought about what they were about to study before they started proved invaluable. When we discussed what they had just read, I noticed that what they thought when they began my courses controlled what they comprehended, what they noticed, when they read. As they read, they recognized stuff that they already thought, for which they had existing schemas.[54] They did not notice stuff they had never thought about before. Or maybe better, they read it, but since they had no place to put it in their brains, no existing schemas, they did not think about it. As a result, they did not remember it.

So there I was, working with bright candidates for a masters degree in education, and what they were learning was pretty much confined to whatever added to or reinforced what they knew when they began the program. I had to help them learn to think about more than what they already knew. I told them, you have got to take what you think and what you read, and place all of it outside yourself and evaluate all of it. But as I challenged them to think about what they were reading, I recalled an old management maxim: "'Ya oughta wanna' is not a universal incentive to action." I had to do more than tell them to want do what I wanted them to do. I had to figure out how to help them do it.

---

[54] Schemas are like files we create in our brains.

I got them started thinking about different learning theories by reading *Perspectives on Learning,* a neat little book by two professors of education, one from Stanford, the other from Teachers College, Columbia University. I also had them read *Thought and Language*, Alex Kozulin's brilliant compilation and translation of Vygotsky's work. They read challenging material, and they worked. And they could not do what I asked. They could not account for what they read unless it reinforced what they already thought. I had to figure out how to help them account for everything they read. And then I got lucky.

For years I had struggled with what Piaget meant by formal reasoning. How it helps us think about what we think made sense, but I could not make sense out of how it helps us account for all of the hypotheses around a topic. Then one day, an epiphany: Kuhn's paradigm gave me not just a new way to think about formal reasoning, but a whole structure of advanced formal reasoning. Kuhn's *The Structure of Scientific Revolutions* became required reading for all of my students.

Kuhn's structure of paradigms provides a way to organize knowledge in a discipline. His structure includes five components: Fundamental Assumptions, Problems and Solutions, Methodology, Instrumentation, and Laws. My students used this way of organizing knowledge about learning theories to organize what they thought and what they were reading.[55]

First they would read a complete text. Get the big picture. Then they would go back and look for these components of a paradigm. First, they asked themselves: What are this author's fundamental assumptions about how children learn? That focused their attention on just the author's fundamental assumptions. And they wrote them down. Then they focused just on the problems and solutions that authors addressed. And so on.

---

[55] There it is, the final component of an epistemology: organization of knowledge. It goes along with the source, structure, and standards of knowledge. A paradigm provides the ultimate organization of knowledge in a discipline.

I talked with them, and together we got better and better at identifying fundamental assumptions, problems and solutions, and methodologies.

After a series of conversations, we changed Kuhn's components of a paradigm a bit.

Fundamental Assumptions stayed the same.

We changed **Problems and Solutions** to **Advantages and Disadvantages Students Bring to Learning** because those were the problems that kept coming up.

Methodology remained but included **solutions**. **Methods solve** the **problems** that both teachers and students encounter. Methods are **solutions**.

Instrumentation remained, but was not at all important in CP 1.0. It became a paradigm changer in CP 2.0.

Laws: In CP 1.0, I had the insight not to focus on laws in education.

Not including laws was fortuitous because I hadn't figured out what Kuhn meant by them. Later, I understood them better.

So my first attempt at constructing an education paradigm, CP 1.0, only included Fundamental Assumptions, Problems and Solutions, and Methodologies. And even those got changed a bit.

We're about to get into CP 1.0, but let's remember what we're doing in general. We're looking at how paradigms provide the organization of knowledge in a social science. CP 1.0 changes how we organize knowledge in education and it changes how we think in education. It has the potential, when fully developed, to unit knowledge in education and to unite the education community.

Using CP 1.0

Kuhn defined scientific paradigms as containing five components. CP 1.0 consists of three:

> Fundamental assumptions about how children learn and how best to teach.

> Advantages and disadvantages that students bring to learning.

> Methodologies teachers and students use to help students maximize advantages and overcome disadvantages.

Let's talk about how I used this mini paradigm to guide my students' learning, and how they used it to think about how they think and to think about what they were studying.

Fundamental Assumptions

I taught my students to study the various theories they read and ask themselves, "What are the author's fundamental assumptions about how children learn?" By focusing just on fundamental assumptions, they began to find them. At first, some would call me and we would talk about the task, how to spot fundamental assumptions. The more they did it, the better and faster they got at identifying the different author's fundamental assumptions.

Then I asked them, What are your fundamental assumptions? And they were able to think about what they think and identify their fundamental assumptions. Of course, as they thought about their fundamental assumptions, they added some of the fundamental assumptions that they had encountered in the reading. Finally!!!! They began to adapt what they thought when they started the course by adding what they were learning in the course.

But how were they supposed to evaluate the different fundamental assumptions that they encountered. They could try to speculate about which would have the greatest predictability and efficacy, but it was hard to tell just by reading them. They did not have criteria, or standards, for evaluating different fundamental assumptions. All of that changed when they had to identify the advantages and disadvantages that those fundamental assumptions told them that children bring to learning.

Advantages and Disadvantages that Students Bring to Learning

My graduate students had to think to figure out the advantages and disadvantages that different students bring to learning. Specifically, they had to think about the fundamental assumptions about how children learn that they had just read. They had to ask themselves, "What do these fundamental assumptions about how children learn tell me about the advantages and disadvantages students bring to learning?" The criteria for evaluating fundamental assumptions is what they tell us about what students bring to learning. Bada Bing Bada Boom. We have begun to build the capacity to distinguish good research from bad, significant from trivial. If a learning theory can't help identify the advantages and disadvantages that students bring to learning, it's either bad or trivial.

Behaviorism explains how to change behavior but not how to aid cognitive development. It says nothing about learning concepts and higher order thinking. Vygotsky, by describing socio-cultural sources and methods of learning explains both the advantages and disadvantages that students bring to learning and what to do about them. We will get to Vygotsky shortly. All we need to know for now is that Vygotsky died young, but many Russian educators expanded his theories and applied them to curriculum and instruction programs which they developed from the 1930s until the fall of the Soviet Union. All of that work made Vygotsky and those who followed him enormously helpful when elaborating the details of CP 2.0.

But it was Feuerstein who explained the problem that Coleman identified but neither he nor subsequent American educators have solved: socio-economic background is the most efficacious predictor of student achievement in American schools. The problem with Coleman's conclusion may not be obvious.

Consider, if socio-economic background is the greatest predictor of student achievement, then nothing teachers do is as significant as what the kids bring to school from their families. That means that if we want to improve education, we must improve the economy and expand participation in it. That's all well and good as an economic goal, but it reduces education to being a dependent variable, not a major source of learning and development.

Understanding Feuerstein's theory of structural cognitive modifiabilty let's us understand the advantages and disadvantages that students bring to learning and do something about them. Feuerstein's theory empowers educators to make a difference in the education of children beyond their socio-economic background. We need to talk about it.

Feuerstein's Theory of Structural Cognitive Modifiability

Feuerstein developed his program of Structural Cognitive Modifiability[56] in Israel. One aspect of his work demonstrates that Coleman was right only because American educators were wrong. How do we account for differentials in cognitive development and learning? Coleman cited socioeconomic background.

Feuerstein distinguishes distal (distant from the center of learning) factors that impact learning from proximate (close to the center of learning) factors. Distal factors include but aren't limited to: heredity/genetics, maturational level, emotional balance, environmental stimuli, socioeconomic status, and cultural differences. Those are the distant factors that impact child development and learning. And they account for Coleman's findings.

What are Feuerstein's proximate factors? There are just two: Mediated Learning and the Lack of Mediated Learning. Those are Feuerstein's two immediate, proximate causes of students learning or not learning: Mediated Learning Experiences and the Lack of Mediated Learning Experiences. But in our discussions of moral development, we recognized a third: Negative Mediated

---

[56] Feuerstein, Reuven, "The Theory of Structural Cognitive Modifiability."

Learning. What are the results? Below, I describe these insights as a formal conceptual framework.

Now, what can we do with Coleman's conclusion that the single greatest variable that impacts learning is socio-economic background and not about schools or teaching? Let's start with students (and adults) who have learned and can learn. They have had the kind of mediated learning experiences that have allowed them to achieve adequate or superior cognitive development which has enhanced their modifiability. They can learn and change whenever they need or want to.

Formal Conceptual Framework of Cognitive Modifiability		
Mediated Learning =====>	Adequate Cognitive Development =====>	Enhanced Modifiability
Lack of Mediated Learning =====>	Inadequate Cognitive Development =====>	Reduced Modifiability
Negative Mediated Learning =====>	Immature Cognitive Development[57] =====>	Negative Modifiability

On the other hand, too many students and adults could learn but have not. They have had inadequate mediated learning experiences which has led to cultural deprivation which occurs as a syndrome of inadequate cognitive development. They labor with inadequate cognitive modifiability. They have difficulty learning or changing when they need to or want to. But individuals who have, for whatever reason, lacked adequate mediated learning experiences are often amenable to adequate mediated learning

---

[57] Feuerstein's full description of Inadequate Cognitive Development is: Inadequate Cognitive Development Syndrome of Cultural Deprivation. My full description of Immature Cognitive Development is: Obdurate Immature Cognitive Development Syndrome of Cultural Deprivation. The shorter versions fit.

experiences. They can and often are willing to learn if they're taught how to learn. If they're given rich and caring mediated leaning experiences. At any age.

Not so victims of negative mediated learning experiences. They have been taught that they cannot or should not learn. The most common negative mediated learning experiences students suffer under in the U.S. have to do with mathematics. They have been taught by parents and other adults to hate mathematics or that they cannot learn mathematics or that they do not have to do the work needed to learn mathematics because it's not important.

Other negative mediated learning experiences deal with moral reasoning. Young people and adults are taught to operate at Stage 3 Tribal moral reasoning by their parents and their community. Racism is taught. This is a well known phenomena, even if the term "negative mediated learning experience" is not known. It's the subject of a song from South Pacific, *You Have Got to be Carefully Taught*:

> "You've got to be taught
> To hate and fear, . . .
> You've got to be taught
> Before it's too late,
> To hate all the people
> Your relatives hate"

The reader may have figured out that Feuerstein defines intelligence as modifiability, the ability to solve problems, often to change how we think or what we do in order to solve problems. Cognitive modifiability is indispensable (*mutatis mutandis*) to learning math or history or to maintaining relationships. And it's essential to being a good person and to performing one's duties well, in whatever roles we play.

But notice, the huge difference between behaviorists on the one hand and Vygotsky and Feuerstein on the other. Behaviorists sought change in behavior as an indication of learning. Vygotsky and Feuerstein also seek change as an indication of learning, but it's change in cognitive structures, changes in how we think that account for changes in behavior.

All of the commonly identified causes of the lack of cognitive and moral development among children and adults as well as difficulty in school, family, work, and society are exacerbated by the lack of adequate mediated learning experiences and are overcome if adequate mediated learning experiences are provided. But negative mediated learning experiences present a whole different set of challenges to educators and society. It's important to notice the impact of negative mediated learning experiences to all that we have been talking about and the importance of developing in schools and society the ability to identify the forces that drive negative mediated learning experiences and the capacity to reverse their impact. With this new understanding of learning theory, we can return to CP 1.0.

Advantages and disadvantages integrate theory with student needs. All students have learning needs. Even good students have needs, they're just different from the needs of students who struggle in school.

Advantages and disadvantages preclude political arguments over the distribution of resources. Should they go to students who have enjoyed effective mediated learning experiences or to those who have not? All children have needs that must be met by teachers and the quality of an education system, its efficacy and its justice, must be judged by how it meets the needs of all of its students. Schools must be funded so that they can meet the needs of all their students.

Advantages and Disadvantages as a Formal Conceptual Framework

We have used two different kinds of formal conceptual frameworks. Our formal conceptual framework for Economic Justice uses the Golden Mean and it is structured with two continua, one on either side of the Mean. Cognitive Development, Moral Development, and Advantages and Disadvantages that Students bring to learning are each structured on a single continuum. Cognitive and Moral Development can each be described on a continuum from immature to mature stages of development. And as we have seen, a lot can go on within each stage. Similarly, Advantages and

Disadvantages that Student Bring to Learning can be structured on a single continuum from some theoretical lowest capacity to learn to a theoretical highest capacity to learn. I call them theoretical capacities because I have no idea how to describe or name them, but it is useful to assume that they exist.

More to the point, using different theories of knowledge, we can describe different continua of Advantages and Disadvantages that Students Bring to Learning, or we can describe different locations along the same continuum. Theories that produce different continua of the advantages and disadvantages that students bring to learning form the starting points of Competing Theoretical Models. CP 2.0 constructs one continuum, one formal conceptual framework, to describe all of the Advantages and Disadvantages that Students Bring to Learning and it uses theory from both Feuerstein and Vygotsky because they are compatible. Obviously, Feuerstein provides content of the continuum that moves from Negative Mediated Learning to Absence of Mediated Learning to Mediated Learning. And each can be elaborated. Descriptions of the specific conditions that occur in students because of specific kinds of negative mediated learning identify different challenges that must be met within the paradigm. The same is true of the different conditions that can be observed in different children because of the lack of mediated learning or due to adequate mediated learning. The more detailed the descriptions of these conditions in students, the more detailed our understanding of different students, the more precise our solutions can be.

Vygotsky helps us get more precise in describing mediated learning and how we use that information. Vygotsky's theory of learning is called a Socio-cultural Theory. Vygotsky described mediated learning providers and mediated learning devices that come from our society and culture. Parents are the most immediate providers of mediated learning to students. The different capacities of parents to mediate their children's development and actual learning accounts for huge differences in the capacity of different students to learn in school. Head Start was created to help students whose parents were not able to provide the mediated learning experiences children need to succeed when they first enter school. Some have criticized Head Start programs for not having staying power. Before or around third grade, the effects of Head Start begin to wear off and the inability of these students to succeed in school that was predicted before they entered Head Start shows up. No kidding.

Parents provide mediated learning experiences to children at all ages. At all ages, the presence or absences of adequate mediated learning experiences at home accounts for some of the ability of students to learn in school. Parents who could not prepare their children for kindergarten are unlikely to provide adequate mediated learning experiences for their children when they reach third or sixth or ninth grade.

Not just parents provide mediated learning experiences to children. So do relatives, neighbors, older siblings, and even peers. That is enough to help the reader think about how different societies and the people within them mediate child development. What about culture?

Does the culture have a rich intellectual tradition? Does the culture provide schools and libraries and free access to the internet? Does the culture provide job training? Get the picture? We start to account for all of the different sources of mediated learning and that helps us account for Coleman's findings about the impact of socio-economic background of students. But more, it tells us how to overcome the impact of socio-economic differences. We must provide the mediated learning experiences that some children receive to virtually all children.

Just think how many doctoral dissertations and major research projects could pursue the goal of fully elaborating the mediated learning experiences that account for all of the advantages and disadvantages that students bring to learning in school. Which take us to our next topic.

Methodology

Good research in education reveals the advantages and disadvantages that students bring to learning. Education research must also tell us what to do for students to help them overcome disadvantages, turn disadvantages into advantages, and maximize advantages. That's what good methodology does.

Methodology is everything the teacher uses: First to figure out (assess) what each student's advantages and disadvantages are, and Second, to develop and provide instruction that maximizes those advantages or overcomes the disadvantages. Good methodology is good mediated learning. Methodology builds both the capacity to learn, and the quantity of knowledge and skills that students do learn.

We can evaluate different theories, distinguish good from bad theories, based on what they reveal about the advantages and disadvantages that students bring to learning. And we can also evaluate different theories based upon what they contributed to what teachers do to teach and what students do to learn. The criteria for the evaluation of education theories and education research include:

> What do they tell us about the advantages and disadvantages that children bring to learning?

And,

> What methodologies do they provide that allow us to maximize the advantages and overcome the disadvantages that students bring to learning?

Now, back to my students. What did they do? They studied various theories in a manner that forced them both to understand each theory and compare, contrast, and evaluate different theories. Their evaluations of different theories were based on obvious criteria: Which fundamental assumptions tell us the most about students? and Which fundamental assumptions help us develop the best methodologies for maximizing advantages and overcoming disadvantages? It kept getting easier and easier for my students to distinguish good research from bad.

CP 1.0 made a major theoretical breakthrough by establishing the capacity of learning theory to reveal the advantages and disadvantages that students bring to learning as the criteria that allowed us to distinguish good from bad theory. It also established the criteria for evaluating methodologies. And it united theory and methodologies. It began to tell us how to increase the instructional tools teachers have in their tool boxes.

And just as we tried to imagine all of the dissertations and research projects that could be conducted to identify all of the advantages and disadvantages that students bring to learning, there could be similar projects aimed at developing all of the methodologies needed to overcome disadvantages, turn disadvantages into advantages, and fully develop advantages. It is a bigger challenge than the human genome project, but if educators were united, working together, how fast could they make huge inroads into the task?

But working to implement CP 1.0 revealed a whole new set of problems. It became clear that implementing CP 1.0 was so complicated as to make it impossible to implement. That had to wait for CP 2.0.

The Stories Behind Conroy's Paradigm 2.0

We have seen that a paradigm is an intellectual achievement that unites knowledge in a discipline and allows its members to form a professional community. By presenting my paradigm, I am claiming an intellectual achievement. It might help the reader to accept such a bold claim if I explain how I did it. By the time I began working on CP 2.0, I knew I was working to elaborate a full blown paradigm. Working with thoughtful graduate students helped me develop CP 1.0. An old friend and a new friend helped me develop CP 2.0. Again, the stories are worth telling. They provide useful insights into CP 2.0 and paradigms in general.

After talking to education faculty and deans at Stanford and Harvard graduate schools of education and a few others, I realized that they were not interested in the problems I was interested in and were certainly not interested in building an education system in the United States based on research developed in Israel and the Soviet Union. So I went to work to fully elaborate CP 1.0. There is no need to report here all the steps I went through other than to say that some of the work I did took a lot of time and effort and yet its products are almost charming in their simplicity. Eventually, I developed a fairly good description of what a fully developed K-12 mathematics program would look like when developed within CP 1.0. It included teaching methods, curriculum, teacher training, teacher guides with model lessons, textbooks, learning materials, implementation supervision, instruction, formative assessment and designs for re-teaching and extensions. All of this vast amount of material grew out of conversations with colleagues at SUNY Binghampton and several Catholic universities.[58]

I believe in planning and am willing to work at it. And I'm glad I did. Because eventually, after a ton of work writing a detailed plan of how to implement just the math project in CP 1.0, the full scope of it hit me. As I wrote increasingly detailed drafts of an implementation plan, the enormity of the changes I was proposing became obvious. I realized that it would be impossible to deliver all of the materials and training involved, or to manage all of the institutional and individual activities and changes that it required. I had no capacity to implement the plan. So, I decided to enjoy my retirement.

Then I got a phone call from an old friend who I thought was living in London. Allan McNichol. Allan had been working for Thomson Reuters. He had led a massive project that integrated all the various information platforms that had evolved over the years in that financial information and news service. It was a huge information technology challenge. The project was up and running. Allan had returned to the U.S. and was looking for something new to do. He had read *ILE* and knew I had been working on a math project. Allan knows math. He thought he could help and that the work would be interesting, challenging, and rewarding.

During that phone call, I explained that I had become overwhelmed by the enormity of the project and was focusing on enjoying retirement. Of course, that just peaked his interest. We made arrangements for him to visit me at my home.

---

[58] Education faculty at Boston College, St. Johns, Loyola of Chicago, and Loyola of Los Angeles were especially helpful.

During our first meeting, I described the project. Allan was impressed. But then I told him that I had no clue how to implement it.

He was not surprised. He explained that I was thinking of it as an education project with textbooks and training materials, workbooks and tests. And then he changed the entire project: You have got to think about it as a cloud based information system.

He explained that everything I was talking about is information and if we think of it that way then we can talk about how to design it so that we don't develop it as paper but as cloud based information. Allan introduced me to information science and technology.

Furthermore, we could reasonably expect that by the time we were ready to deliver our program, school district instructional leaders, teachers, and students would all have access to it on laptops and hand held devices. Allan convinced me that the project is doable.

But I knew that I would have to dig far deeper into the details of the instructional program and teacher training than I had. That too seemed overwhelming.

Until I got to know Alex Gorodinsky. Alex is from Latvia and is something of a legend in Soviet education. He had several books published in Russian and was the principal of a fantastic school in Riga, Latvia. His story is worth telling.

Alex's school was a highly developed Vygotskian center of learning and had two distinctive facilities. One was a dormitory for girls whose parents sent them in from the country but wanted them in a safe environment. The other was a cafeteria that was no ordinary cafeteria. His school had a woodworking department, and over the years the teachers in that department had cleverly directed their students in projects that became permanent features of the cafeteria. The cafeteria was a show place. And the school was renowned. Representatives of the U.S. State Department had visited it.

Then the Soviet Union collapsed. Latvia and other satellite states became independent. And what we think of as the Russian mafia emerged throughout the old Soviet Union. One day Alex had visitors to his school from the local mafia. They only wanted two things. His girls dormitory for a brothel and his cafeteria for a restaurant. He politely declined. They politely departed. A few days later, he got a phone call. "Hello Alex, do you know where your children are?" They were holding them. He negotiated their return, called a couple from the U.S. State Department who had recently visited his school, and made arrangements for the immediate flight of his son and daughter to the United States. He soon followed. As it turned out, they all settled in Colorado. I met Alex a few years later. Elana Bodrova introduced us.

Alex and I talked. I listened to him as he introduced me to what had been done in the Soviet Union since Vygotsky's death. Enormous work on curriculum and instruction, teacher training, everything. Alex and I got to work expanding CP 1.0 into CP 2.0.

Using Conroy's Paradigm 2.0

In moving from 1.0 to 2.0, the fundamental assumptions and advantages and disadvantages did not change, but methodologies exploded. But that explosion did not represent any changes in my thinking. Rather, Alex brought to the project work on methodology that had been developed in the Soviet Union. But Instrumentation changed.

Methodology works with fundamental assumptions and advantages and disadvantages to define the educational components of CP 2.0. Instrumentation makes its implementation practical.

Methodology

Earlier I mentioned all the content of our methodology: pedagogy (curriculum and instruction), teacher training materials and plans, teacher guides with model lessons, textbooks, learning materials, implementation supervision, formative assessment and designs for re-teaching and extensions, and summative assessment. As Alex and I began to think of all of this material as information, it took off.

This is where Alex had one of his greatest impacts on my thinking. "Pat," he said in his Russian accent, "All instruction is individual instruction." Alex insisted that even when we talk to the whole group, students listen and process information individually. And we have to know how they process it. I remembered how talking on the telephone with each of my graduate students had contributed to my understanding of how and what they thought. What Alex said made sense. Without thinking about it, I had done individualized instruction and I could see its value. As Alex explained what he meant, I realized that some of my best teaching had occurred when I was doing individualized instruction.

The most striking work we did involved the model lessons Alex developed to help teachers understand and use CP 2.0. Sheer genius. The specifics of these model lessons . . . Let me put it this way. I have an oral presentation that Alex and I developed to describe model lessons. I have never given it in less than seven hours. But let me mention a few elements of Alex's model lessons in mathematics. First, it puts enormous emphasis on learning concepts and algorithms, proofs and practice. They learn to be accurate and precise. Students learn to identify ways the concepts occur in their experiences outside of school and learn to write problems that use them. They learn "problematics" associated with different concepts in different contexts, where they can expect to make mistakes. And it includes teaching students to learn and to study independently. The study independently piece is fascinating. Like Alex says, it is ridiculous to assign homework before we know that students can work independently. That's a hint at what Soviet educators did to advance Vygosky's theories of leaning, to put them into practice. It reminds us of what American educators have missed by ignoring what Soviet educators have done to improve the education of all their children.

We both understood that the huge challenge with individualized instruction is finding the time it takes with each student to learn what and how they think, how they process what is being taught, and how they use it, correctly but especially incorrectly. We knew that we were forming an information company and our whole goal was not just to disseminate information, but also to collect, process, analyze and evolve it. Allan knew it could be done. We could monitor what teachers and students both think and do and collect that information, analyze it, and put it into feedback loops that both teachers and students can use to enhance what they are doing. Our company could provide feedback to teachers and students in real time that act as a form of individualized instruction.

Now of course, the huge game changer is that with CP 2.0, every school district that bought our program would commit to our paradigm, CP 2.0. Each district would commit to having all of their teachers trained and committed to it. Now think about that and compare it with what we know goes on in schools. Teachers don't agree on how children learn and how best to teach different children. So they think about their students differently and they teach them differently. And they teach them different values and habits, which is why children who need teachers to help them develop appropriate learning values and habits have so much trouble in school. Think of the teachers who tell their students that as adults they have never used any math except what is needed to balance their check books. Nice. Negative mediated learning. Kids who must pay attention in algebra and geometry classes and work at learning those subjects are told by some of their teachers that they don't need them. In such schools, it's useless to try to collect information.

It's also important that when university schools of education and school districts operate within one education paradigm, schools of education and teacher training programs support the goals and practices of school districts. Teacher educators prepare teachers for the work they will do. And more, education research and practice are conducted within the same paradigm. That has a huge two way effect. Teachers can go to their local education researchers with questions, problems they have encountered with their students that they can't figure out how to solve. The local education researchers can agree to work on those problems or contact education researchers at another university who work within the same paradigm and seek their assistance. So researchers can solve problems that they know teachers face which means they know that teachers will use what they discover and develop.

Also important, in any classroom, some students learn more, some less. That means that many students develop gaps in their learning. These gaps become significant barriers to learning later when what they did not learn is a prerequisite to what they're about to learn. It's impossible for teachers in different grade levels to keep track of all that information to say nothing of finding the time with each student to do something about it. Our cloud-based information analysis and feedback system could do that for teachers and students. But all teachers would have to work within the same paradigm, operate with the same fundamental assumptions and methodology for useful information to exist.

When teachers do not operate within the same paradigm, their standards and practices are the accident of each teacher. When that happens, it's impossible for them to develop shared information.

The point for us is that there is no place for instrumentation, for information technology, in a district that generates noise not information. For information technology to be useful, worth the expense, cost efficient, the district's instructional program must generate information, and that requires common standards and practice: a paradigm they have all accepted and to which they have all committed. When a school district commits to work in our program, commits to CP 2.0, it generates valuable, actionable information.

Instrumentation

Technology and information enabled instrumentation that collects useful information on how teachers teach and how different students learn. We began to think of CP 2.0 as an information collection, analysis, and dissemination system. We knew that there is an enormous amount of information that we could collect on each student's knowledge. But we were also interested in the information we could collect from teachers about how they teach. Which unique activities they brought to their students that worked and which did not work. We decided to collect that information but also to develop teacher chat groups that our members could join. And we decided to develop student chat groups in which kids could talk to each other about math, how they use it, their ideas about it.

What were we going to do with all this information? Collect and analyze it, of course. And some we would analyze in real time to give students immediate feedback, and for teachers to use on a daily basis. Teachers and administrators could also use this information to help improve their instructional programs and we could use it to improve the content of our program. And some we would collect and analyze to verify that our program was being implemented as we intended. And some we would collect to help provide the evaluation of students at the end of semesters and years. All of that information would be placed in feedback loops. And all of the information we collected would be stored to be mined later when we had new techniques for processing it or new questions that we needed to answer.

Laws and Intellectual Authority in Education

The last component of Kuhn's paradigm is laws. We identify laws in education when we account for all of the hypotheses around learning and teaching. Our laws include: This is what we know works, are able to do, and must do; and this is what we know does not work or even harms children and we must not do. Those are our laws. And by fully developing our paradigm and getting school districts to commit to it, we institutionalize the intellectual authority needed to implement and sustain the paradigm and the program the teachers use. We institutionalize intellectual authority in education and moral certitude.

Our intellectual authority also comes into play in the other two ways we account for all of the hypotheses around education: This is what we don't know but are studying confident of finding out; and this is what we don't even know how to study and can't be asked to do. The first justifies, even demands, funding of education research and development. It asserts education's intellectual authority in federal and state government, the sources of funding for public schools.

The second is the stance we take as a professional community that keeps parents, politicians, and pundits off our backs. It establishes education's intellectual authority in the governance of public schools. When kids are in junior high school they develop the capacity for a kind of magical thinking. They see all kinds of stuff in the world that they do not have and know that if they were their parents they would provide those things to their children (to me). Most of them out grow that, much to their parents' relief. But the capacity has a way of raising its troublesome head. Like with fans who cannot imagine why their team does not win the championship. Or with parents, pundits, and politicians who cannot imagine why educators cannot do whatever they can imagine in their magical minds. Being able to say, as a united community that includes everyone from classroom teachers to education researchers that we do not even know how to study that is enormously important.

Evaluation in Education

We have mentioned evaluation in education and socialist enterprises. Now we can elaborate important principles.

First, the goal of evaluation is to collect information that allows us to improve whatever we are evaluating. It is not to reward or punish which are behaviorist goals. Let's quickly dismiss merit pay in socialist institutions. The problem with merit pay is that no matter how well anyone in a socialist institution performs, they do not increase revenue for their institution. What the institution does can win public support for it and the public can agree to increase funding for the institution, but that has nothing to do with merit pay. Merit pay is great for salesmen in capitalist organizations because their sales directly impact revenue and huge sales numbers warrant financial rewards.

Second, everyone and everything educators do gets evaluated. Researchers and their research get evaluated. Teacher educators and trainers and their programs get evaluated. Administrators and their strategies and plans get evaluated. School teachers and their teaching get evaluated. Student work and learning gets evaluated. All of those evaluations have the primary goal of improving whom and what is being evaluated.

Third, evaluations must be conducted as part of the overall information gathering system. Evaluation information is analyzed and enters feedback loops to aid improvement.

Competition plays a major role in capitalism. Does it have a place in socialism? Competition awakens our imagination and motivates us to seek excellence. Competition teaches us that work is important and reveals the benefits of work. But we have to keep our heads screwed on straight about competition. It has got to be fair. We do not give greater resources to some and then celebrate their ability to achieve more than others. It has to be fair and it has to be properly ordered. The goals we pursue must meet the standards of morally grounded purposes. Then we have solid criteria for evaluation and competition.

Competition is a major feature of capitalism and it can help socialist institutions. All of the members of socialist institutions benefit from competition. They all must be committed to doing their job better, providing better service, improving their institution. A great evaluation system helps everyone improve what they are doing and allows leaders and participants to notice and celebrate outstanding achievement. Achievement that improves how institutions serve their clients and the nation.

I have mentioned that CP 2.0 is not really a paradigm because it has not been adopted by the education community. More to the point, no other paradigms have been presented within the education community that would allow CP 2.0 to compete. The education community only has two choices: Develop different theoretical models, set them in competition, and adopt the one that wins. Or adopt CP 2.O and fully elaborate it. And that means fully articulating it in research, teacher education and training, administrator education and training, curriculum development and implementation, instructional program and material development, student assessment development, the whole ball of wax.

A paradigm unites knowledge in a discipline and the community of scholars and practitioners in that discipline. It completes the epistemology of education that we developed for the social sciences by organizing knowledge in education and uniting the community of educators. With that organization and unity, educators can unite in their commitment to the morally grounded purposes of our liberal democracy and can lead students to commit to them also.

Imagine what American educators could do if they were united in a single paradigm. For one thing, they would become the intellectual leaders regarding education in all of the social sciences in universities all across the country. They should be the intellectual leaders in education, in universities. They are the educators, for god's sake. Other social scientists may know their content areas, but they should all come to schools of education to learn, to improve how they educate their students.

American education should and could become the most effective and efficient socialist enterprise in the world.

We the People would conduct productive arguments about which areas of our economy would be best served by capitalist enterprises and which would be best served by socialist enterprises.

So there we have it, CP 2.0, a paradigm and its enormous potential to assure:

The full intellectual development of education as a profession,

The establishment of education's intellectual authority,

The capacity of education to achieve the full development of students,

The success of education as a socialist enterprise, and

Education's demonstration of the capacity of socialist enterprises to balance capitalist enterprises in the American economic system.

All of the potential power and production of CP 2.0 work to the benefit of all of our educators and all of our children. We can realistically expect all American children to learn far more than anyone currently recognizes as their capacity to learn. They can learn what they need to go to work and continue to learn in the world of work. They can learn what they need to go on to college and continue to learn in ever more challenging classrooms. But also, they can leave high school with well developed domains of their humanity: the individual, the person, and the self; and the capacity to continue to develop those domains as adults. And to the point of this book, they can leave high school with the capacity fully to participate in our liberal democracy and join other mature members of We the People in the public square. We can heal our fractured body politic.

We can achieve our goal:

> To conduct discourse in the public square that allows us to agree on what is right and what is wrong in public life so that we can make laws and develop public policies that support what is right and reject what is wrong.

We just need:

> A critical mass of Americans to show up in the public square and support our arguments. Religious humanists who believe that social responsibility is a prerequisite to redemption. Secular humanists who believe that a good life requires that they help others. Americans who believe that they're members of and responsible for our community and our liberal democracy.

11
Women's Reproductive Rights

I wrote early drafts of this chapter during the summer of 2017 and completed the fourth draft during the winter of 2017-2018. I sent the fourth draft to my friend Ron Messina in South Carolina to get a second opinion. Ron argued against my including this chapter in the book because it makes such a drastic shift from the public moral reasoning I use in the other chapters. He used my own argument against me: Theology and religious moral philosophy belong in the Religious Square, not in a book about discourse in the public square. Barb Conroy, my wife, agreed, so I took it out.

But then Justice Kennedy resigned from the Supreme Court and I had no doubt that Donald Trump would appoint a new justice who would form the majority needed to reverse Roe v. Wade, either at the federal or state level. I decided that this chapter is important. It refutes the religious arguments that have dominated arguments in the public square regarding women's health, and I believe it improves the public moral arguments that support a woman's right to choose. Ron and Barb agreed.

The reader may also find this chapter interesting and valuable because it deals with the enormously emotional topic of abortion in a calm and rational manner. It demonstrates that we can have civil discourse in the public square. But we need to use mature moral reason. So what do we do? In order to counter the religious moral arguments against a woman's right to choose, we subject the Catholic moral arguments to rational scrutiny.[59] But as we have learned, we cannot conduct productive arguments unless we operate from a foundation of agreement. So we delve into Catholic moral reasoning and subject Catholic arguments to Catholic rational scrutiny. Well, rational scrutiny that comes out of the Catholic intellectual tradition. They are not supported by the Vatican.

Then we turn to public moral philosophy, social science, and psychology to make our public moral arguments for a woman's right to choose. Our public moral philosophy uses phenomenology, metaphysics, and teleology. Social science contributes data on the realities of abortion, why women choose to have them, when they make their choices, and why they make their choices when they do. Psychology helps us understand that the vast majority of women who have abortions experience trauma. These women need and deserve our love and support.

But before we get to my arguments, it's important to notice the makeup of the Supreme Court and why it threatens Roe v. Wade. Otherwise, there would be no need for me to drag the reader through our discussion of Catholic moral philosophy, or for the reader to pay attention to it.

The Supreme Court and Religious Moral Arguments on Abortion

Religion and gender prove to be predictive of the conservative or liberal bent of the current Supreme Court. All conservatives are Catholic men: Chief Justice Roberts (Harvard and Harvard Law), Neil Gorsuch (raised Catholic, went to Georgetown Prep in Washington D.C., then Columbia and Harvard Law), Samuel Alito (Princeton and Yale Law), Brett Kavanaugh (Georgetown Prep, Yale, and Yale Law). None of these justices received a Catholic education beyond high school where students are taught

---

[59] We would have done the same with the arguments made by Status Christians, but they do not have an intellectual tradition that would allow them to make rational arguments. Their moral arguments are based on a fundamentalist reading of scripture, not reason.

what to think far more than how to think. It is reasonable to expect that they bring doctrines felt as facts to discussions of abortion rather than mature rational arguments.

These are all really smart men. But they have not been educated in moral philosophy. We need to recall that moral philosophy at Columbia and Yale was influenced by the writings of Harvard's esteemed philosopher Willard Quine who insisted that the only valid philosophy is the philosophy of science. There was virtually no moral philosophy for any of these men to learn as undergraduates or in law school. They were stuck with the doctrines felt as facts they brought with them from their families. These men are all really smart, but they operate with immature moral development.

Clarence Thomas's education deserves special attention. Thomas went to a majority black Catholic high school for two years before transferring to St. John Vianney's minor seminary.[60] He then briefly attended Conception Seminary College in Missouri[61] and graduated from Holy Cross College. Holy Cross is a fine Jesuit school in Massachusetts from which Thomas graduated cum laude in English lit. He graduated from Yale Law in 1974. Thomas was born in a small all black town in Georgia and grew up speaking Gullah as his first language. Gullah is a creole-like language based on different varieties of English and languages from West and Central Africa. He chose to major in English lit at Holy Cross to help him refine his understanding of English and his speech.

He attended school from the early 60s to 1974. We know that the nature and quality of the education we receive begins with our relationships with other students. At Holy Cross and Yale, Thomas lived in an inhospitable climate. He had to overcome a ton of

---

[60] Catholic men study to be priests in seminaries. Some seminaries are divided between minor seminaries (first year of high school through second year of college), and major seminaries (third year of college through fourth year of theology). The last two years of college focus largely on philosophy.

[61] In the early 1960s, I had a theology professor at Notre Dame who had been released from Conception Abbey for teaching views that were too liberal.

prejudice, and more, the absence of close supportive relationships from white students. That's hard. In addition, the Yale Law School Dean, Louis Pollak, had written in 1969 that Yale Law had expanded its quota for black students, de-emphasizing grades and LSAT scores. Although Thomas had graduated in the middle of his class, thus proving that he surely belonged there, law firms that interviewed him were blatant in expressing their skepticism that he belonged in Yale Law and that his grades were indicative of his intelligence. These experiences led Thomas to develop views that prefer that the government and courts stay out of social programs and that the poor and minorities lift themselves up.[62] That in his view (if I may presume to state his view) would allow those who do achieve to get credit for their achievements. I wonder how he would have turned out if he had grown up in an American city and had seen highly educated blacks working as janitors. But one thing is clear, his opinions are based on his experiences as a black man in the America he grew up in, not on his education as a Catholic. We can expect that he too brings doctrines felt as facts to discussions of abortion, not mature reasoned moral arguments.

Gorsuch replaced Antonin Scalia who was also Catholic and conservative. Kavanaugh replaced Anthony Kennedy who was also Catholic but a moderate on social issues. Kavanaugh represents a major swing to the right on the Supreme Court. A swing orchestrated in untoward ways by Senate majority leader Mitch McConnell. He used Stage 3 Tribal moral reasoning to justify his abuse of power as the Senate Majority Leader. He would raise holy hell if a Democratic Senate Majority Leader did the same thing he has done. Democracy is not perfect. Can we hope that the people of Kentucky will recognize and act upon McConnell's gross misuse of legislative power? No way if they are stuck in Stage 3 Tribal moral reasoning and agree with what he did. But if

---

[62] I freely admit that after reading up on Justice Thomas so that I could accurately describe his background and education, I have increased my admiration for him. I still don't agree with him on many things, but I respect him.

they grow up, which we all must do, there is hope. But back to the court that is.

Five Catholic male Supreme Court justices argue with four liberals about the morality of abortion. The liberals are either Jewish: Ruth Bader Ginsberg, Stephen Breyer, Elena Kagan or a Catholic woman, Soniya Sotomeyor.

Again, all laws are moral laws. The Justices argue about the morality of abortion. And the Vatican, a bunch of old celibate Catholic men, dominates religious moral arguments against abortion. The majority of the Supreme Court thinks in these Catholic male morale arguments as justifications for their doctrines felt as fact when discussing the legal right of women to choose to have an abortion. That fact alone begs some attention to the Catholic arguments.[63]

Around 20 states can be expected to adopt laws that terminate a woman's right to have an abortion, either de jur or defacto. They will either prohibit it outright or make it inaccessible, and the majority of the Supreme Court will support them. These eventualities make it necessary for We the People to know the Catholic arguments and subject them to rational scrutiny. Arguments must be grounded in agreement. You cannot rationally confront the Catholic arguments with secular arguments. If there is no foundation of agreement in an argument, the two sides cannot engage each other. Figuratively, they just yell at each other as if they were eight year olds on a playground: Is so. Is not. Is so. Is not.

Few American liberals understand how vulnerable the religious arguments against abortion are as religious moral arguments. Nor, seemly, do the Catholics and Status Christians who make them. We the People need to subject those arguments to rational scrutiny.

---

[63] I was raised Catholic and educated in Catholic elementary schools, Jesuit High School in Beaverton, Oregon, and the University of Notre Dame. I criticize the Vatican for failing to lead a great Christian church, committing existential suicide, undermining political discourse in Western democracies, and doing enormous harm to women. It is hard to remember the good the church has done and is doing today.

On the other hand, to claim that a woman has the right to choose raises questions. First, it's a conclusion, not the argument that supports that conclusion. Put it this way. It's a conclusion, not a syllogism. Second, to choose is a transitive verb. It has an object. Choose . . . a baseball glove. Choose . . . a hair spray. A woman's right to choose . . . what? "A woman has the right to choose to terminate an unwanted pregnancy before the fetus is viable" is a very different claim from, "A woman has the right to choose to murder her unborn child." We need mature rational public moral arguments about the nature of the fetus and a woman's right to choose to have an abortion. And we need to clean up our language.

Before Roe v. Wade

Before Roe v Wade, the enormous problems created by laws that prohibited abortion caused wide spread agreement that something had to be done. Even the Southern Baptist Convention (SBC) supported abortion before Roe v. Wade.

> A 1971 SBC resolution on abortion appeared to capture the consensus. It stated that "society has a responsibility to affirm through the laws of the state a high view of the sanctity of human life, including fetal life."

> But the resolution added, "We call upon Southern Baptists to work for legislation that will allow the possibility of abortion under such conditions as rape, incest, clear evidence of fetal deformity, and carefully ascertained evidence of the likelihood of damage to the emotional, mental, and physical health of the mother."[64]

In 1971, The Southern Baptist Convention could have written Roe V. Wade. Southern Baptists gave precedence to the life of the mother over the life of the fetus. And they recognized the

---

[64] David Roach; "How Southern Baptists became pro-life," *Baptist Press; January 16, 2015.*

three domains of the mother: individual (physical), person (social), and self (mental). Southern Baptists thought of abortion as a Catholic issue. There they are again. Those Catholic arguments.

The evolution of Baptists into a pro-life/anti-choice position was supported by two references in scripture to an unborn child as a "baby." That supports the phenomenological experiences of women who have wanted to be pregnant and whose pregnancies produced healthy children. It does not get into deeper issues that confront women who need abortions or women who have walked the mental and emotional road that led to the support of a woman's right to choose to terminate an unwanted or unhealthy pregnancy.

So I will conduct four different arguments.

First, because Catholic arguments against a woman's right to choose are based on Catholic theology and religious moral philosophy, I will confront them using arguments grounded in Catholic theology and religious moral philosophy.

Second, I will develop public moral arguments that support a woman's right to choose using public moral philosophy, public moral reasoning, and psychology and science that deal with fetal and human development.

Third, I will draw a line between pre and post viability pregnancies: Before the fetus can survive outside the womb, and after the fetus can survive outside the womb with medical assistance. This is important. Arguments regarding a woman's right to choose to terminate pregnancy once the fetus has become viable are the same for both religious moral philosophy and public moral philosophy.

Fourth I will conduct arguments that defend and limit a woman's right to choose to terminate a viable fetus using public moral philosophy, social science, and medical science. Again, religious and public moral arguments regarding a woman's right to choose are the same once the fetus is viable.

But before I discuss abortion, I need to address birth control, for we can expect it too to come under attack by the new Supreme Court. Access to free an easily available means of birth control impacts issues that surround abortion. Arguments against artificial means of birth control are entirely religious but are played out in the public square where Catholics and Status Christians team up with radical capitalists to form a powerful political block that supports conservative political purposes. But these are Catholic arguments that are adopted by Status Christians. They work their way into electoral politics and away from the vast majority of women. We can't allow Catholics and Status Christians to avoid responsibility for the targeted injustice they create. What target? You ask. Poor women.

Again, religious arguments against artificial birth control come from the Vatican. Status Christians have adopted the Vatican's arguments because they cannot make any of their own. Fundamentalist Christianity has no Thomas Aquinas. It's impossible to conduct rational arguments if you cannot think rationally. We cannot argue with claims made by Status Christians because their claims have no rational foundation. Their arguments are based on a fundamentalist interpretation of scripture. But we can argue with Catholic arguments.[65]

Catholic Arguments against Artificial Birth Control

We find Catholic moral arguments in the *Catechism of the Catholic Church* (CCC) which has Vatican approval.

CCC 2351 . . . sexual pleasure is morally disordered when sought for itself, isolated from its procreative and unitive [between spouses] purposes.

CCC 1643 . . . conjugal love . . . aims at a deeply personal unity, a unity that, beyond union in one flesh, leads to forming one heart and soul.

---

[65] Major Protestant churches and other religions either support both birth control and a woman's right to choose or remain silent in the public square.

Purposes. Teloi. Teleological reasoning. We like that. And we know that just because an argument has a teleological structure does not mean that it's correct. The purpose must have the rational clarity of an axiom or withstand the scrutiny that any premise of any syllogism must withstand.

It's abundantly clear to anyone who has any kind of sex life at all that sex has to do with far more than procreation and unity. Indeed, procreation is seldom the purpose of sex. So obviously, there are other, more important purposes that must be accounted for if we're going to develop a teleological argument regarding the morality of sex.

So why do we have sex? Let's see. It's fun and feels really good ("all over my body"). And it has all kinds of potential layers of intensity, including but not limited to creating a profound sense of unity for the couple. We learn a lot about our partner during sex: their comfort with their body and physical competence; the level of their sexual interest and passion and importantly if their sexuality matches ours; their sense of themselves as human beings, their sense of humor, and their interest in us. We learn to pay attention to each other.

And even before all those mature sexual purposes kick in, there are the introductory purposes. Getting to know my body with a partner. Getting to know how my partner's body works. Even how my body works. Becoming a great lover is a process, like becoming highly literate and well read.

Those are just a few purposes that come to mind, off the top of my head. Others, I am sure could add to this list. I should mention that the choices individuals make about their sexuality and how they are going to live it are essential social freedoms that we are committed to protect. The rights of the LGBT community have finally been accepted by a majority of the country and are increasingly protected. The narrow definition of the purposes of sex asserted by the Vatican supports their opposition to sexual freedom and fun. The absurdity of their rules warrants a sense of humor.

The celibate moral philosophers in the Vatican think about sex as only celibate moral philosophers could. They suffer from a kind of sexual illiteracy. They aren't that different from regular folks who have had disappointing experiences with sex and don't know what they have missed. They too can be thought of as sexually illiterate.

It only takes a minute to make a mockery of the teachings on sex that have been issued by the Vatican to justify their prohibition of any artificial means of birth control.[66] But there is a more practical argument that may be even more compelling.

The real point against any argument the Vatican may make against artificial means of birth control is that virtually no Catholic women and (this is huge) no Catholic priests support that view. Catholic women and priests make the ultimate argument against the Vatican's teachings on artificial birth control. Catholic women use artificial means of birth control to prevent pregnancies and Catholic priests don't even ask them to confess it. Catholic pastoral moral philosophy, the moral philosophy used by pastors, by priests, working with women, approves of artificial means of birth control. Sorry Rome. You have lost the argument to Catholic women where it matters most.

As for Status Christians, they have no arguments. They have, in an historically astonishing turnabout, latched onto the teachings that come out of Rome. You know, Roman Catholics who, according to Status Christians, aren't Christian; and the Pope who, according to Status Christians, is the anti-Christ. Yes. They love the Catholic arguments against birth control. Being anti-intellectual they can adopt contradictory positions without noticing what they're doing.

Political Arguments against Birth Control

Some rich Catholic men enjoy turning birth control into a political cause célèbre. But they use the same arguments as the celibates in the Vatican which we already have seen deserve to be ignored. But we can be vocal in or refutation of these men and their political opportunism. Many are radical capitalists using birth control to broaden their base, but more important, they're hypocrites.

---

[66] Eliminating procreation as the purpose of sex makes heterosexual and homosexual sex morally equivalent.

Their Catholic wives use birth control or they aren't getting any love at home. We need to take any opportunity available to express public opprobrium toward them. Shame them. Even laugh at them. Nothing is much funnier than a man who opposes artificial means of birth control and is not getting any love at home. They aren't pure and chaste. They're funny. As we proceed, they become offensive.

There are absolutely no arguments for the prohibition of a woman's right to birth control that can withstand the slightest scrutiny. But let's follow the trail of political arguments and see where it leads.

Early on it became clear that religious arguments for public laws against birth control carried no weight because nothing prohibits religious communities from denying this right to women in their communities. But as we have seen, there is no way for religious authorities to monitor the behavior of women. Catholic women and priests ignore those Catholic laws. So religious leaders who wanted to prohibit birth control needed public laws.

They sought to prohibit the sale of birth control devices. But that train left the station years ago. There is no way that politicians can ban the manufacture, sale, and purchase of artificial means of birth control.

But radical capitalists must do whatever they can to maintain the support of Americans who oppose birth control or just want to vote against liberals. So they sought to prohibit the government from funding the means of birth control. But most birth control is not provided through public funding. It's included in health insurance benefits or is purchased outright by women who can afford it.

But they had to do something. So they targeted the few beneficiaries of public funding for birth control. Organizations like Planned Parenthood provide medical services to women who can't afford to purchase them on their own. Poor women.

Nice. Radical capitalists, Catholics, and Status Christians have taken their gigantic fight against access to birth control to the weakest, most vulnerable women in our country, poor women. They know full well that the vast majority of American women have access to artificial means of birth control and use them. And they give public speeches and political candidates win elections on probably the most overtly scandalous treatment of a group of Americans since slavery, Andrew Jackson's Indian Removal Act, and Jim Crow.

This denial of women's health care to the most vulnerable women in our country demands that all Americans of good will overcome their indifference and fight this disgraceful political conduct. Racism and these attacks on poor women are a blight on the American conscience today. How can we expect our nation to care about economic justice, the environment, or world peace if we don't have the moral fiber, the soul, the conscience required to preserve and protect the rights, the dignity and worth of all of our people.

Birth control is not even difficult. If there were not all these political motives, it would not be an issue. Abortion is more difficult. It requires serious intellectual attention.

Abortion – Women's Rights and Public Responsibilities

It's important to recognize that we can ease the tensions in this debate by respecting the different experiences different women have with pregnancy and r recognizing that those experiences support different attitudes toward abortion. We acknowledge and discuss abortion issues respectfully. And we establish the contexts that allow women with different experiences to talk with each other.[67]

What are those contexts? First, women who view abortion from a religious context. Second women who view abortion from only their personal experiences, whether happy or desperate. And last, women who view abortion from a Civil Rights standpoint, women's rights. We will acknowledge these contexts as we discuss

---

[67] Most men support a woman's right to choose. If they oppose it rationally, the arguments in this text could help them change. If they do not oppose it rationally, I suspect that they oppose women's rights in general, which means that the deny the full dignity and rights of women. Women might stop rewarding them for their mean, childish beliefs.

abortion, but they will not define our arguments. Rather our arguments will focus, as we stated above, on:

1. Catholic Moral Arguments against Abortion.
2. Public Moral Arguments Regarding Pre Fetal Viability Abortions.
3. Pre and Post Fetal Viability Issues.
4. Public Moral Arguments Regarding Post Fetal Viability Abortions.

Catholic Moral Arguments against Abortion

I submit the religious moral arguments against abortion to religious moral scrutiny. Now think about that. We must make religious arguments against religious arguments. Otherwise, we risk being as silly as religious fundamentalists who make religious arguments against scientific evidence: creationism[68] vs evolution. Creationism may constitute a meaningful belief within a religious community, but it makes no sense as a scientific argument. We must keep our intellectual contexts clear, well defined, in order.

Since the only fully developed religious arguments against abortion come out of the Vatican, I address them. Now all you non believers out there and all you traditional Christians, work with me on this. We walk down a path less traveled, and it makes all the difference. We're going to get into religion and make a religious argument. Our path is the theology of the soul.

Soul, who believes in the soul? Heck we don't even think about the mind anymore. We think about the brain. Biology. Facts. Well, do you think about dark matter and dark energy? Astrophysicists sure do. And arguments about the soul are no less illusive than arguments about dark energy and dark matter.

But even more important to this discussion, to this religious argument, is the importance of the immortality of the soul to Christianity and virtually all religions. Immortality. The most profound

---

[68] Creationism: the belief that the universe and living organisms originate from specific acts of divine creation, as in the biblical account, rather than by natural processes such as evolution.

question that any religion must answer is: What meaning can my life have when I know that I am going to die? When I know our sun is going to die? When I know that the human race will eventually disappear? Religious teachers answer: Your body dies, man dies, but our souls live forever. Our souls are immortal.

Different religions and different sects within religions have different answers about what precisely happens to souls after death, but everything begins, in any religious explanation of the meaning of life in the face of death, with assurances about life after death and the immortality of the soul.

This is no small matter. Any religion in which the immortality of the soul provides a core belief, a pillar of faith, must have an adequately developed theology and moral philosophy regarding the soul to answer essential questions raised about the soul. Religions can't make everything depend on the immortality of the soul and then ignore its existence when dealing with critical moral issues such as abortion. And any religion that destroys its theology of the soul to win its political arguments regarding abortion, destroys itself in practice. It commits existential suicide because it destroys its core beliefs, its identity, *its raison d'etre.* For what? To advance a legal argument that contributes nothing to its core beliefs. Destroy your theology of the soul, and there is no reason to believe or care about anything you say about anything. If I am going to die and disappear, I am going to listen to Sartre and Camus, not some priest or preacher.

William James (1842-1910) is one of American's most esteemed intellectuals. He virtually founded psychology and pragmatism in America. During a series of lectures at Harvard on pragmatism, James was repeatedly asked if he believed in God. He had not intended to discuss the existence of God in that set of lectures. Finally, out of frustration, he told his audience that he believed in God as a practical necessity, for without God, he quoted Arthur James Balfour (1849-1930):

> The energies of our system will decay, the glory of the sun will be dimmed, and the earth, tideless and inert, will no longer tolerate the race which has for a moment disturbed its solitude. Man will go down into the pit,

and all his thoughts will perish. The uneasy consciousness which in this obscure corner has for a brief space
broken the contented silence of the universe, will be at
rest. Matter will know itself no longer. "Imperishable
monuments" and "immortal deeds," death itself, and
love stronger than death, will be as if they had not been.
Nor will anything that is be better or worse for all that
the labor, genius, devotion, and suffering of man have
striven through countless ages to effect.[69]

Now when we are young and healthy and having a great old
time, these questions may not trouble us. But they do if we are in
a foxhole getting shot at, and they do when we bury loved ones,
and they do when we get old and are trying to make sense of our
lives. This discussion of the soul may seem ridiculous to innocent,
young readers but it goes to the heart of anyone's belief in the
existence of God and the authenticity of any religion.

The Soul and Abortion

If a child is conceived, comes to term, and is born; there is no
need to bother with questions of when the soul entered the body.
There is wide agreement that by birth, the soul is in the body. But
abortions occur before birth. So any religious arguments about a
woman's right to choose an abortion must begin with answers to
the question, When does the soul enter the body?

But let's not start with abortion when constructing our
argument. Let's start with conception and events that follow.
Medical science tells us that around 31% of all conceptions end in
miscarriages. That's an estimate because it includes chemical
pregnancies in which the pregnancy is usually lost before the
woman is scheduled to have her first period after implantation.
She often does not even know that she was pregnant. But many
arguments against a woman's right to choose limit that right at
conception, even before a woman knows that she is pregnant.

---

[69] In James, *Pragmatism*, p. 76; from Balfour, *The Foundations of
Belief,* p. 30.

10% to 25% of all clinically recognized pregnancies end in miscarriage. That's also only an estimate because not all women who have their pregnancies clinically confirmed continue to have prenatal care sufficient for these pregnancies to be tracked. Miscarriage is defined as a pregnancy that ends before the fetus can live independent of the mother when supported by up to date medicine. The earliest that a fetus can survive is after 24 weeks, with a debate emerging to move that date back to 22 weeks. Those dates will matter more in later discussions. But for now, we can assume that if a fetus can live outside the mother, the soul has entered the body. We can't prove any of this, but it's rational to assume that if the fetus is viable, the soul has entered.

But what about chemical pregnancies? Pregnancies that never had a chemical chance of developing. And what about the 10% to 25% of clinically recognized pregnancies that end in miscarriage. What about the estimated 31% of all pregnancies that end in misarranges? Has the soul entered the body in all or some or none of them?

OK. Take a breath. We have to be able to talk about God a bit. We have to venture into theology: the study of God and the nature of religious belief. Here we go.

God creates the soul and puts it in the body. In Christian theology, that's axiomatic. But step back. God created the universe, made the earth be what it is, and created humans and gives each human a soul. To do all that, theologians assume that God is really powerful, all powerful, Omnipotent. And God is really smart, knows everything, Omniscient. Alright, hold those two thoughts: God is omnipotent, and God is omniscient.

Back to our miscarriages. If the soul is in the fetus when the fetus dies, what happens to the soul? Eastern religions have a different answer than the three Semitic religions, Christianity, Islam, and Judaism. Virtually all eastern religions include teachings around **Samsara**, the cycle of life and death through which the soul travels. Reincarnation. The consequence of the death of an embryo or fetus is not so great when an entire culture believes that the soul continues to live and has multiple opportunities to live a life that gains Nirvana. And not only believes that, but has elaborate teachings regarding what happens to these and all souls after death.

Virtually all Semitic religions teach that God creates the soul, places it in the unborn child, that the soul is immortal, and that the soul faces judgment after death. One life, one soul, eternal salvation or damnation. Everything is at stake in the theology of the soul. So the theology of the soul better answer some serious questions.

Here are some questions that Catholic theology used to be able to answer:

Q: Is the soul somehow a physical, biological thing that exists at conception, like DNA?
A: No. The soul is not physical. It does not come from the father and mother. It comes from God.

Q: Is the soul spiritual and immortal, created by God and infused into the body by God, endowing each person with the chance of eternal life?
A: Yes.

Q: Does the soul travel through a cycle of life and death, is it reincarnated in multiple lives as the Eastern religions teach, or does each soul have only one chance at full development with one body?
A: One life, one body, one chance.

If the soul is spiritual and immortal and can't reincarnate, which is the traditional belief in Semitic religions, then everything is at stake in its one life.

If that's what we believe, then to even think about abortion as a moral issue, we must answer one additional question: When does God place the soul in the body? Now remember, any under-standing at all of a living God, creator of the universe, maker of humans, includes that God is omnipotent and omniscient.

Q_1: Does this omnipotent and omniscient God know-ingly place souls in fertilized eggs that will not survive naturally, through no action by the mother or anyone else?

Q_2: If so, then what happens to those souls?

It's easy to answer "Yes" to Q_1. It's not so easy to answer the second question, What happens to those souls? And of course, anti-intellectual Status Christians don't even attempt to answer that question.

The Catholic Church used to say the souls of the unborn and the souls of children that died before they were baptized went to Limbo. But they abandoned the entire teachings on Limbo along with much of the theology of the soul of the unborn around the time they revved up their political opposition to abortion. Now the Vatican just files the theology of the soul under "Mystery," topics that we cannot know, understand, or explain but that Catholics must believe as an act of faith. Of course, the fact that the soul is mysterious does not keep the Vatican from making assumptions necessary to support their moral laws. We will get to that weakness in their arguments in a bit.

Status Christians have never been bothered by such theological questions that aren't addressed in the bible. They just declare that humans enjoy full humanity from conception, that fetuses have superior rights to the mother, and that all abortions must be illegal. They use these doctrines felt as facts to insist that no harm be done to the fetus while allowing enormous harm to be done to the mother. Without further argument. There is no way to conduct rational discourse with anyone who holds such anti-intellectual claims. Rather, we resort to our rules of engagement: those are arguments that must be confined to religious communities for they can't be part of rational discourse in the public square. Notice, they can teach those beliefs and insist that they be followed by women who volunteer to be members of their communities. They simply can't bring those beliefs into the public square and make laws that affect all women that are based on those irrational religious beliefs.

However, the Catholic Church does theology and philosophy in a thousand year old intellectual tradition that makes its claims subject to rational scrutiny. One can rationally challenge the Catholic stance on the two major questions theology must answer regarding abortion:

1. When does God place the soul in the body?
2. On what basis can a woman claim to have the right to make the decision to terminate her pregnancy?

It's helpful to notice that the Catholic intellectual tradition is grounded in metaphysical and teleological reasoning. Our arguments with Catholic moral philosophers must slide into their mode of reasoning or risk being incompatible and incommensurable. It's useless to make arguments against the Catholic arguments unless we address the Catholics arguments. We start with the metaphysical[70] premises of Catholic arguments.

Both the Nicene Creed and the Apostles Creed promise the resurrection of the body, eternal life, although they don't mention the soul. The Catechism of the Catholic Church (CCC) frames the issues that must be scrutinized:

CCC 362   The human person, created in the image of God, is a being at once corporeal and spiritual. The biblical account expresses this reality in symbolic language[71] when it affirms

---

[70] Let's avoid the long discussion about what metaphysics was to Aristotle and what it can possibly mean today. Let's just distinguish metaphysical arguments from teleological arguments. Metaphysical arguments build from *a priori* assumptions. Teleological arguments build toward ends, for us, morally grounded purposes.

[71] "The biblical account expresses this reality in symbolic language . . ." Symbolic language. Language that cannot be taken literally. Scripture scholars must work to discern its symbolic meaning. This is the heart of the argument the fundamentalist theologians at Princeton Divinity School lost to Yale in the late 1800s. Right there in the Catholic argument against abortion. Status Christians have adopted the conclusion of this argument without noticing that the argument that supports this conclusion also rejects fundamentalism and the literal interpretation of the bible, irreplaceable foundations of Status Christianity.

that "then the Lord God formed man of dust from the ground, and breathed into his nostrils the breath of life; and man became a living being." Man, whole and entire, is therefore *willed* by God.

"Man, whole and entire, is therefore *willed* by God," but not produced. The parents produce the child. God produces the soul.

CCC 366   The Church teaches that every spiritual soul is created immediately by God – it's not "produced" by the parents – and also that it is immortal: it does not perish when it separates from the body at death, and it will be reunited with the body at the final Resurrection.

The soul provides human persons with immortality, life after death. Yes, the soul and body will be reunited, but it's the soul that's immortal. When the Church refers to "Man, whole and entire," it refers to body and soul. But when does God create the soul? Immediately is a bit vague, for reasons already cited (the high percentage of conceptions that end in miscarriage). God breathed life into the fully formed Adam, ". . . breathed into his nostrils the breath of life . . ."

So to our Fist Question: When does God place the soul in the body?

On the one hand, the Vatican is clear on the existence and importance of the body and soul, but it seems careless at best in deciding when the soul enters the body. There is no biblical source or rational argument supporting the view that God creates the soul at conception. It makes more sense to believe that God creates the soul of the unborn, rather like he did with Adam, and breathes it into the child when fully formed, "whole and entire," at birth, or for our purposes, at the earliest, when the fetus could survive outside the womb.

That's our answer: God places the soul in the fetus after it has become viable.

Notwithstanding doctrines treated as facts by the Vatican, a religious woman's right to choose to terminate her pregnancy is obvious and unqualified if she makes the decision before her fetus is viable. Nothing really is at stake. There is no soul, just physical matter with the potential to become human, but not yet human, not yet fully developed as body and soul. Such an abortion has no greater moral consequence than a miscarriage. No laws can prohibit miscarriages. No laws can justly deny a woman the right to choose to have an abortion that's morally equivalent to a miscarriage.

A Woman's Capacity to Make Moral Decisions

Let's talk about a woman's agency. Her capacity and right to make any moral decision for herself. Does she depend upon permission from her father or husband or confessor or the Church? Or is a woman capable of making moral choices for herself? That's a huge question that does not receive adequate intellectual attention. Rather, it's either assumed to be true or flat denied. Fortunately, the Vatican has given it serious intellectual (albeit theological) attention.

CCC 1704   The human person participates in the light and power of the divine Spirit. By his reason, he is capable of understanding the order of things established by the Creator. By free will, he is capable of directing himself toward his true good. He finds his perfection "in seeking and loving what is true and good."

An important note on grammar. The men in the Vatican who wrote the Catechism are big on traditional concepts of gender and pronouns that they got from Latin grammar. The use of the male personal pronoun is assumed, in these contexts, to apply to both men and women. That assumption is not casual. It has legal standing. But we only feel the power of that truth when we restate these assertions using the female pronoun.

221

CCC 1704   The human person participates in the light and power of the divine Spirit. By her reason, she is capable of understanding the order of things established by the Creator. By free will, she is capable of directing herself toward her true good. She finds her perfection "in seeking and loving what is true and good."

Catholic moral philosophy is grounded in reason and free will because it's each person's free will, their capacity for free will, both to know what is right and to act rightly, that establishes personal moral responsibility. Reason and free will make humans able, responsible, and accountable to act rightly. Without reason and free will there could be no consequences for doing evil. Reason is a gift from the divine, a participation by humans in the divine, and the source of human capacity for free will. A whole arena of Catholic moral theology and philosophy depends on those three assumptions: reason, freedom, and will. They're the basis of merit and guilt.

So faced with the decision to keep or not keep a pregnancy, what can a Catholic woman do?

CCC 1706   By his reason, man recognizes the voice of God which urges him "to do what is good and avoid what is evil." Everyone is obliged to follow this law, which makes itself heard in conscience and is fulfilled in the love of God and of neighbor. Living a moral life bears witness to the dignity of the person.

Again, we need to see and hear the female pronouns in this statement to feel the full weight of what it grants to women.

CCC 1706   By her reason, (every) woman recognizes the voice of God which urges her "to do what is good and avoid what is evil." Every woman is obliged to follow this law, which

> makes itself heard in her conscience and is
> fulfilled in her love of God and of neighbor.
> Living a moral life bears witness to the
> dignity of every woman.

By her reason a woman recognizes the voice of God which urges her to do what is good. This law makes itself heard in her conscience. So a Catholic woman has a choice: listen to her own inner voice and the voice of God within her or listen to those celibate old men in the Vatican. According to Catholic teaching, her inner voice is informed by her knowledge that God participates in the creation of every human. And it's totally rational and responsible for a woman to conclude that God's participation in the creation of the life of her fetus occurs around the time the fetus becomes viable and not before. And it's totally rational for a woman to conclude that the Vatican's insistence that the soul enters the body at conception is absurd, especially since it doesn't provide any rational argument for this doctrine and doesn't explain what happens to the souls of fetuses that miscarry.

A woman can listen to the voice of God within her or the voice of a bunch of celibate bishops who are terrified of women for at least two obvious reasons. One, there is no more intimate relationship between humans and God than that of women when they bring life into the world. Women and God work together to make humans, to maintain the existence of the human race. There is something to be said for the high priest of the Catholic Church to be a woman, and the men in the Vatican fear that argument. It's an existential threat to male authority and power.

Second, women are mothers who relate to the earth and nature as an extension of themselves. Let women have a prominent place in church ritual, like saying mass, and the next thing you know, everyone will start dancing. And once everyone starts dancing, they will dance themselves outdoors and the next thing you know mass will be celebrated in a grove of trees. Back to the druids. Many women in Ireland are probably closer to the ancient Celtic rituals than to anything resembling male dominated Catholic ritual. There is a lot more going on in this struggle for male Catholic authority than men want Catholics to talk about. Catholic bishops fear Catholic women, and their fear causes them to repress women. And the Catholic men on the U.S. Supreme Court appear set to make rulings that codify in American law the Vatican's fear of women and their moral arguments against a woman's right to choose. Women are free and able and responsible to listen to the voice of God within them and ignore all of the men who fear them. These justices cannot defend their stupid commitment to ignorance.

Early term abortions have the same moral significance as a miscarriage and a Catholic woman has the right to choose an early term abortion at will and no one has the right to interfere with her reason, her freedom, and her will.

And since it's the Catholic church that has led the fight for laws that prohibit abortion, these arguments for a woman's right and capacity to choose not only defeat the Catholic Church's arguments for laws prohibiting abortion, they defeat all political demands made by Status Christians who have no rational arguments to support those demands.

What can we say about a Catholic woman's choice? Her choices are never easy, but they can be more or less complex. Her choice is difficult but not terribly complex if it's made before the 24th or possibly the 22nd week. It's much more complex if it's made after the 22nd or 24th week.

The highly politicized arguments against a woman's right to choose regarding early term abortions made by Catholics isn't just built on sand, it undermines pillars of Catholic faith and has no place in the public square. The *Catechism of the Catholic Church* actually makes better arguments for a woman's right of choice during early term pregnancies than of the Church's right to intervene in that choice. So choice and early term abortions are off the table. A woman of faith has the ability and right to choose to terminate an unwanted pregnancy before the fetus is viable.

We have used Catholic moral reasoning both to refute Catholic arguments against early term abortions and to establish a woman's right to make that choice. But look at what we have also done. We have used Catholic moral reasoning to reclaim and reassert moral certitude on a major moral issue that has confounded

We the People. It's just a beginning, but it's important. Radical capitalists are beginning to lose their claim to the moral high ground in political discourse and We the People are beginning to reclaim and reassert our public moral certitude.

Oh, and by the way, all those Catholic men on the U. S. Supreme Court, they must abandon their opposition to Roe v. Wade or expose themselves as inveterate supporters of radical capitalists or subjects of Roman Catholic Papal authority. Once they're forced to admit either of those positions, We the People can question the legitimacy of any rulings they make. For they will have admitted that they are not guided by a sound reading of the U.S. Constitution.

Before we turn to public moral reasoning and a woman's right to choose, we must give attention to the phenomenological issues that impact how many women think about abortion, irrespective of their religious backgrounds.

Early Term Abortion and the Phenomenology of Pregnancy

I mentioned phenomenology when we were talking about modern philosophies and used a quotation from Luigi Pirandello's play *Six Characters in Search of an Author* which I paraphrase again:

> How can we ever come to an understanding, if I put in the words I utter, the sense and value of things as I see them? While you who listens to me, must inevitably, translate them according to the things you see? We think we understand each other, but we never really do.

It's ineffective in the extreme, actually totally irrational, to claim that a woman has a right to choose without defining and defending exactly what it is that she has a right to choose. And to discuss that choice, we must anticipate and care about the different experiences different women bring to that discussion. A friend of mine who has only been pregnant twice and whose pregnancies produced her two healthy children, told me that from the moment

225

she knew she was pregnant, she was excited about the "child she bore." She was a little embarrassed by the old fashioned language, but she remembers being excited "to be with child" and about the "child she bore." She never for a moment thought of her fetus. She only thought of her child.

Women like her, and they're innumerable, have some work to do even to sympathize with let alone agree with the idea that any woman has the right to choose to end the life of her child. We must help her. We have to help her think at Stage 5 moral reasoning, and we must help her think about and feel the vastly different experiences other women have when they find out that they're pregnant. We must help these women develop "the sense and value" of the things other women put into the words they use when they talk about abortion.

Like the young single teacher who knows she will lose her job as soon as her principal finds out that she is pregnant.

Or the mother of five who does not know how she will care for the children she already has.

Or the woman who has been told that one more pregnancy will debilitate her physically or mentally for life.

Or any of the many nurses who worked in hospitals before Roe v. Wade and remember the wards that cared for women who had "back alley abortions" (that's what they were called) and were in hospital receiving critical care. Whole wards were set aside for these women, there were so many of them, and many of them died. And many of those who survived could never have children. These nurses remember those experiences and have told their stories to their daughters and granddaughters. These are just some of the women for whom Roe v. Wade was written.

Different women have different experiences with pregnancy and we must bridge those highly emotional differences in order to conduct rational arguments. We can't expect rational arguments to replace or refute profound emotional experiences. We need to stop and ponder what we're saying and recognize that any time we address the public morality of abortion, we do what Pirandello warned us about. We put into our words the sense and value of things as we see them, and many listening to us, will interpret them according to their feelings. Phenomenology matters in human relationships. It helps us understand each other, connect at both emotional and rational levels.

As I have mentioned, if we talk to virtually any woman who has had a child she wanted, she will describe her getting pregnant in terms similar to the old, "I am with child." There is no, "I am with fetus." Or, "I am with individual that's not yet even potentially a person or self." From the moment a woman who wants to be pregnant finds out that she is pregnant, she invests in her child all of the hopes and dreams that mothers have for their children, as a new born, toddler, youngster, teenager, young adult, and adult. The whole spectrum of the child's potential and her hopes for it come alive as soon as she finds out that she is pregnant. And all of our talk of the changing status of the fetus compared to that of the mother may seem at best strange and unfamiliar to her; and at worst downright offensive. We must respect those feelings.

And we need to ask these women to stop and think about, imagine, the feelings of a woman who is shocked and frightened and even desperate when she finds out that she is pregnant. She simply can't have this baby. She doesn't imagine all of the wonderful potential of the child. She imagines all of the harm that this pregnancy will cause her and others at this time in her life.

These two different experiences of finding out "I am pregnant" are so different that we might think that women simply can't imagine what other woman feel. But that's complete nonsense. Of course they can. Well, most of them can. They're women and they have experienced excitement and fear in society. Men may not be able to imagine what different women feel, but women can. And we ask these women who have never thought about the women who must make these choices to think about them with care and love. And we must ask these women who must make these choices to think about the women who have not had to make these decisions with care and love.

And we can ask these women to do even more. We can't start any conversations in the public square about women's health by only focusing on the different feelings different women or different men have about women's rights and women's health care. We must start public discourse using mature reasoning and mature moral reasoning. We have developed the capacity to conduct mature public moral reasoning. We begin by establishing the morally grounded purposes of our society, of our body politic. And then we study which laws and policies and programs help us achieve those purposes, and which laws and policies and programs prevent us from achieving those purposes. We commit to those that help us achieve our morally grounded purposes and we reject those that prevent us from achieving those purposes. Once again, we need to state the morally grounded purposes of our liberal democracy.

The Morally Grounded Purposes of America's Liberal Democracy

Recognize, preserve, and promote the dignity and worth of all humans.

Preserve and protect essential social freedoms of all humans.

Provide for life, liberty, and the pursuit of happiness for all humans.

Guarantee justice and peace for all humans.

Make no laws that give happiness or benefit to some at the cost of doing harm to any other humans.

And we think about these morally grounded purposes using Stage 5 moral reasoning: we use universal moral principles. When we think of either men or women in our society, we begin with the assumption that they're free.

> . . . civil freedom of the citizen under a government whose powers are limited, and under a rule of law whose reach is likewise limited, chiefly by the axiom that the constraints of law must serve the cause of essential social freedom.

We don't start with the assumptions that others must feel the way we feel. And as we have seen, the ability to rise above our feelings and to use reason to order our lives, to direct our actions and discipline our will, to control our actions are essential human capacities that we all must develop and to which we all must commit. No woman who has only experienced the thrill of mother-hood can impose those feelings on women whose experiences of being pregnant are entirely different. We can respect each other's feeling and we can talk about each other's feelings. But we cannot conduct the arguments needed to make good and just laws if we only focus on feelings. We must use mature cognitive develop-ment and mature moral reasoning.

Now we turn to public moral reasoning and the question of a woman's right to choose to terminate an unwanted pregnancy before the fetus is viable.

Early Term Abortion and Mature Public Moral Reasoning

Public moral philosophy does not consider the soul at all, and therefore when the soul enters the body is of no interest to public moral philosophers. Public moral philosophy has been unable to identify a stage in the development of the fetus that's as dramatic and impactful as when the soul enters the body. Indeed, all of the DNA that makes the fetus an individual and the infant an individ-ual and the adult an individual is there at conception. So how does public moral philosophy justify terminating the life of a fetus at any stage, unless the mother's life is at risk? We can take a moral stand that prefers the life of the mother over the life of the fetus, at any stage of the fetus's development. But how do we make any argument to terminate the life of a fetus if the mother's life is not threatened? We will get to that discussion and it turns out that there is a point in the development of the fetus that is as dramatic in public moral philosophy as it is in religious moral philosophy, and they are the same: fetal viability. But the moral philosophy that supports the two are significantly different. We will get to that discussion soon.

It's helpful to note the reasons why women have abortions. Abort73, an online Christian education service that opposes abortion, provides useful statistics. In 2004, they tell us, the Guttmacher Institute surveyed 1,209 women who had recently had abortions with these results:

7.5% of the abortions involved reasons over which the woman had no control:

- 0.5% Rape
- 3% Fetal health problems
- 4% Mother's health problems caused by the pregnancy

92% dealt with known conditions that would allow a woman to avoid pregnancy through the use of birth control:

- 25% Not ready for a child
- 23% Can't afford a child
- 19% Done having children
- 8% Don't want to be a single mother
- 7% Not mature enough to be a mother
- 4% A child now would interfere with education or career
- 6% Other

In 92% of these abortions, the mother should never have become pregnant in the first place. Opposition to free and easy access to birth control is so counterproductive to the realities of abortion and women's health as to be totally indefensible. Only the raw, irrational political power of misguided Catholics and Status Christians have created the conditions that have made birth control inaccessible. However, even when using birth control, some women become pregnant. So access to birth control does not completely resolve this issue.

From a public moral reasoning point of view, the underlying moral issues don't change from early to late term, if the mother's life is at risk. That is why few arguments are brought to the public square proscribing abortion when a mother's life is at stake. So our first job is to establish the underlying moral foundations for terminating any pregnancy using mature public moral reasoning if the mother's life is not at stake. How do we even have such a conversation? Not surprisingly, we need interdisciplinary assistance. This is a great example of moral philosophy not being able to do its job alone. It needs social science and psychology.

When comparing the rights of the fetus to the rights of the mother, it's necessary to deepen our understanding of what it means to be a fully developed human being. Psychology tells us, and we need only recall, that each person's humanity is experienced, lived, in three domains: the individual, the person, and the self.

Individual: The biological human, the DNA and physical makeup which is unique to each human.

Person: The individual in society, all of the commitments and relationships the individual has developed living in society.

Self: The intellectual, psychological, aesthetic and spiritual development of the human.

A woman is at once an individual, a person, and a self. A fetus is just an individual. A fetus has all of the DNA it will have as an adult. But as long as the fetus can't live outside the mother, it isn't even potentially a person or self. Before a fetus is viable, it cannot live outside the mother's body and therefore it has no independent potential to establish social relationships or develop its own inner self. But once it becomes viable, it gains that potentiality. Once the fetus becomes viable, he or she can become a self and a person.

Moral philosophy often conducts moral arguments using deductive reason. We have referred to metaphysical arguments made by the Vatican. We can do the same thing. Establish *a priori*[72] assumptions and build arguments from them.

A Priori Assumptions (APA) of Public Moral Arguments Regarding Abortion

APA 1: In considering the rights of the fetus and the rights of the mother we consider each as an individual, person, and self, and evaluate their status and rights to the extent that each of those three is developed.

Many religious traditions as well as psychologists make the distinction between the individual that's born and the complex nature of the self and person the individual becomes, grows into. Paying attention to these three domains of each human, we notice that there is little difference between the individual of the fetus and the individual of the mother. The DNA of any human was set at conception. It's unchanged either in late term pregnancies or in living human beings. So as an individual, in terms of one's genetic nature, one can't distinguish the fetus from the mother.

But of course, that only helps us understand the enormous difference between the person and the self of the fetus and the person and the self of the mother. It's absurd to equate the person and the self of the fetus with the person and the self and of the mother. The fetus has had no social relationships and has had no intellectual, psychological, or spiritual development at all. And as long as the fetus cannot live outside the mother, it has no potential to develop either. It has no person or self. But the mother has whole networks of family, friends, coworkers and acquaintances, lives connected to and dependent upon her. And the mother has an inner life that makes up her special and unique self.

---

[72] Deductive reason uses *a priori* assumptions or premises which are different. To keep this discussion simple, I just refer to *a priori* assumptions. My apologies to logicians who find this too casual. They could also argue that I have stopped doing metaphysics. Same. Let's keep it simple. It is already a complex topic. We are just walking over the bridge. We are not the engineers who designed it.

APA 2: Although the individual of the fetus and the individual of the mother are indistinguishable, the person of the mother and the self of the mother are so superior to those of the fetus as to be incommensurate with the self and person of a fetus that is not viable.

If the fetus can't live outside the mother; if the fetus is entirely dependent upon the mother for its existence, then it has not even developed the potential for a unique person or self. If the fetus cannot live independent of the mother, the fetus has no person or self. It does not even have a potential person or self. Not even having a potential person or self creates the same calculus for the standing of a fetus in public moral philosophy as a fetus not having a soul creates in religious moral philosophy. Abortions of such fetuses are morally equivalent to miscarriages.

It is important to give due consideration to this argument. Any argument that attempts to equate the rights of a fetus that is not viable with the rights of a mother undermines any sense of the full humanity of the mother, the dignity and worth of the mother as a human being. Any such argument also attacks the full humanity of all women, the dignity and worth of all women as human beings. Arguments that equate the rights of a fetus that is not viable with the rights of the mother reduce women to their roles. They are not full human beings. They are mothers or wives or housekeepers or secretaries or providers of sex or there to bring men a beer when they are watching a football game. Whatever. But they are not full human beings and they do not deserve to be treated with the full dignity and worth of a human being. All of those arguments violate our morally grounded purposes as they apply to all humans, not just to women. They must be rejected. They violate our identity as Americans. And they open the door to racism and every form of the inhumanity of man to man. They must be rejected in our private lives, the public square, and in the voting booth.

APA 3: The fetus has no independent rights until it is viable, able to live independent of the mother with medical assistance.

Conclusion 1: A woman has unrestrained rights to terminate any pregnancy up until the time the fetus becomes viable, can live outside the mother with medical assistance.

Conclusion 2: Every woman has the right to and must be provided access to the full range of choices to complete or terminate her pregnancy before the fetus becomes viable, and must receive the information and health care required to assist her in choosing the one best suited to her.

Once the fetus can live outside the mother, removing and saving the fetus becomes an alternative to abortion. Once the fetus is viable, the choice to abort a pregnancy becomes a choice that a mother alone can't make. Once the fetus becomes viable, We the People have the right and duty to represent the welfare of both the mother and the fetus. So we have a third rationally established conclusion.

Conclusion 3: Once the fetus becomes viable, the mother's right to choose to terminate her pregnancy becomes limited and the public has the right to be involved in the decision in order to serve the cause of essential social freedom for both the mother and the fetus.

Using Our A Priori Assumptions

Using our work in deductive reasoning, we can now make three recommendations:

First, avoid unwanted pregnancies with responsible use of free, accessible birth control.

Second, should a pregnancy occur, the mother has the right to choose to terminate it, for any reason, up until the time the fetus becomes viable.

Now, different religious communities may make their own rules and different families may make different decisions about abortion, but they can only make those rules for their religious communities and decisions for their families. Similarly, individual women can make decisions in consultation with doctors, and husbands, and lovers. No law can prohibit that. But no law can proscribe the freedom of a woman to make her own decisions on whether or not to sustain a pregnancy before the fetus is viable. And since medical science is incapable of predicting when any fetus actually becomes viable, that decision must be left to the woman's doctor.

Third, once the fetus is viable, once the fetus can live outside the mother with medical assistance, a pregnancy can be terminated and the life of the child can be saved. The child gains a right to its own life. At this point, far more is involved in the choice to terminate the pregnancy than the woman's choice, for at this point our morally grounded purposes apply to both the mother and the child. At this point we all must be concerned that the constraints of law must serve the cause of essential social freedom of both the mother and the child.

Fetal Viability and the Morality of Abortion

It's really interesting and important to notice that once the fetus becomes viable, both religious moral philosophy and public moral philosophy merge. The presence of the soul and the viability of the fetus occur at the same stage of fetal development, when the fetus becomes viable. At this point, religious and public moral philosophy must deal with the same issues and must come up with the same solutions.

It's important to notice that fetal viability outside the mother is the key stage of development when talking about the rights of the fetus and the rights of the mother. The divisions of the trimesters aren't at all helpful. The first trimester is from conception to the 12th week of pregnancy. The second trimester is from the 13th to the 27th week. And the third trimester is from the 28th week until birth. It makes no sense to distinguish the woman's right to choose in the first trimester from the second trimester. The key time is fetal viability and that occurs around the 22nd or 24th week, at least 10 weeks into the second trimester. So a woman loses no rights when the pregnancy enters the second trimester, only at around 22 or 24 weeks when the fetus becomes viable.

The third trimester starts at 28 weeks, four to six weeks after the fetus becomes viable, six weeks after the mother's right to choose has been restrained by public laws. It's better to use early and late term abortions when discussing the mother's rights and responsibilities and society's rights and responsibilities. Early term occurs before the fetus is viable outside the mother; late term, after the fetus is viable. All of the arguments around the moral rights and responsibilities that concern our discourse in the public square deal with late term abortions. And as daunting as the topic may seem, by establishing our system of mature public moral reasoning and by agreeing on our *a priori* assumptions, we have constructed the foundation of agreement that allows us to conduct productive arguments. Once again, establishing agreement does not eliminate the need for arguments. It makes it possible to conduct productive arguments.

Mature Religious and Public Moral Reasoning and Late Term Abortions

First, we need to understand late term abortions, get the facts, and know the stories. Again, public moral philosophy can't operate without social science, medical science, and phenomenology to gain this understanding.

Social Science: Our first fact comes from social science. Only about 1.0% of abortions occur at or after 21 weeks, 1.3% according to *Abort 73*. 1.3% is a statistical fact that comes from social science and has been published by a religious cite that opposes abortion. Even *Abort 73* acknowledges that only about 1.3% of abortions involve Late Term Abortions. We have established in both religious moral philosophy and public moral philosophy that women have unlimited rights to choose to have early term abortions but can be restrained by public laws from having late term abortions. All this noise about the legal right of a mother to choose to have an abortion only applies, at the most, to 1.3% of abortions.

And late term abortions involve far more than the simple fact regarding the viability of the fetus. Why do women wait until after 20 weeks to have an abortion? It's far easier and safer and cheaper to have an early term abortion than a late term abortion? We need to know these facts. We need to know what causes women to choose to have late term abortions so that we can think about what laws, policies, and programs we must make and not make. Once again, We the People must be smart.

Medical Science: The 20 week scan (also called the anomaly scan, or mid-pregnancy scan) is the last critical test for the diagnosis of fetal abnormalities and explains many late term abortions. The mother did not know about her fetus's abnormalities until she had the 20 week scan. This explains why some women don't confront the decision to abort a pregnancy until after the fetus becomes viable. There is little time between the 20 week scan and when the fetus becomes viable, only about two to four weeks. That is not much time to make this kind of decision. There is even less time to make this decision if a woman's and her doctors' schedules did not permit the woman the opportunity to have the scan until later than 20 weeks. And time is needed for a woman to process the shocking new information she receives about the abnormalities of her fetus. And that's why it's important to at least have a sense of the personal narratives of women who have faced the facts that impacted their decisions to terminate a late term pregnancy.

The Phenomenology of Late Term Abortions: Our commitment to "recognize, preserve, and promote the dignity and worth of all humans" includes the mother. Any talk of preserving the dignity of the mother assumes that we at least have a sense of the stories of these mothers, know what they have experienced that has led them to require a late term abortion. We need to know more than the fact that the fetus is or may be viable or even the social science and medical science facts.

Women don't go into the 20 week scan hoping for an excuse to abort their pregnancy. Heck, some mothers bring their children along so that they can see the wonderful pictures of their little brother or sister. By the 20th week, they have told everyone about their baby, his or her name, and have begun preparing the nursery.

Scheduled time off from work. Talked their mother-in-law into coming or not coming to help.

The only reason these women face late term abortion decisions is that they got terrible, shocking, unexpected bad news from the 20 week scan. And they only have, at the most, two to four weeks to make a decision and schedule the abortion before the child becomes viable, this child who is already existentially viable in their hearts and minds. Hell, the mother spends at least three days crying before the doctor can explain the nature and the extent and the consequences of the baby's abnormalities. And it takes a good three or four days for her and her husband and family to process that information so that they can begin to consider their options. Imagine, a woman is twenty weeks pregnant, getting more and more excited about and connected to the life growing within her. She goes in for this last routine scan and finds out that her child's brain has not developed, that and or other life threatening conditions. All of a sudden, she faces a horrifying decision that will impact her child, her family, and herself. Who but that woman and her family should make the decision that she faces?

On the other hand, even if it's unnecessary, it seems appropriate that reasonable people operating with medical facts sort out the issues and make laws that protect the viable fetus and the mother. A child who will be born without a forearm can have a full life. No mother should have the right to terminate the life of that child. But no mother who is carrying a fetus that will be born without a brain or that will never be able to eat or sleep and will live in constant pain should be told by the state that she must carry that child to term and care for it until it dies. She is not seeking pleasure for herself at the expense of her child. She is allowing her child to die before entering a short life, a life with no potential for development, a life defined only by suffering.

Virtually all late term abortions are performed on women who wanted the child but decided that the child had no chance of surviving until birth, no chance of surviving for any length of time if removed early, or would only survive natural birth for a short painful life. Even if unnecessary as a practical matter, it's appropriate for states to make laws proscribing the abortion of healthy fetuses once they have become viable. But attempts to remove the mother and doctor and husband's choice to end the pregnancy of a child who is about to die in the womb or can't survive being removed or will not survive a natural birth and faces only increasing pain; those attempts at law making can't survive scrutiny in the public square. They don't, can't, serve the cause of essential social freedom.

But back to the fetus with only one arm. That child has a right to live. How about a child with cerebral palsy or muscular dystrophy. My younger brother Brian had muscular dystrophy. He sat in his wheel chair and watched me play basketball and run races. I still can't talk about him in public. But I will tell one story.

My dad had a floor covering store that he kept open until 9:00 PM every week night. My mother often joined him there in the late afternoon to work on the books, sell, and so that they could enjoy being together. I fixed or simply heated up dinner and Brian and I ate together then hung out a bit. Studying rarely interfered with my time with Brian. So it was after dinner and we were in the living room talking. He in his wheel chair. Picture him. Dark blonde hair that looked like Joe Palooka's. It was not a fashion statement. If he needed to scratch his nose or an eye, he would drop his head, hook his hair with is thumb and forefinger, and using his head, lift up his arm until his elbow rested on the arm of his wheel chair. He would scratch his eye and then let his arm fall. Dark blonde hair and piercing blue eyes.

So this night as we were talking, I was pacing. Finally he said, "What are you doing?"

"What?" I asked.

"All this pacing. What is wrong with you?"

"I have a big race tomorrow."

"You have a big game or race all the time. Why are you pacing tonight?"

"I could lose this one," I said, expecting him to understand.

He thought for a minute, and then he said, "It seems to me that if you could not lose a race, it would not even be interesting."

Get that. A kid in eighth grade who had muscular dystrophy, who from the time he was four years old only got weaker, who sat in a wheel chair and couldn't lift his hand to scratch his eye, had a brilliant insight into athletic competition.

He died a couple months before his 18th birthday. I was a senior at Notre Dame and was inconsolable. For years, I believed in the immortality of the soul and eternal life in heaven because I simply could not come to terms with the anguish I felt at the thought of his living his short life in such a diminished and constantly diminishing state and yet with courage and humor and a brilliant mind. And all of it gone before he could experience life even as a young adult. I could make no sense of his life without immortality. But there were larger issues than mine. Caring for him completely changed my parents' lives.

If parents know that their fetus will have no chance at a full life, do they have the right to terminate the pregnancy? These will be important arguments that will tear at the heart of any moral discourse. I will sit them out, unless someone wants to insist that the lives of these children can't be important, that they're flawed as individuals and have no hope to develop a worthy self or become a person who matters. For me, right now, I say save them, care for them, good luck at trying to love them more than they love you. Go ahead. Encourage them while they inspire you. But one thing I do know. If the parents bring these children into the world, they should not be left alone to care for them. We as a society must help the parents.

That's no small matter, helping the parents. These children must receive complete health care and physical therapy, prostheses, wheel chairs, and other equipment; counseling, school, and day care. We the people have no right to compel parents to bring children into this world who will be an enormous financial, emotional, and physical challenge if we're not willing to provide substantial help to both the child and the parents.

What do we know? What are we able to do? These are discussions that must be held in the public square, and they must be supported by research and development in the social sciences and medicine. What care can We the People give these children? What is best provided in a loving home? What is best provided in public facilities? Is there a place for private facilities? Can any of these services be privatized without making commodities out of these children and their families? Even after all of the agreement we have established in this context, agreement that has escaped public discourse until now, even after all of this, as promised, there is room for much more argument and work.

Again, religious communities can proscribe abortion in any contexts they choose and women can choose to subject themselves to those proscriptions, including transferring the decision to one's husband or father, but those laws only apply within those religious communities and to women who voluntarily subject themselves to them. They only apply to the women who make that choice. Those religious laws have no place in public law for they can't be sustained by any rational arguments.

We the People can win any argument regarding a woman's right to choose to have an abortion before the fetus becomes viable. And we have simplified the decisions that must be made regarding to terminate or not terminate the pregnancies of viable fetuses. We have simplified these decisions, but not the roles and responsibilities attendant to them.

I am glad I included this chapter. I learned a lot about Justice Thomas, and I am grateful for that. And it has made the book better in ways I had not anticipated. Women's Reproductive Rights is a major topic in social justice. But our chapter on social justice deals almost entirely with what economic enterprises, community groups and individuals need to do to promote social justice. Women's Reproductive Rights has dealt with the religious and moral reasoning that must be brought to the public square to guide the writing of laws and public policies.

Reviewing this chapter, it is pretty amazing all of the moral philosophy we have used. Of course, we had to use our morally grounded purposes, and we had to use Stage 5 moral reasoning. We had to think of all of our people, develop laws and policies that protect the essential social freedom of all of our people. And that required a profound study of the difference between a fetus that is not viable and the mother. That discussion reminded us of what we have observed throughout this book. A fully developed human being consists of the individual, the person, and the self. And a fetus that is not viable does not even exist in potential as a person or self. To equate the rights of a fetus that is not viable with the rights of a woman who is pregnant requires that we deny the existence of the woman as a person and self. Any arguments that so profoundly deny the full dignity and worth of a woman would be the same arguments used to support racism or any other form of Stage 3 Tribal moral reasoning. This should be no surprise to us. Any denial of the rights of pregnant women as full human beings is a denial of the rights of all men and women as full human beings.

This chapter has also been interesting for how it integrates moral philosophy and social science (as well as psychology, mathematics, and medicine). That was cool and it helps make all that work we did relevant and valuable.

And I am delighted and somewhat relieved by the intellectual tools we have talked about in moral philosophy and how useful they have been. We have stressed that social and natural science do not have the intellectual tools to conduct moral reasoning, to help us decide what we ought to do. Well, we sure used moral philosophy's intellectual tools in this chapter. We used metaphysical moral reasoning and teleological moral reasoning and we used Stage 5 moral reasoning to judge our conclusions. This has been one hell of a chapter and it all ended with the astonishingly powerful conclusion that any arguments that equate the rights of a fetus that is not viable with the rights of a woman who is pregnant must be rejected outright. They must be rejected because they deny the full humanity of pregnant women and in doing so they deny the full humanity of all men and women. Like I say, I am glad I wrote this chapter and included it in this book. But writing it and reading it are not enough.

We can achieve our goal:

> To conduct discourse in the public square that allows us to agree on what is right and what is wrong in public life so that we can make laws and develop public policies that support what is right and reject what is wrong.

And we need to work and fight. We need:

A critical mass of Americans to show up in the public square and support our arguments. Religious humanists who believe that social responsibility is a prerequisite to redemption. Secular humanists who believe that a good life requires that they help others. Americans who believe that they're members of and responsible for our community and our liberal democracy.

12
Social Justice

We begin thinking about social justice by keeping in mind the morally grounded purpose of our liberal democracy.

The Morally Grounded Purposes of America's Liberal Democracy

Recognize, preserve, and promote the dignity and worth of all humans.

Preserve and protect essential social freedom of all humans.

Provide for life, liberty, and the pursuit of happiness for all humans.

Pursue justice and peace for all humans.

Make no laws that give happiness or benefit to some at the cost of doing harm to any other humans.

We know that education justice and economic justice provide the foundations of social justice. If we don't provide education justice we leave a large segment of our society living lives governed by low intellectual and human development, without the knowledge and skills needed to participate in our economic system. And that matters because our economic system allows us to meet our basic needs and pursue our full development. These two systems have such a profound impact on social justice that it's difficult to think about how to provide social justice at all without them. So we must assume that we're committed to providing education and economic justice, that our educators and economists can figure out how to do it, and that We the People will pass laws and policies that provide it. That being said, what should seem obvious becomes obvious. If we want to achieve social justice, we will need a ton of help from the social sciences.

This was by far the most difficult chapter to write. In the other chapters, I knew how to think. I had to flush out some major concepts and details, but I always felt like I knew what I was doing.

But in this chapter, I had no idea how to think. I will save the reader my stumbling journey and just tell you a couple things. I spent a lot of time developing a Golden Mean that accounts for individualism and communiarianism, how we act in society as individuals and how we act as members of our community. But when I addressed the social justice challenges we face, I did not use any of that work. So I cut all ten pages of it. You're very welcome.

Rather, I used a way of thinking that we learned when discussing Economic Justice: That We the People need to decide which economic challenges are best met by capitalist enterprises and which are best me by socialist enterprises.

In this chapter I used the list of challenges The American Association of Social Work and Social Workers (AASWSW) published. Their list is organized in three categories: Individual and Family Well Being, Stronger Social Fabric, and Just Society. I found it invaluable because it brought topics to my attention that I could not have thought of on my own. However, as I worked through their list, it made more sense to organize their challenges in the categories we have talked about, Capitalist Solutions and Socialist Solutions. And it just made sense to add Individual/Community Solutions. As it turned out, we can talk about individual and community solutions without getting into the weeds of what it means to be an individual or community, individualism and communitarianism.

So here is what we do. We list huge social justice challenges (thank you AASWSW) in categories that clarify how we will address them. We answer the question: Which of these challenges can best be met within Capitalist Enterprises? Which can best be met within Socialist Enterprises? Which can best be met by Individuals and Community? And with the clarity provided by knowing the sources of our solutions, we are able to discuss what some of the solutions might be. Of course, agreeing to have this discussion in this way leaves room for plenty of arguments, but the entire framework of the topic promises calm, productive arguments.

Social Justice Challenges that Demand Capitalist Solutions

Advance Long and Productive Lives

Throughout the life span, fuller engagement in education and paid and unpaid productive activities can generate a wealth of benefits, including better health and well-being, greater financial security, and a more vital society.[73]

This is an interesting issue because it contains aspects of economic justice, education justice, and social justice. It deals with how we live better lives as individuals and in our community and how our community contributes to our living better lives. A whole range of the social sciences could contribute to how we think and what we decide to do to live better lives. But as an old guy, I am aware of the enormous impact that financial independence has upon one's ability to live a long a productive life. Universal health care is vital. So is discretionary income. At least for now, I think this is an economic justice issue. If everyone who works had health care and received a living wage that includes some discretionary income, our social scientists would have

---

[73] Descriptive paragraphs that follow topics are in bold if I have taken them directly from the AASWSW list of challenges. If the descriptive paragraph is not in bold, I changed it.

something to study to help us maximize our opportunities to live full and productive lives alone or in community.

End Homelessness

> **During the course of a year, nearly 1.5 million Americans will experience homelessness for at least one night. Our challenge is to expand proven approaches that have worked in communities across the country, develop new service innovations and technologies, and adopt policies that promote affordable housing and basic income security.**

Homelessness is first an economic issue. Full employment and living wages are the first step to ending homelessness. But so is mental health care. We know or can imagine how to provide universal housing and universal mental health care. But radical capitalists have convinced us that we can't afford it.

Consider affordable housing. Housing is a basic human need. We are not pursuing our morally grounded purposes if we are not actively working to provide affordable housing.

This topic presents a useful example of where capitalists and socialists can conduct a morally grounded pragmatic dialectic and find balance. At this time, real estate operates almost totally as a capitalist enterprise. Real-estate has commercial value, but we can't make commodities out of affordable housing. A socialist solution may be needed. The government can build affordable housing and control it so that it never enters the free market. Maybe there is a break point where houses can become commodities, and below which they must be treated as a socialist enterprise, protected, and kept affordable.

In the meantime, mortgage banks and regular banks must conduct appropriate due diligence and act with fiduciary responsibility. Individuals may want homes they cannot afford and fail to understand the risks they take in buying them. Banks need to take fiduciary responsibility in their lending practices. The 2008 housing crisis damn near destroyed our economy. Individuals were responsible and so were banks and hedge funds. I tend to place most of the blame on financial organizations because they have the knowledge and sophistication to run their programs responsibly, control risks, and evaluate the efficacy of other organizations such as financial insurance companies, credit rating companies, and sub-prime lenders. They should prevent borrowers from making bad decisions.

None of this is easy, but we can conduct productive arguments about them and we can tell the difference between good solutions and bad, significant and trivial.

Build Financial Capability for All

Nearly half of all American households are financially insecure, without adequate savings to meet basic living expenses for three months. We can significantly reduce economic hardship and the debilitating effects of poverty by adopting social policies that bolster lifelong income generation and safe retirement accounts; expand workforce training and re-training; and provide financial literacy and access to quality affordable financial services.

Good jobs and fair wages. Capitalists and socialists finding solutions in our morally grounded pragmatic dialectic. What solutions can the free market economy provide? What solutions can only socialist laws and programs provide? Balance. And we must have a far better understanding of our people who can't work. Social scientists need to study our people, examine what is going on with people who are poor and don't or can't work. But again, it's unproductive and intellectually dishonest to treat all people out of work as if they are the problem. So I treat this topic as primarily a topic of economic justice that capitalists must address. What they can't achieve will be met with socialist solutions. Those solutions can include regulations that require capitalist organizations to do the right thing. The more we provide work to people who only lack opportunities to work, the easier it is to identify people who cannot work. Medical and mental health care professionals can step in and work with those who can't help themselves.

And I should add that it seems brutally unrealistic to expect people with modest incomes to provide for their retirement. Social Security can and must be strengthened. Now there is a topic that needs mature moral reasoning and a ton of civil discourse. We can be civil if we all commit to and keep our eyes on our morally grounded purposes and pay attention to what works and what does not work to achieve those ends.

Reduce Extreme Economic Inequality

The top 1% of the American population owns nearly half of the total wealth in the U. S, while one in five children live in poverty. We can correct the broad inequality of wealth and income through a variety of innovative means related to wages and tax benefits associated with capital gains, retirement accounts, inheritance taxes, and home ownership.

We have dealt with this topic in Economic Justice. But it's important to notice that AASWSW has listed it as one of the major challenges facing Social Work and Social Welfare professionals. Extreme economic inequality has significant social consequences and they must be addressed by We the People because radical capitalists have written the laws and policies that have created this inequality. There is no evidence that capitalists are capable of fixing these problems. We the People must fix it without doing more harm to our capitalist system than good. I like that. Our capitalist system. Not sure I have used that term before.

Social Justice Challenges that Demand Socialist Solutions

Ensure Healthy Development for All Youth

Each year, more than six million young people receive treatment for severe mental, emotional, or behavioral problems. Strong evidence shows us how

to prevent many behavioral health problems before they emerge.[74]

AASWSW describes the healthy development of all youth as a mental health issue. It includes physical health issues, social health issues, and psychological health issues. All three work together: the individual, the person, and the self. Let's look at all three.

Physical Health of All Children

The foundation of physical health is laid with nutrition and exercise. Nutrition depends on knowledge and resources. Years ago the state of Washington implemented a program that taught poor mothers to shop for good food and cook tasty meals. The program administrators kept track of what their staff did and their results. When they published the findings of their study, they created a political problem. Poor children were eating better tasting and more nutritious meals than many working and middle class children. The program was terminated.[75] We know what to do and how to do it. We need a critical mass of people who care and will fund and develop the socialist programs that will meet the needs of mothers and children. Washington might have expanded their program to include more parents rather than eliminating it. And we should not ignore the fact that the program worked in Washington and could work throughout the country.

Exercise. Physical education in public schools every day through 10th grade and expanded programs in parks and recreation. Just do it!

---

[74] Bold text is taken from the report by The American Academy of Social Work and Social Welfare (AASWSW). I don't use bold text in some places so as to acknowledge where I have changed the language used by AAWSW.

[75] Source: Firsthand account by one of the staff who I met while camping on the Pacific side of the Olympic Peninsula south of Forks, Washington in 2000.

Social Health of All Children

Physical activities at schools and in parks and recreation often create opportunities for social as well as physical development of children. Social development should be treated as an important goal along with physical development. I am not familiar with research on child social development, which I must admit constitutes a serious gap in my adult development. It is an important topic for parents and educators to understand and be competent in. We need the social sciences to weigh in and We the People must fund and support them.

But some children need programs that target their social needs. Children do not run away from home. Children run away from what is happening in their homes. Physical abuse. Sexual abuse. Neglect. Until 2010, runaway children who engaged in prostitution were arrested and placed in the criminal justice system. Now, some states place them in child services and treat the crimes associated with them as they should be: Adult sex trafficking. Society must care for children whose families cannot or do not care for them, We must get to know them, love them, and care for them. We just need . . .

Mental Health of Children

We know a lot about how to aid the mental development of all youth. Clearly, it's appropriate and necessary to establish socialized mental health services to meet the needs of all Americans, including our youth.

As we learned with education, socialist programs don't automatically develop adequate professional leadership, supervision and evaluation of services and providers. Like education, intellectual leaders in psychology have some work to do if a socialist system is to be formed to meet the mental health needs of all children. A socialist system will be supported by tax revenue, and the system must be accountable to taxpayers as well as clients.

Currently, psychologists typically work alone with individuals who have the freedom to choose their psychologist and methods. In order to create a socialist approach in the development of mental health solutions for our youth, psychology needs a paradigm that unites the profession's knowledge and the community of psychologists in serving the needs of their clients. Their services must assure predictability, establish a clear relationship between the advantages and disadvantages various clients bring to their development of mental health, and the methodologies used to address them. My work on paradigms in education can help psychologists think about how to think about unifying knowledge in psychology.

By building agreement that mental health is a major issue in social justice that demands socialist solutions, we pave the way for necessary agreement and inevitable but productive arguments in the public square. Those arguments will be guided by our morally grounded purposes.

For example, what right do We the People have to intervene in the care of children? When do our responsibilities to children trump the rights of parents? And who decides the location of care: in the home, in a psychologist's office, in a school counselor's office, or in an institution? None of this is easy. But it does not have to be impossibly complex.

Close the Health Gap

Until the Affordable Care Act was implemented, millions of Americans had inadequate access to basic health care while also enduring the effects of discrimination, poverty, and dangerous environments that accelerate higher rates of illness. We must defeat and end the arguments from radical capitalists that the market can provide health care to all Americans who can afford it and those who can't afford it don't deserve it. And we must build an effective and efficient health care system that helps individuals live healthy lives, avoids unhealthy behaviors, and supports innovative, scientific strategies that improve health care and lead to broad gains in the health of our entire society.[76]

Medicine is a highly developed science and profession. It can tell good research from bad, good practice from bad. For all its problems as currently played out in our courts, medical malpractice lawsuits demonstrate that the medical professionals can tell good practice from bad. We know how to close the health care gap. It's a matter of economic justice that can be accomplished in a socialist enterprise that accommodates but is not dominated by capitalist enterprises. We must bring mature moral reasoning to discourse in the public square regarding health care. No Stage 3 Tribal arguments allowed. And our morally grounded pragmatic dialectic will work because it does not create a dichotomy between capitalist and socialist solutions in health care. It works to find balance.

Promote Smart Decarceration[77]

The United States has the world's largest proportion of people behind bars. Our challenge is to develop a proactive, comprehensive, evidence-based "smart decarceration" strategy that will dramatically reduce the number of people who are imprisoned and enable the nation to embrace a more effective and just approach to public safety.

This topic calls for discourse in the public square that produces sufficient agreement on what is right and what is wrong to enable us to make good laws and develop sound public policies regarding incarceration. But I want to discuss the entire law enforcement system: our laws and policies, police training and

---

[76] I changed the AASWSW description of the topic to reflect the changing political conversations.

[77] Incarceration is in my spell check. Decarceration is not. That indicates how little thought we have given to decarceration, how little has been written about it.

supervision, police conduct, jail policies, district attorneys, judges, jails and prisons. Law enforcement is a socialist enterprise. We the People authorize its existence and the collection of taxes to pay for it. It's not a capitalist enterprise. We the People are responsible for it. We the People must participate in and take responsibility for its governance.

Stage 5 moral reasoning drives us to recognize that we incarcerate humans and our morally grounded purposes demand that we care about how we treat them. Americans do not lose their dignity as human beings or their rights under the Constitution when they enter the legal system. Once We the People make the cognitive modification, the intellectual leap, needed to commit to our morally grounded purposes, we can argue productively about such critical questions as:

Who will be incarcerated and who will not?

Who will decide the length of sentences?

How will different prisoners be categorized?

How will those different categories of prisoners be housed and treated?

How will we decide to release individuals who are incarcerated?

Once we shift from Stage 3 moral reasoning to Stage 5 moral reasoning when thinking about the humans we incarcerate and how to keep our communities safe, what is wrong and what is right becomes abundantly clear. Then all we must do is stop doing what is indefensible and start doing what is right.

Among all of the items in our list of social justice issues, this is the one for which we know what to do and have the resources to do it. I say we know what to do because in the late 1960s I worked in the most effective prison in the world at the time, the U. S. Air Force Retraining Group. Since then, I have been shocked at the extent to which state and federal governments have ignored what was known and done in that prison. It wasn't a military secret but it also wasn't run on the cheap. We had significant resources. But when we consider how much we spend on our current prison system, how little good it does, and how much harm it does; we can at least agree that the money we spend can be put to better use. For those incarcerated and for society.

More recently, Norway has developed the most humane prison system in the world. So maybe I should say that clearly there is much to be known about what to do in, and how to structure and conduct our criminal justice system. Where do we start? We stop dehumanizing people before and after we arrest them and after we incarcerate them.

We the People must take responsibility for the criminal justice system run by our government. The police officer who arrests a person is operating with the rules, regulations, and training that We the People provide through our local, state, and federal government. We don't get to live in a liberal democracy, enjoy all its freedoms and benefits, and then claim no responsibility for how our government and government employees work in our socialist enterprises. We the People approve the expenditure of enormous tax dollars for our socialist criminal justice system. We can't shrug off responsibility for the fact that too often our criminal justice system uses these revenues in ways that are intellectually indefensible. Too often they're stupid and immoral. "Too often" does not mean that they happen all the time. It means that any occurrence is unacceptable, and unacceptable behavior happens too often.

We must insist that we do what is right. We must insist that the academic and professional leaders of our socialist criminal justice system recognize that they are the leaders of a major socialist system and its success depends upon their intellectual leadership. They lead a huge socialist program that must make decisions and implement programs that pursue our morally grounded purposes with significant levels of predictability and morality.

We must change laws and judicial policies and practices that incarcerate too many people, too many black and brown people, and too many people for too long.

We must change police practices that are unjust, while supporting and protecting our police officers. Those aren't mutually exclusive goals. Indeed, they support each other.

We must change police training, supervision, and leadership. Police aren't regular, ordinary citizens. Police officers must meet a high standard of courage. We give them badges and guns so that they can protect all of us from danger. When they sense danger, they must meet it with courage and sound judgment. Our laws and policies must prohibit police officers from using deadly force unless they're confronted by clear and present danger as defined by trained professional police officers, not by the standards of frightened, untrained citizens who sit on juries.

Obviously police officers cannot be cowards. Equally obviously, they're not. But sometimes some police officers act like cowards. We must be interested in why. Social scientists could study this, but we have a pretty good idea what is going on.

First, too often police departments get caught up in Stage 3 moral reasoning. The whole department identifies groups of citizens as others, as not deserving to be treated like full human beings. We have seen that racism can infect whole departments. Sometimes individual police officers shoot an innocent victim and the entire department and office of the district attorney work to protect them. How else can we explain juries finding police officers innocent who are clearly guilty of using unwarranted deadly force. "He scared me!" is not a defense that protects police officers. But district attorneys fail to defeat that argument and judges allow juries to treat police officers as if they must meet the same standard of courage as the members of the jury would be expected to meet if they faced the same threat.

Cowardice in armed police officers is criminal conduct. It's not criminal for police officers to feel fear. It's criminal for police officers to act like cowards. And what makes all this even more infuriating is that we know police officers are not cowards. They prove their courage when the life of another officer is at risk or when the members of the community they are committed to protecting are at risk. But We the People have allowed too many police departments to develop an entirely different standard of courage when dealing with citizens from groups they see as others: African Americans, Hispanics, and Muslims.

Police departments and district attorneys' offices are filled with people and people are susceptible to human error and immature moral development. We the People must do our duty and require the full intellectual development of those who lead law enforcement and train law enforcement personnel.

And let's be clear. We must end violence in prisons! Again, human beings do not lose their right to the dignity and worth of a human being by entering the legal or prison systems. We must change the laws and policies that currently cause that to happen. We must create laws and policies that make sure that these human beings are safe and secure. This includes ending the practice of treating prisoners like slave labor.

Mean people have created mean laws. Good people have supported them with their indifference. We the People can't deny the humanity of others without denying our own humanity.

Social Justice Challenges that Demand Individual and Community Solutions

Eradicate Social Isolation

Social isolation is a silent killer, as dangerous to health as smoking. Our challenge is to educate the public on this health hazard, encourage health and human service professionals to address social isolation, and promote effective ways to deepen social connections and community for people of all ages.

This seems like a problem that could best be solved by family and community. I would have to learn a lot more from social workers about what is and is not harmful social isolation. We need to know who needs help and who thrives when left alone. And we need to know what interventions work, what we can do as a community. But I would think that caring local communities could figure out how to meet this basic need of our people, at least make opportunities available. And maybe families and friends would do more if they knew more.

Again, this topic seems to demand more information from the social sciences.

Stop Family Violence

Assaults by parents, intimate partners, and adult children frequently result in serious injury and even death. Proven interventions can prevent abuse, identify abuse sooner, break the cycle of violence, or find safe alternatives.

The most important part of the statement describing family violence is: "Proven interventions can prevent abuse, identify abuse sooner, break the cycle of violence, or find safe alternatives." Proven interventions! We don't see that claim made regularly in the AASWSW description of these Challenges. That clarifies our discussion. We must do what we know how to do to assure peace and safety to all of our people.

Family violence is a local issue. Local law enforcement and social services, working together, seem best equipped to intervene if the police are well trained and the two departments are guided by clear and mature policies and practices. Both police departments and departments of social services are socialist enterprises. They are organized and directed locally. Their success depends upon the academics and professionals who lead them and their relationship with each other and their communities.

We ended our discussion of Education Justice by addressing evaluation of education personnel and programs. We need to address the same issue here. When We the People create socialist programs, we must assure that the personnel and the programs implemented undergo regular, thorough evaluation aimed at improving the personnel and programs. Obviously, some personnel will be removed and some programs will be eliminated, but the efficacy and efficiency of any evaluation system is measured by its capacity to improve personnel and programs. The development of professional evaluation systems constitutes a major challenge and responsibility for the social sciences. But they must rely on moral philosophy to help identify the criteria by which they judge personnel and programs.

Achieve Equal Opportunity and Justice

Historic and current prejudice and injustice bars access to success in education and employment. Addressing racial and social injustices, deconstructing stereotypes, dismantling inequality, exposing unfair practices, and accepting the super diversity of our population will advance this challenge.

Racism should have nothing to do with the government. Racism occurs in the minds and hearts of individuals and that's the only place where it can be cured. We have seen attempts by the federal government and courts to reverse institutional racism, most obviously in Brown v. Board of Education, the Civil Rights Act, the Voting Rights Act, and the 14th Amendment. All of these efforts have improved the condition of African Americans and other targeted groups, but none of them have addressed the minds and hearts of Americans who benefit financially or psychologically from their hatred and dehumanization of others. Securing equality through quota systems and equal opportunity legislation constitute a legitimate strategy that addresses an important goal. But as we learned from the experiences of Justice Thomas, they can have negative unintended consequences if the hearts and minds of people in power reject both the goal and the strategy. I don't know if Justice Thomas would have been accepted to Yale Law School if the dean had not implemented a quota system for African Americans, but the fact that he finished in the middle of his class proves that he was qualified. Consider how qualified all of the white students at Yale Law were. And Justice Thomas finished ahead of half of them. A little humility is in order. How many readers of this book could have been admitted to Yale in any field of study? Justice Thomas did more than get admitted. He did damn well. And white law firms looked at him, saw his black skin, and refused to recognize what were his obvious achievements. Clearly, equal opportunity and justice can be pursued in law but ultimately must be achieved in the minds and hearts of individual Americans. Again, we are talking about structural cognitive modification.

We need community groups to form among the majority of Americans to overcome the vast indifference we have to racism and to attack the overt racism in our communities. This is a personal and community moral issue that can no longer be ignored. Individuals and community groups must demand Stage 5 moral reasoning in how we think and feel and act toward one another. Yes, how we think and feel. Doctrines felt as facts drive feelings. We can examine, criticize, reject, and replace doctrines felt as facts that are grounded in Stage 3 moral reasoning.

And one of the doctrines felt as fact that we need to change is how we think about the source and legitimacy of our feelings. How we feel is impacted by our body's chemistry. Events create chemical reactions that impact our feelings. We have known that for around two thousand years without getting into the weeds of biochemistry. But we have also known that reason allows us to order and control both our feelings and our behavior. Structural cognitive development of how we reason and how we reason morally allows us to order and control our feelings and actions. Somehow the truth of human agency has been lost in our universities and society, and excessive credit has been given to biological determinism. We must get over that, for everyone's sake.

Racism can be changed through the mediated learning experiences that provide morally grounded structural cognitive modification. That's what happens when we grow up. That's what happens when our grandmother or grandfather share their wisdom with us. That's what happens in great homes and schools and communities: good mediated learning. There is nothing more absurd, nothing more dehumanizing, than the assumption that feelings are immutable. Good feelings are great and to be enjoyed. Feelings that lead us to hurting others must be overcome and replaced.

Racism is rooted in education injustice, economic injustice, and social injustice. But most of all it's rooted in Stage 3 moral reasoning, doctrines felt as facts that are taught in civil society, in our most uncivil civil associations.

A lot of the work that needs to be done to end racism must be done in families and churches, and as much as they're beyond the reach of public laws and policies, they aren't beyond the reach of public opprobrium. Racism is America's Original Sin. It has stained our country and our people for over 400 years. At best, white Americans have inherited indifference, the great American sin of omission. And then there are the mindless acts of commission. Americans who wave and carry and display the Confederate flag are the greatest proof operating today of the fact that there is no such thing as white supremacy. The Confederate flag never represented a nation or state. And since its emergence as a major southern symbol in the 1920's it has only signified white racism. Those who display it today are white and they prove the capacity for white ignorance, cruelty, and inhumanity. Their galactic stupidity has them stuck in vicious ignorance.

Now that's harsh, and I don't apologize for it, for these Americans deserve public opprobrium. But I can't leave my comments there. Racists deserve opprobrium, but they don't lose their place and rights as human beings by being wrong. A ton of money is spent every year providing negative mediated learning experiences to poor and working class white men and women convincing them to believe in stuff that in the end hurts them. Like racism. They're taught that there are people in our society who don't deserve to be treated as fully human. When they support that argument against African Americans they also support it when it applies to themselves. Again, we can't deny the humanity of others without denying our own humanity.

When the economic system is conducted with no regard for the well being of these white Americans. When they have no jobs or only lousy jobs with low wages and no benefits. When they do not have the health care their family needs. When they live in a degraded environment, exposed to unsafe food or water or air. When they cannot afford a car or its maintenance or gas for it and have no public transportation available that will get them to a job in a reasonable amount of time. When they are denied jobs that they're totally capable of doing because arbitrary education standards have been created for employment, standards that reward class rather than competence. When they experience any of those things, they experience the same denial of their humanity that they deny to African Americans, Hispanics, immigrants, and whomever else they chose to hate.

The more we think about it, the more we realize that a lot of white men and women who behave badly deserve our empathy, along with our opprobrium. Admittedly, it's hard to feel sympathy when we think about these Americans as harming themselves by insisting on their racist views, by voting for racist policies and racist politicians. But it's not hard to feel sympathy for them when we focus on the fact that they too are human beings whose immature cognitive and moral development has been imposed on them through negative mediated learning experiences. Teach your children well. Yes, and teach them good.

But back to white indifference, America's great sin of omission. When we add up all the good we do for one another in this country and subtract the cruelty of our treatment of all women, poor women,[78] black and brown Americans, and other groups that don't get so much attention, we're forced to admit that we reside low on a scale of humanity among developed countries.

And here is the killer. We know of the overt cruelty: poor women who are denied health care, women who are sexually assaulted or denied equal pay for equal work, black and brown men who are denied apprenticeships in technology and skilled labor, denied jobs, and then imprisoned or murdered with impunity, black Americans who don't feel safe anywhere in public. We know about all that.

We go tut tut to the cruelty but remain indifferent. And moral philosophers and social scientists in our universities earn tenure and live in comfort while enabling such behavior. After all, none of them can make a moral claim that applies to anyone but their

---

[78] I think of poor women as requiring special attention, separate from all women, but I am willing to stand corrected if I am presented with evidence that they receive equal moral and political attention to that received by "all women." I am impatient with anyone who has fought against their health care in general and especially their reproductive health care.

selves. And, according to them, none of us can either. They have institutionalized the moral indifference that's killing the American soul, our identity and sense of self.

And what white church fights for the dignity and worth of poor women and black Americans? They too, by their indifference, kill the American soul.

All of this cruelty and consequence result directly from our failure adequately to take an obvious, irrefutable moral stance. All of this cruelty and consequence because of our inability to think and act like mature moral adults. All of this because we haven't attained the moral reasoning of which we became capable when we were still in or just out of high school. We should all spend a moment in shame, then shake it off and begin the work to grow up and take responsibility for our own, our community's, and our nation's moral development.

Public laws and policies must assure justice throughout all of society. Yes, we need moral philosophers and social scientists to provide better intellectual leadership. But we can't expect the federal government to be of much help until major changes are made by voters. And we can't expect any help for justice or human dignity from the Supreme Court where appointments were made to assure that the goals of radical capitalists are protected. Courts that will outlast two generations of Americans. We the People must come together using mature moral reasoning and fight for liberty and justice for all.

Social Justice Challenges that Require Capitalist, Socialist, and Individual/Community Solutions

Create Social Responses to a Changing Environment

Climate change and urban development threaten health, undermine coping, and deepen existing social and environmental inequities. A changing global environment requires transformative social responses: new partnerships, deep engagement with local

communities, and innovations to strengthen individual and collective assets.

Cute. We can cope with the effects of climate change. Does anyone want to talk about the point at which we can no longer cope, no matter what we do, with the effects of global climate change? Do we dare think or talk about how close we are to that breaking point? Plenty of information is available from climate scientists. Let me share something that is not widely known. Chaos theory mathematicians paint a scary picture. Chaos theory mathematicians warn us that complex systems, like weather, can maintain order through an enormous amount of change. But! After all that change, one small, unpredicted change can cause the system to collapse into total disorder, total chaos. Those of us who expect climate change to proceed in a predictable, orderly fashion until it becomes just too inconvenient, at which time we can do something about it, take a huge risk. They mistake the Sword of Damocles held by a single hair for a manageable challenge.

We can add two rules to our list of intellectual tools:

1. Scientists, be damned sure you're right when you bring scientific facts to the public square. We depend on you for scientific facts. Fear being wrong. The public's trust is at stake.

2. We the People must listen to scientists and mathematicians when they have gathered scientific facts that impact our lives. We must treat what they're telling us as true because we have no other source of valid information on what they study. If they tell us that what they say is supported by compelling scientific evidence, we must listen.

We must build conscious commitment to saving human life and the life of mother earth. Then we can argue about how to do it. And we must shame and defeat radical capitalists' use of propaganda, negative mediated learning experiences, to oppose solutions that are at hand. In reality, the environment is not just a health issue; it's a justice, peace, security, and survival issue that can only be solved by nations working together.

I have to admit, Social Justice was such a complex, difficult topic when I started writing about it that I almost abandoned it. But once I figured out that we already knew how to approach it, writing it became straightforward. Our morally grounded purposes, our morally grounded pragmatic dialectic, and our categories of capitalist solutions, socialist solutions, and individual/community solutions have set the stage for productive discourse by We the People on these topics.

Clearly, we can achieve our goal:

To conduct discourse in the public square that allows us to agree on what is right and what is wrong in public life so that we can make laws and develop public policies that support what is right and reject what is wrong.

Of course, we need:

A critical mass of Americans to show up in the public square and support our arguments. Religious humanists who believe that social responsibility is a prerequisite to redemption. Secular humanists who believe that a good life requires that they help others. Americans who believe that they're members of and responsible for our community and our liberal democracy.

13
Conclusion

The United States is a liberal democracy with a remarkable story of success. But we're going through a rough patch right now. Our public square and our body politic are fractured, unable to function the way our Founding Fathers intended. We have set out to heal our fractures. Of course there is far more work to do than we have done in this book, but at least we have figured out how to do it. We haven't solved all of our problems but we have simplified them so that we can talk about them and solve them. Simple. Not easy, but simple. So what have we done?

We have investigated both how we think and what we think and we have discovered that what makes our challenges seem so complex and intractable is the result of how we think even more than what we think. So most of our attention has focused on improving how we think, which will change how we talk to each other. We have investigated and repaired how We the People conduct political arguments in the public square.

We started by looking at cognitive and moral development. Right away we established that Learning Leads Development. This assumption is enormously important because it puts us (society, teachers, parents, friends and neighbors) in a dynamic relationship with each other and especially young people. We know that people learn to be who they become, they learn to think both how and what they think.

We also assumed early on and later demonstrated that intellectual development consists of both cognitive development and moral development. That's huge and should be obvious, but we do not take it for granted. It's one of the major assumptions used in our work. Cognitive and moral development proceed through stages that are associated with our biological development that occurs at different ages. We all must go through each stage to get to the next. And we learn that by the time we get to about our senior year of high school or shortly thereafter, we have attained the biological maturity required for the highest levels of cognitive and moral development. But, far too few of us actually achieve the levels of cognitive and moral development that we need to function as mature adults, even though we're able to. We lack both the cognitive development and moral development we need to achieve full intellectual development.

The key to both full cognitive development and moral development lies in cognitive modification, modification of how we think, not behavior modification. Behavior modification works well when training pets or helping children deal with simple tasks. But it is totally inadequate at helping humans achieve full cognitive development, the ability to reason, and full moral development, the ability to reason morally.

We modify our cognition, how we reason, and that allows us to modify our behavior. The behavior that interests us is how we talk to each other, specifically how we conduct arguments in the public square. Our goal is to conduct discourse in the public square that allows us to agree on what is right and what is wrong in public life so that we can make laws and develop public policies that support what is right and reject what is wrong. In order to achieve that goal, we all must operate with mature cognition and mature moral reasoning.

Why do some of us reach full intellectual development? And why do most of us not reach full intellectual development? How is it that our Founding Fathers who wrote the Declaration of Independence and the Constitution of the United States, had reached full intellectual development, but we as a nation seem to have slipped back into immature levels of cognitive and moral development?

We have taken two approaches to answering those questions. First, we looked and the forces that promote and teach immature levels of cognitive and moral development because immature adults allow them, and sometimes help them, achieve their selfish goals. We have observed how the benign capitalism that our Founding Fathers embraced has degenerated into radical capitalism. Not in all of our capitalists enterprises and not among all capitalists. But rather in too many of our richest and most powerful capitalist organizations and individuals. Obviously, those organizations are rich and powerful, but there are too few of them to establish the political capacity to achieve their greedy goals. Our democratic form of government makes that impossible. They need help, they need voters who support them and they found those voters in the religious right, specifically among many Catholics and Status Christians.

We have observed how Christian and Jewish humanism, religious humanism, has been a force for good in our society. But it has been trumped by right wing Catholics and Status Christians. Status Christians, Christians who celebrate their personal salvation as a status and make no commitment to improving the lot of their fellow Americans. Radical capitalists, right wing Catholics, and Status Christians oppose and undermine the full cognitive and moral development of the American people because their goals are incompatible with full cognitive and moral development. What they believe can't withstand mature rational and moral scrutiny. In short, we have identified the enemies of the full cognitive and moral development of our people, the enemies of rational discourse in the public square of our liberal democracy. They threaten the foundations and future of our liberal democracy.

But then we had to ask, How is it possible that in the United States of America, the greatest nation in the history of the world, the richest and most powerful nation in the history of the world, the United States with the first free universal public school system and the greatest universities in the world, how did the forces for ignorance prevail over the forces of enlightenment, of full intellectual development in the United States of America?

As we have seen, our decline started when we began to make remarkable progress toward the full moral development of our nation, in the 1950s and 60s. The Civil Rights Movement, the Free Speech Movement, the Anti-Vietnam War Movement, the Women's Rights Movement, all of the movements for expanded

Civil Rights and social justice that began in the middle of the 20th century. All of the great social activism of the 1950s and 60s aimed at the full development of all of our people and the recognition of their full humanity in public and private life. What stopped this striving for justice and the recognition of the full dignity and worth of all humans? What stopped our attempts to redeem the promissory note made by our Founding Fathers and written in our Constitution? The promissory note that guaranteed us that all humans are created equal and endowed by their creator with the right to life, liberty, and the pursuit of happiness. Our Founding Fathers could not hold the union together, could not adopt our Constitution, without compromising with slave owning states. But they did compromise. They talked to each other and they created a liberal democracy that could heal itself. But to fix our country, we had to end slavery.

Slavery. America's Original Sin. And that original sin has corrupted every generation of Americans. Slavery became racism. And racism has survived as doctrines felt as facts that corrupts our moral reasoning. The lingering effect of slavery is racism in its most extreme form and indifference in its most insidious form.

But again, how is it possible for a great nation, a great liberal democracy, to fracture and not to heal itself? Not to overcome the forces of evil, and let's not prevaricate. Racism is evil. But we don't fix our public square by pointing out the evil of racism or other evils that may exist in society. We must win the fight for justice and the good that virtually all of us want in society. How do we do that? How do we get America back on track? How do we heal our fractured body politic?

We must simplify the problems. The big problem is our fractured public square. If we could talk, if we could conduct rational discourse in the public square, we could solve our problems. Reason is the key. Full cognitive development means mature reasoning. Full moral development means mature moral reasoning. Reason. How do we recover the place of reason in our public mind?

We dipped into history and noticed that the golden age of Islamic culture ended in the 13th century, around the time Aquinas made the West safe for reason. At around that time, the Islamic

269

world abandoned reason in favor of religious fundamentalism that took control of political and civic life, every aspect of Islamic life. Islam has still not recovered. So this is no small thing that we're having to reassert reason's central place in our public mind. In our universities, journalism, how We the People conduct discourse in the public square, and ultimately how our political leaders make laws and adopt public policies.

We give a lot of attention to the rise and fall of American humanism, the hope and victories of the 50s and 60s and the despair and defeat of the 70s and 80s. It's an important story because it reaffirms what we can be. We can be driven to activism in the belief that all men and women are created equal. We can be activists and we can win economic justice and social justice. We can have education justice. And we can guarantee women justice in their health care. But the 50s and 60s also reveal the forces that oppose hope and humanism. But that reflection on our past does not tell us what to do, for the most striking achievement of the past has been to fracture our public square. We must look to solutions.

The solution is to bring full intellectual development to discourse in the public square. And as we have seen, learning leads development. It's not the job of the public square to provide the intellectual leadership that guides our peoples' cognitive and moral development. That's the job of our universities. The university is where We the People go to learn to think. The university is supposed to guide our learning so that we achieve full intellectual development: both cognitive development and moral development.

The strongest, most self-confident, most compelling departments in the university inquire into and teach natural science. But natural science studies what is, not what ought to be. The natural sciences can aid our cognitive development but not our moral development. The natural sciences study what is, not what ought to be. We appreciate the natural sciences for all that they have contributed to our lives in science, engineering, technology, and medicine. We appreciate the enormous wealth science has created by taking research and development into product development, the partnership between science and business. We appreciate that, and we're committed to listening when science warns us that dangers lurk in our world. But science can't tell us what We the People ought to do in our society.

When we ask, What ought to be? We're asking, What should we do? And that's a moral question. Who can answer public moral questions? Most obviously, moral philosophers, but they have lost their way. It has been a long time since anyone listened to moral philosophers, so we fixed public moral philosophy. We'll get to that in a minute. But first, let's go ahead and jump right into our most important work. Public moral philosophy must tell us **what ought to be** in society. But it does not have the tools to tell us **what we ought to do** in society.

Notice we have focused our questions. We're asking about what ought to be in society and we're asking what we ought to do in society. The public square is where we decide what ought to be and what we ought to do in order to become who we ought to be. We're not talking about personal life or community life. Those are areas of our life that operate independent of government, of our laws and public policies. Our personal and community behavior attracts public attention, but only when it does harm to others. Then that behavior ceases to be private or communal and becomes public. Tidy little clarification to our thinking. Do harm, you have gone public.

Back to the public square. We want to know what we ought to be as a society and what we must do and not do so that we can become what we ought to be. Two sets of questions: What ought we to be in society? And what must we do and not do in society to become what we ought to be.

Here we go.

Moral philosophy has the tools to tell us what we ought to be in society. But moral philosophy fell into increasing levels of chaos after the Reformation and during the Wars of Religion that followed the Reformation. It was not the fault of Luther (one of my heroes), Calvin, or Henry the VIII who set the Protestant Reformation in motion. It was the fault of moral philosophers who got stuck in Stage 3 Tribal moral reasoning.

So just when Copernicus, Galileo, Newton, et al invented natural science and advanced mathematics and created the astonishingly productive scientific revolution that continues today; moral philosophy fell into disrepair. Moral philosophy failed so badly that what we call the social sciences divorced themselves from moral philosophy. The divorce weakened both. Neither can help We the People answer our most pressing questions. Neither can help We the People conduct productive arguments so that we can agree on what we must be and what we must do to become what we must be.

Importantly, moral philosophers and social scientists don't perceive themselves as having failed. But then, they evaluate themselves, and as Francis Bacon (1561-1626) pointed out long ago, a discipline that evaluates itself "will never be found wanting." Indeed, they thrive. They teach, write, get tenure, earn substantial salaries, and look forward to retirements that most Americans can hardly imagine. No, they're in fat city, not useless. So where is the problem? In the public square. How does all this stuff fit together?

Because the social sciences have divorced themselves from moral philosophy, moral philosophy can't reach full development. It can't figure out what is in society, so it does not know what moral questions need to be answered. Moral philosophy cannot reach full development without the social sciences.

Because the social sciences have divorced themselves from moral philosophy, the social sciences can't reach full development. They can't figure out what ought to be in society. Therefore they have no criteria, no standards, to judge what is right or what is wrong in society. This is a bit subtle. The social sciences do not have the intellectual tools needed to study moral questions, like, What should we do? What is right and what is wrong in society? Because social scientists have no way of knowing what ought to be in society, they have no criteria, no standards, to apply to the study of what is in society. They have no standards that would allow them to discern what in society is good and must be maintained and what is bad and must be removed from society. Therefore, they have no way of saying what we ought to do to fix society. Oh, they can have all kinds of personal opinions, but that does not help anyone. They are incapable of bringing moral certitude to the public square and therefore they have none of the intellectual authority needed to tell We the People what we should be doing. There you go: No intellectual authority, no moral authority. Full intellectual development consists of both full cognitive development and full moral development.

See how simple the problem is. Yea, looks simple, but it took us over a hundred pages to get there.

So what do we do? Well, obviously, we have dug into how moral philosophers and social scientists think, their theories of knowledge, and we have found their theories of knowledge wanting.

That's why our public square and our body politic is fractured. Because moral philosophy and the social sciences are responsible for the full development of our public mind and body politic: how we think in the public square (mind politic), and how we conduct discourse in the public square (body politic). As long as moral philosophy and the social sciences can't reach full intellectual development, full cognitive and moral development; they can't aid the full intellectual development of We the People.

So we fixed moral philosophy and the social sciences. We fixed moral philosophy's and the social sciences' theories of knowledge (they're related, interdependent, but not identical) and that allowed us to fix the social science method. That allowed us to show moral philosophers and social scientists how to integrate their work, reach full intellectual development, and assert leadership, both cognitive and moral leadership, and intellectual authority (both cognitive and moral authority) in the public square. We allowed moral philosophers and social scientists to help We the People bring moral certitude back to our mind politic, body politic, and back to the public square. We the People can tell right from wrong in public life and fix it.

In a nut shell, moral philosophy uses a system of mature moral reasoning to tell social science what ought to be in society. They describe what ought to be in society as the Morally Grounded Purposes of a Liberal Democracy.

The morally grounded purposes of our society provide social scientists with the criteria for evaluating what is in society, which they do as scientists (study what is), and to conduct the research and development required to figure out what we can and must do as well as what we must not do in society to achieve our morally grounded purposes. That's what social scientists are supposed to do. Social scientists must be able to say with a significant level of predictability: If we do A we will get B, and B is good.

Obviously, then, the social science method employs moral philosophy's morally grounded purposes as its criteria, its standards of knowledge. And it uses both the structure of scientific research and reasoning to decide what works, and the structure of moral reasoning to decide if what works is good. Social science integrates both the theory of knowledge in natural science and the theory of knowledge in moral philosophy to develop its unique theory of knowledge for social science.

As we stepped back and looked at what we had done, we realized that we could make our conclusions a bit more recognizable and acceptable by noting that we were being Pragmatic, we were paying attention to results. But we had also overcome a major weakness of Pragmatism which has always focused on results but was incapable of deciding and was therefore silent about the moral status of what was being sought. Pragmatists paid attention to scientific predictability: if I do A, I will get B, but they could not say if B is good or not good. So we're doing more. We're doing Morally Grounded Pragmatism. We work to achieve morally grounded purposes and therefore we evaluate what we do in terms of its efficacy (does it do what it says it will do?), its efficiency (does it use the fewest possible resources?) and its morality (is it good)? Does it help us achieve our morally grounded purposes? Or is it bad? Does it undermine or prevent us from achieving our morally grounded purposes?

That was pretty powerful stuff. And we took all of what we had learned and applied it to major challenges that confront We the People in the public square.

Let us recall what we did with Economic Justice so that we can make use of our Morally Grounded Pragmatic Dialectic. In discussing Economic Justice we developed a formal conceptual framework which one must have to conduct formal reasoning, the most mature level of cognitive development. And we want to operate with the most mature reasoning we can. Kind of like, we're taking on serious issues and we want to be smart not stupid, grownups not immature.

No need to revisit our formal conceptual framework of Economics here. But we do want to notice that it places capitalism and socialism in a dialectic. We don't know how to construct the perfect economic system, but we do know that we can create a process in which we match capitalistic solutions with socialist solutions. We moved from using our Morally Grounded Pragmatism to using our Morally Grounded Pragmatic Dialectic. And we used our morally grounded pragmatic dialectic to help us simplify and solve major challenges in economics. Well, at least we got the conversation started in a way that's amenable to mature rational discourse in the public square.

Our chapter on Education Justice demonstrates how the inability of education's intellectual leaders to lead has undermined America's most prominent socialist enterprise and thereby has undermined how We the People think about socialism. That's a big deal.

But education's intellectual leaders have also failed to provide the intellectual leadership needed for school administrators and school teachers to reach full development as educators and as a professional community. That matters, again for the harm it does to education as a socialist enterprise. But more important, it matters because of the harm it does to children who depend on school teachers to learn and to develop their full humanity.

Because education's intellectual leaders do not lead, school teachers cannot agree on how students learn and how best to teach. Individual teachers make those decisions for themselves. "No one knows better than the teacher in a classroom what the students in that classroom need." Great. Try that with your doctor who only knows what he has taught him or herself about medicine. Try that with your attorney. Or the aeronautical engineers who designed the plane you are about to get on or the structural engineers who designed the bridge you are about to drive over. They don't agree, but somehow or other they will practice medicine or law or design planes or bridges.

I showed education's intellectual leaders how to provide intellectual leadership by explaining paradigms and describing one I have developed for education. A paradigm is an intellectual achievement that unites knowledge in a discipline and unites the community of scholars and practitioners in that discipline. A paradigm allows members of its community to operate at the highest level of formal operations, the highest level of cognitive development. It makes everyone in the community a whole lot smarter. Education's intellectual leaders must either adopt my paradigm or a version of it or advance their own. They need to get their act together so that the entire community of educators can agree on what and how they think.

But the larger point is that after seeing the enormous harm education's intellectual leaders have done to teachers, administrators, and students, we get a sense of the importance of intellectual leadership not just in education but also in society. We realize that the failure of moral philosophers and social scientists to provide intellectual leadership in the public square does enormous harm to our mind politic and our body politic. Moral philosophers and social scientists also do harm to We the People and to the socialist institutions that our country needs to be effective and efficient.

Next we addressed Women's Reproductive Rights. I had written this chapter and then removed it because it gives so much attention to religious moral reasoning that it seemed out of place in a book that deals with the public square and public morality. But the recent changes in the U.S. Supreme Court have created a majority of male Catholic justices who at least appear bound to vastly reduce women's reproductive rights. At least regarding this topic, they appear to have allowed their strange alliance with the Vatican to trump their commitment to the U.S. Constitution. So we took the little time and intellectual attention needed to defeat and replace the Catholic arguments against artificial birth control and a woman's right to choose to terminate an unwanted pregnancy before the fetus becomes viable. In our discussion, we demonstrated our understanding of women who have only had healthy, happy pregnancies from women who are terrified at the prospect of carrying an unwanted, unanticipated pregnancy to term.

And then we talked about late term abortions and noticed how few there. Noticing how few they are relieved some of the hysteria around the topic, but it did not eliminate its importance. We also listened to some of the compelling stories of women who have faced this urgent, unexpected, and unwanted choice. We established the right and duty of We the People to have a voice that protects the mother and the viable fetus, the child. And we framed some of the conversations that are required when these tragic questions confront mothers.

Social Justice required a lot of work because it has received so little intellectual and political attention. We were able to use concepts we developed in Economic Justice when discussing major social challenges that were identified by the American Association of Social Work and Social Workers. Not only did it help us discuss those challenges rationally, it allowed us to distinguish which challenges are best addressed by government run programs, either capitalist or socialist, and which are best met in communities and families. It's a pretty cool chapter.

All of this work tells We the People what to expect of ourselves as mature members of our body politic. And it tells our moral philosophers and social scientists what they must do to fulfill the vast potential they have to help heal and lead the public square of our liberal democracy.

Now what do we need to get started to achieve our goal?

To conduct discourse in the public square that allows us to agree on what is right and what is wrong in public life so that we can make laws and develop public policies that support what is right and reject what is wrong.

We need:

A critical mass of Americans to show up in the public square and support our arguments. Religious humanists who believe that social responsibility is a prerequisite to redemption. Secular humanists who believe that a good life requires that they help others. Americans who believe that they're members of and responsible for our community and our liberal democracy.

Bibliography

Aristotle; "Nichomachean Ethics;" *The Complete Works of Aristotle*, The Revised Oxford Translation, Jonathan Barnes Editor, Vol. 1; Princeton University Press, 1991.

Bacon, Francis; *Essays, Advancement of Learning, New Atlantis, and Other Pieces;* (Selected and Edited by Richard Foster Jones) The Odyssey Press, Inc., New York, 1937.

Bodrova, Elena and Deborah J. Leong; *Tools of the Mind: The Vygotskian Approach to Early Childhood Education*; Pearson Education, Inc., Upper Saddle River, New Jersey; 1996, 2007.

Bonhoeffer, Dietrich; *Ethics*; A Touchstone Book, Simon and Schuster, New York, 1995.

Boyer, Ernest L.; *Scholarship Reconsidered: Priorities of the Professoriate*; The Carnegie Foundation for the Advancement of Teaching, Princeton, NJ, 1992.

Burtt, Edwin A. (editor); *The English Philosophers from Bacon to Mill*; The Modern Library, New York, 1939.

Clark, Thomas D. And Albert D. Kirwan; *The South Since Appomattox*; Oxford University Press, New York, 1967.

Conroy, Barbara J.; *Teachers' Moral Reasoning and their Attitudes and Behaviors Regarding Discipline*; Unpublished doctoral dissertation, University of Tulsa, 1986.

Conroy, J. Patrick; *The Effect on the Job Descriptive Index Used for Measuring Teacher Job Satisfaction when a Student Area is Added*; Unpublished doctoral dissertation, University of Denver, 1979.

———. *Intellectual Leadership in Education*; Kluwer Academic Publishers; Dordrecht, the Netherlands, 1999.

Dewey, John and James H. Tufts; *Ethics*; American Science Series; Henry Holt and Company, New York, 1908.

El'konin, D.B.; "Toward the Problem of Stages in the Mental Development of Children"; (Nikolai Veresov, translator) *Voprosy psikhologii,* No. 4. 6-20, Soviet Psychology, 1971.

El'konin, D.B. and V. V. Davydov (editors, Anne Bigelow translator) "Learning Capacity and Age Level: Introduction"; from *Learning Capacity and Age Level: Primary Grades*; Prosveshchenie, Moscow, 1966.

Epstein, Herman T.; "Growth Spurts during Brain Development: Implications for Educational Policy and Practice"; *Education and the Brain*, The Seventy-seventh Yearbook of the National Society for the Study of Education, Editors: Jeanne S. Chall and Allan F. Mirsky, University of Chicago Press, Chicago Illinois, 1978.

Evans, Richard I.; *Dialogue with Jean Piaget*; Praeger Publishing, New York, 1981.

Feuerstein, Reuven, Ya'acov Rand, Mildred B. Hoffman, and Ronald Miller; *Instrumental Enrichment: An Intervention Program for Cognitive Modifiability*; University Park Press, Baltimore, 1980.

Feuerstein, Reuven and Mildred B. Hoffman; *Instrumental Enrichment: A Word of Introduction*; Hadassh-Wizo-Canada-Research Institute, Jerusalem.

Feuerstein, Reuven; *Instrumental Enrichment: A Selected Sample of Materials for Review Purposes*; Hadassh-Wizo-Canada-Research Institute, Jerusalem.

Feuerstein, Reuven and Mildred B. Hoffman; "Intergenerational Conflict of Rights: Cultural Imposition and Self-Realization", in *Viewpoints in Teaching and Learning*, Journal of the School of Education, Indiana University, Vol. 58, No 1, Winter, 1982.

Feuerstein, Reuven; "The Theory of Structural Cognitive Modifiability", in *Learning and Thinking Styles: Classroom Interaction*; Robert McClure, editor; National Education Association, Washington, D.C., 1990.

279

Fischer, David H.; *Historians' Fallacies: Toward a Logic of Historical Thought*; Harper Torchbooks, Harper & Row, New York, 1970.

Foster, Richard J. and James Bryan Smith (editors); *Devotional Classics: Selected Readings for Individuals and Groups*; HarperOne, HarperCollins Publishers, New York, 1993.

Hauerwas, Stanley with Richard Bondi and David B. Burrell; *Truthfulness and Tragedy: Further Investigations into Christian Ethics;* University of Notre Dame Press, Notre Dame, Indiana, 1977.

Huxley, Aldous; *The Perennial Philosophy;* Perennial Library, HarperCollins Publishers, New York, 1990.

James, William; *Pragmatism and four essays from The Meaning of Truth;* Meridian Books, The World Publishing Company, New York, 1964.

Kant, Immanuel; The Critique of Pure Reason, The Critique of Practical Reason, Preface and Introduction to the Metaphysical Elements of Ethics, With a Note on Conscience, General Introduction to the Metaphysic of Morals. In *Great Books of the Western World*, Robert Maynard Hutchins, General Editor, Encyclopaedia Britannica, Inc, Chicago, 1952.

Karpov, Yuriy V. And John D. Bransford; "L. S. Vygotsky and the Doctrine of Empirical and Theoretical Learning"; *Educational Psychologist*, 30(2), 61-66, Lawrence Erlbaum Associates, Inc., 1966.

Karpov, Yuriy V. and H. Carl Haywood; "Two Ways to Elaborate Vygotsky's Concept of Mediation: Implications for Instruction"; *American Psychologist*, the American Psychological Association, Vol. 53, No.1, (p. 27-36) January, 1998.

Kaufmann, Walter; *Nietzsche: Philosopher, Psychologist, and Antichrist*; Meridian Books, The World Publishing Company, New York, 1962.

Kohlberg, L.; "From Is to Ought: How to Commit the Naturalistic Fallacy and Get Away with it in the Study of Moral Development"; in *Cognitive Development and Epistemology*, T. Michael editor; Academic Press, New York, 1971.

——. "The Contribution of Developmental Psychology to Education"; *Education Psychologist*, 10, No. 1, 1973.

——. "Development as the Aim of Education"; *Stage Theories of Cognitive and Moral Development: Criticism and Application*, Harvard Educational Review, 1978.

——. *The Meaning and Measurement of Moral Development*; Clark University Press, Worcester, MA, 1976.

Kozulin, Alex; "Book Review: Vygotsky and Education: Instructional Implications and Applications of Sociohistorical Psychology", (Edited by Luis C. Moll, New York: Cambridge University Press, 1990) in *American Journal of Psychology*, Vol. 105, No. 3, pp 510-516, Fall, 1992.

——. "Literature as a Psychological Tool", in *Educational Psychologist*, 28(3), 253-264; Lawrence Erlbaum Associates, Inc., 1993.

Kozulin, Alex and Boris Gindis, Vladimir S. Ageyev, and Suzanne M. Miller, Editors; *Vygotsky's Educational Theory in Cultural Context*; Cambridge University Press, New York, 2003.

Kuhn, Thomas S.; *The Structure of Scientific Revolutions*, Second Edition, Enlarged; The University of Chicago Press, Chicago, 1970.

Lagemann, Ellen Condliffe and Lee S. Shulman; *Issues in Education Research: Problems and Possibilities*; Jossey-Bass, San Francisco, 1999.

Lagemann, Ellen Condliffe and Lee S. Shulman, Co-Chairs; *Next Steps: Reflections on Education Research and Ways the National Academy of Education Might Help Further Strengthen It*; National Academy of Education Commission on the Improvement of Education Research; September, 1999.

Leontyev, A. N.; *Problems of the Development of the Mind*; Progress Publishers, Moscow, Union of Soviet Socialist Republics; 1981.

Lezotte, Lawrence W.; "School Improvement Based on Effective Schools Research"; Unpublished Paper, National Center for Effective Schools Research and Development, Okemos, Michigan; 1989.

---. "Effective Schools Research Model for Planned Change"; Unpublished Paper, National Center for Effective Schools Research and Development, Okemos, Michigan; 1989.

---. "Strategic Assumptions of the Effective Schools Process"; Unpublished Paper, National Center for Effective Schools Research and Development, Okemos, Michigan; 1989.

---. "Correlates of Effective Schools"; Unpublished Paper, National Center for Effective Schools Research and Development, Okemos, Michigan; 1989.

Lezotte, Lawrence W. and Michelle L. Maksimowicz; *Workbook for Developing A District Plan for School Improvement Based on the Effective Schools Research*; Michigan Institute for Educational Management, Lansing, Michigan; 1989.

Locke, John; *An Essay Concerning Human Understanding*; In Great Books of the Western World, Robert Maynard Hutchins, General Editor, Encyclopaedia Britannica, Inc, Chicago; 1952.

---. *An Essay Concerning the True Original, Extent and End of Civil Government*, (The second of Two Treatises of Government published together in 1690) in The English Philosophers from Bacon to Mill, Edwin A. Burtt, editor; The Modern Library, New York, 1939.

Luria, A. R.; *The Making of Mind, A Personal Account of Soviet Psychology*; Editors, Michael Cole and Sheila Cole; Harvard University Press, Cambridge, MA, 1979.

Maslow, Abraham H.; *Toward a Psychology of Being*, Second Edition; D Van Nostrand Company, New York, 1968.

MacIntyre, Alasdair C.; *Three Rival Versions of Moral Enquiry: Encyclopaedia, Genealogy, and Tradition*; University of Notre Dame Press, Notre Dame, IN, 1990.

---. *After Virtue: A Study in Moral Theory*; University of Notre Dame Press, Notre Dame, IN, 1981.

Mann, Dale, Editor; *Making Change Happen?*; Teachers College Press, Columbia University, New York, 1978.

Marx, Karl; *Capital*; Great Books of the Western World, vol. 50; Encyclopaedia Britannica, Inc., London, 1952.

Marx, Karl and Friedrich Engels; *Manifesto of the Communist Party,* Great Books of the Western World, vol. 50; Encyclopaedia Britannica, Inc., London, 1952.

Mill, John Stuart; *On Liberty*; The Liberal Arts Press, New York, 1956.

———. *The Six Great Humanistic Essays of John Stuart Mill*; Washington Square Press, New York, 1969

Mischell, Theodore (editor); *Cognitive Development and Epistemology*; Academic Press, New York, 1971.

Montaigne, Michel de; *In Defense of Raymond Sebond*; Translated by Arthur H. Beattie; Milestones of Thought, Frederick Ungar Publishing Co., New York, 1959.

———. *The Essays of Michel de Montaigne,* in three volumes; Translated by George B. Ives, 1925, Harvard University Press; with an Introduction by Andre Gide, translated by Dorothy Bussy, Longmans Green and Co, 1939; and an accompanying Handbook by Grace Norton; The Heritage Press, New York, 1946.

Murray, John Courtney S.J.; *We Hold These Truths: Catholic Reflections on the American Proposition*; Sheed and Ward; New York, 1960.

Naughton, Barry; "Is China Socialists?", *Journal of Economic Perspectives,* Journal of the American Economic Association, Volume 31, Number 1, Winter, 2017.

Nehamas, Alexander; "Trends in Recent American Philosophy", *Daedalus: Journal of the American Academy of the Arts and Sciences*, Winter, 1997.

Newman, John Henry Cardinal; *An Essay in Aid of A Grammar of Assent*; University of Notre Dame Press, Notre Dame, IN, 1979

Newton, Sir Isaac; *Mathematical Principals of Natural Philosophy*; in Great Books of the Western World, Robert Maynard Hutchins, General Editor, Encyclopaedia Britannica, Inc, Chicago, 1952.

Nietzsche, Friedrich; *Beyond Good and Evil*; Translation by Walter Kaufmann; Vintage Books, Random House, New York, 1966.

————. *The Birth of Tragedy* and *The Genealogy of Morals;* Translation by Francis Golffing; An Anchor Book by Doubleday, New York, 1956.

Phillips, D. C. and Jonas F. Soltis; *Perspectives on Learning,* Second Edition; Teachers College Press, New York, 1991.

Presseisen, Barbara Z. (et al); *Learning and Thinking Styles: Classroom Interaction*; National Education Association, Washington, D.C., 1990.

Putnam, Hilary; "A Half Century of Philosophy Viewed from Within", *Daedalus. Journal of the American Academy of the Arts and Sciences*, Winter, 1997.

Ratner, Joseph; *The Philosophy of John Dewey* (Writings by John Dewey, selected and edited by Joseph Ratner, Columbia University); Henry Holt and Company, New York, 1928.

Sapolsky, Robert M.; Behave: *The Biology of Humans at Our Best and Worst*; Penguin Press, New York, 2017.

Singer, D and T. A. Revenson; A Piaget Primer: *How a Child Thinks*; A Plum Book, New American Library, Times Mirror, 1996.

Smith, Adam; *An Inquiry into the Nature and Causes of the Wealth of Nations;* Great Books of the Western World, vol. 39; Encyclopaedia Britannica, London, 1952.

Steele, David N. and Curtis C. Thomas; *The Five Points of Calvinism: Defined, Defended, Documented*; The Presbyterian and Reformed Publishing Co., Philadelphia, 1963.

Stout, Jeffrey; *Democracy and Tradition;* Princeton University Press, Princeton, N.J., 2004.

Teilhard de Chardin, Pierre S.J.; *The Phenomenon of Man;* (Translated by Bernard Wall with an Introduction by Julian Huxley), Harper Torchbooks, The Cloister Library, Harper and Brothers, New York, 1959.

————. *Activation of Energy*; (Translated by René Hague), Harcourt Brace Jovanovich, Publishers, New York, 1970.

————. *Christianity and Evolution;* (Translated by René Hague), A Harvest Book, Harcourt, Inc., New York, 1974.

————. *The Heart of Matter*; (Translated by René Hague), Harcourt Brace & Company, New York, 1976.

Vygotsky, L. S,; "The Problem of the Cultural Development of the Child", *Journal of Genetic Psychology*, Vol. 36, pp 415-434, 1929.

———. "The Problem of Age-periodization of Child Development"; Translated by Mary A. Zender and F. F. Zender, Human Development, N.17, 1974.

———. *Thought and Language*; Alex Kozulin, editor and translator; The MIT Press, Cambridge, Massachusetts, 1993.

Willard, Dallas; *The Divine Conspiracy: Rediscovering Our Hidden Life in God;* HarperCollins Publishers, San Francisco, 1998.

Willey, Basil; *The Seventeenth Century Background: The Thought of the Age in Relation to Religion and Poetry*; Doubleday Anchor Books, Garden City, New Jersey, 1953. (First published in 1935 by Columbia University Press.)

CPSIA information can be obtained
at www.ICGtesting.com
Printed in the USA
BVHW080140090519
547805BV00001B/33/P